T0326426

Re-balancing China

Re-balancing China

Essays on the Global Financial Crisis, Industrial Policy and International Relations

Peter Nolan

ANTHEM PRESS
LONDON · NEW YORK · DELHI

Anthem Press
An imprint of Wimbledon Publishing Company
www.anthempress.com

This edition first published in UK and USA 2014
by ANTHEM PRESS
75–76 Blackfriars Road, London SE1 8HA, UK
or PO Box 9779, London SW19 7ZG, UK
and
244 Madison Ave #116, New York, NY 10016, USA

British Library Cataloguing-in-Publication Data
A catalogue record for this book is available from the British Library.

Library of Congress Cataloging-in-Publication Data
Nolan, Peter, 1949–
Re-balancing China : essays on the global financial crisis,
industrial policy and international relations / Peter Nolan.
pages cm
Includes bibliographical references and index.
ISBN 978-1-78308-126-4 (hardback : alk. paper)
1. China–Economic policy–2000– 2. Industrial policy–China. 3.
China–Foreign relations. 4. Global Financial Crisis, 2008–2009. I.
Title.
HC427.95.N655 2013
330.951–dc23
2013041421

ISBN-13: 978 1 78308 126 4 (Hbk)
ISBN-10: 1 78308 126 0 (Hbk)

This title is also available as an ebook.

For Deirdre, Fionuala, Niam and Siobain

CONTENTS

ACKNOWLEDGEMENTS

I am most grateful to Elizabeth Briggs, for her expert editing of this volume. I am most grateful also to Bob Ash, Peter Garnsey and Jonathan Pincus, for their comments on earlier drafts of Chapter 5.

LIST OF ABBREVIATIONS

ASEAN	Association of Southeast Asian Nations
AVIC	Aviation Industry of China
BAC	British Aircraft Corporation
BAe	British Aerospace
BERR	Department for Business Enterprise and Regulatory Reform (UK)
BIS	Department of Business, Innovation and Skills (UK)
BOC	Bank of China
CASA	Constructiones Aeronáutica SA
CAT	Caterpillar
CBRC	China Banking Regulatory Commission
CCB	China Construction Bank
CFIUS	Committee on Foreign Investment in the United States
CIC	China Investment Corporation
CIS	Commonwealth of Independent States
CNPC	China National Petroleum Corporation
COMAC	Commercial Aircraft Company of China
DASA	Deutsche Aerospace AG/DaimlerChrysler Aerospace
DPJ	Democratic Party (Japan)
DTI	Department of Trade and Industry (UK)
EADS	European Aeronautic Defence and Space Company
EDF	Électricité de France
EEZ	Exclusive economic zone
FDI	Foreign direct investment
FSB	Financial Stability Board
FT	*Financial Times*
GDE	Guangdong Enterprises
GDF	Gaz de France
GDP	Gross domestic product
GE	General Electric
GITIC	Guangdong International Trust and Investment Corporation

GM	General Motors
GW	Gigawatt
ICBC	Industrial and Commercial Bank of China
ICOR	Incremental capital–output ratio
IEA	International Energy Agency
IISS	International Institute for Strategic Studies
IMF	International Monetary Fund
IPD	Integrated product development
IPO	Initial public offering
LMIEs	Low- and middle-income economies
LNG	Liquefied natural gas
LPG	Liquefied petroleum gas
MCP	Malayan Communist Party
MW	Megawatt
NAFTA	North American Free Trade Agreement
NPL	Non-performing loans
OECD	Organisation for Economic Co-operation and Development
PPP	Purchasing power parity
PRC	People's Republic of China
PWR	Pressurized water reactor
R&D	Research and development
SAFE	State Administration of Foreign Exchange (China)
SAIC	Shanghai Automobile Industry Corporation
SASAC	State-owned Assets Supervision and Administration Commission (China)
SIC	SAFE Investment Company
SME	Small- or medium-sized enterprise
SOE	State-owned enterprise
SSB	State Statistical Bureau (China)
TNC	Transnational corporation
UNCLOS	United Nations Convention on the Law of the Sea
UNCTAD	United Nations Conference on Trade and Development
USCESRC	US–China Economic and Security Review Commission
WB	World Bank
WTO	World Trade Organization

LIST OF TABLES

INTRODUCTION

Part I analyses the impact of the global financial crisis upon China and the way in which China's policymakers responded to the crisis.

Chapter 1 ('Re-balancing in the Face of the Global Financial Crisis (1): November 2008') was written at the outset of the global financial crisis. In a world of weakly regulated financial institutions and freely flowing capital across national boundaries, the high-income economies were fundamentally susceptible to speculative activity. This was itself the consequence of structures created by their own governments, supported by the mass of the population. Government regulatory policies in the high-income countries were 'captured' by the giant global banks that had been created as the twin brother of the global business revolution (see Chapters 4 and 5). Deregulation was welcomed by households and voters. They watched happily as their paper wealth rose and they were able to steadily increase their debt based on their illusory increase in wealth. Across the high-income countries voters elected governments that pursued these policies.

The crisis caused enormous difficulties for China, exceeding even those of the Asian financial crisis. China's long-term policy of 'reform and opening up' had led China to be far more deeply integrated into the global economic system than other developing countries. It had moved from an exceptionally low foreign trade ratio at the start of the reform process, to an exceptionally high foreign trade ratio. Such an 'unbalanced' pattern of development carried high risks. The coastal provinces of eastern and southern China were especially deeply integrated into the global trading system, with a large number of jobs directly dependent on exports. The collapse of global trade in 2008–2009 had a severe impact on output and employment, especially in the coastal provinces. The impact of the crisis helped greatly to reinforce the determination of China's policymakers to re-balance demand away from the international economy and towards the domestic economy. Managing the impact of the global financial crisis was a severe challenge to the policymaking capability of the Chinese political system. This was a profound policy challenge for China's leaders. The paper concluded: 'The government will need to adopt a comprehensive package of ameliorative and preventive measures to deal with the coming difficulties in these areas. The Yangtze and Pearl River deltas are criss-crossed with complex water control facilities. If a dyke bursts at its most vulnerable point, in the face of the "rising water level" of the global economic crisis, the central government will need to ensure that it "piles the sandbags to save the dyke and prevent it bursting".'

Chapter 2 ('Re-balancing in the Face of the Global Financial Crisis (2): November 2011') was written three years after the initial impact of the global financial crisis. China's policymakers were remarkably successful in stabilizing the economy in the face of the global crisis. At the core of the stabilization effort was a massive financial injection achieved mainly by the expansion of credit from state-owned banks. The fact that the Chinese government was able to stabilize its own economy was centrally important in preventing an even deeper collapse in the global economy after 2008. The fact that the Chinese government had followed its own path in the reform of its financial institutions proved vitally important to the stabilization of the whole global economy during the crisis. The West has reason to be thankful for the good judgment of China's policymakers in the face of intense international pressure to liberalize and open up the Chinese financial system, including breaking up and privatizing the main banks, allowing global banks free rein in China, and letting the *renminbi* float freely.

Three years after the onset of the global financial crisis, the high-income countries had barely advanced beyond their peak level of output prior to the crisis. Some degree of stabilization in the economies of the high-income countries has only been possible due to a huge increase in public debt. There remained a large overhang of private debt. In the face of widespread public resistance to increased taxation, one after the other, the high-income countries have had no choice but to cut public spending if they wish to cut government deficits and avoid punishment from global 'markets' and the 'death spiral' of high interest rates and economic stagnation. The latest report from the Bank of International Settlements (November 2012) estimates that in most high-income countries the fiscal budget, excluding interest payments, would need 20 consecutive years of surplus exceeding 2 per cent of GDP simply to bring the debt-to-GDP ratio back to its pre-crisis level. Far from pulling out of the crisis quickly, as many experts had predicted, the high-income economies are locked into a prolonged period of economic stagnation, with high levels of both private and public debt, accompanied by profound social and political difficulties. The 'euro crisis' has diverted attention from the much deeper problems across the OECD as a whole, including both the UK and the USA. Japan's situation after 1990 was ameliorated by the fact that the other high-income economies were growing robustly. Today, the OECD as a whole is locked into a situation analogous to that of Japan.

The global financial crisis may turn out to have been a critical turning point in the evolution of the global political economy. The contrast between the relatively successful regulation of the market in China since the 1970s with the disastrous deregulation pursued in the high-income countries since then, may set the scene for a profound transformation of the philosophy for organizing the world economy in the twenty-first century. The tone among the mainstream of Western politicians and in the international media has changed markedly as the crisis in the West has continued and China has continued to achieve a high rate of growth. The level of GDP in the West as a whole is no higher than it was before the crisis, while China's is 50 per cent greater. If the world is able to avoid military confrontation between the West and China, then China's approach to policymaking may make a fundamental contribution to the intelligent regulation of the global economy, in a fashion that sustains the benefits of market competition, but regulates the market in a non-ideological fashion to the common benefit of the whole of humanity.

Part II analyses China's industrial policy in the face of the global business revolution.

Chapter 3 ('China's Industrial Policy at the Crossroads') examines the way in which China's leaders have persisted in attempting to construct a group of globally competitive giant firms to rival those of the high-income countries. After the 1970s the world economy entered a new phase of capitalist globalization. This involved revolutionary changes in information technology, widespread privatization, liberalization of international trade and investment flows, opening up of the former communist 'planned' economies, and comprehensive policy change in the formerly 'inward-looking' non-communist developing countries. The liberalization promoted across the world by the policies of the Washington Consensus led to profound changes in the nature of the large corporation. Large firms with their headquarters in the high-income countries built global production systems, through both organic growth and explosive merger and acquisition. Their suppliers, also typically with their headquarters in the high-income countries, frequently followed them by themselves building global production systems. This period witnessed explosive industrial concentration among both giant 'systems integrator' firms and their supply chains.

Throughout China's economic reforms since the 1980s the central plank of the country's industrial policy has been the attempt to transform its giant state-owned enterprises into globally competitive firms. A large fraction of the world's leading firms were supported in one way or another by their national governments at some stage in their development. The avenues of state support included full or partial state ownership, protection from international competition through tariffs and import quotas, government procurement policy, government support for research and development, and preferential loans from state-owned banks. China's planners studied the experience of other countries and adapted their policies to their own situation. The structure and operational mechanism of the country's state-owned enterprises have been comprehensively transformed since the 1980s. The results have been remarkable. China's state-owned enterprises have grown at high speed and are highly profitable. China now has a large group of state-owned enterprises in the *FT* 500 and *Fortune* 500 global rankings.

However, behind this apparent success, there are deep problems that are widely acknowledged within the Chinese government. The success of China's SOEs has been based heavily on their privileged position within the fast-growing domestic market. The country's banks lend primarily to the SOEs. Insofar as the country's SOEs have built international businesses, these are mainly in developing countries, selling low-technology and low-value-added products. China's SOEs have made a negligible impact within the markets of the high-income countries, either in terms of sales or in foreign direct investment (FDI). At the same time, in a wide range of high-technology and heavily branded industrial sectors, global firms have rapidly built their production base within China, both for the domestic market and for export. After 30 years of industrial policy the blunt reality is that China's giant SOEs have failed to build globally competitive firms. Their high market capitalization masks their fundamental weakness in global competition. It is widely acknowledged that China's SOEs will enter a new round of system reform under the incoming leadership. However, the direction and content of that reform is an open question.

Throughout the period of 'transition' from the centrally planned economies, the Washington Consensus institutions have argued unceasingly that state-owned enterprises are inherently inefficient. At the start of the modern era of capitalist globalization large parts of the Western European economy were dominated by state-owned enterprises selling mainly within their domestic market, often to other SOEs. Over the past three decades many of these have been transformed into leading global firms at the forefront of innovation in their respective sectors. It is widely thought that the essential precursor of this transformation was comprehensive privatization. In fact the process of ownership change and its relationship to the transformation of Europe's former state-owned enterprises has been much more complex. In some cases there was comprehensive privatization. In the case of others the state maintained a substantial minority equity share, which permitted the company to pursue a long-term growth strategy without the possibility of being acquired by another company. In other cases the state orchestrated a merger between a state-owned national champion and a private sector company. In the case of the European Aeronautic Defence and Space Company (EADS), a combination of European governments launched a complex cross-border industrial restructuring, involving a substantial minority state equity share right through to the present day.

Chapter 4 ('Globalization and Competition in Financial Services') examines the relationship between China and the global financial system. Global financial institutions are an essential part of the structure of globalization, providing the financial 'cement' to knit together the activities of global non-financial firms and their value chains, spread across the whole world. During the global business revolution the process of industrial consolidation affected the financial sector at least as strongly as it affected other sectors of the economy. The share of the world's top 25 banks in the total assets of the Global 1000 banks increased from 28 per cent in 1997 to 45 per cent in 2009 (*The Banker*, July 1998 and July 2010). In 2010 the world's top 500 asset managers had a total of $64 trillion under management (Towers Watson 2010). The top 50 asset managers account for 61 per cent of the total assets under management. In 2011 a total of $4 trillion of foreign exchange was traded daily. The top 10 global banks, all from the high-income countries account for 81 per cent of the total (*FT*, 10 May 2012).

As global financial institutions became larger so their influence on policymakers in the high-income countries increased. Their influence was felt through a wide variety of channels. A small minority of analysts warned of the dangers of 'regulatory capture'. The global mass media, university researchers and a wide array of analysts established the mainstream view that freely functioning financial markets are inherently rational and self-regulating. Those who disagreed with this view were ignored, or even ridiculed, in the face of 'overwhelming evidence' that 'this time is different'. An asset bubble of unprecedented proportions developed after the 1970s, with house prices its most important component. The asset bubble fuelled and was mutually stimulated by an uncontrolled expansion of household debt in the high-income countries.

From the late 1990s onwards international bankers and international institutions strongly lobbied China to privatize and break up the major national banks. They argued that China should establish a freely floating, fully convertible national currency, with free movement of capital into and out of the country. However, China's policymakers had long warned of the dangers of financial deregulation that had taken place in the high-income countries after the 1970s. They argued that it would be extremely dangerous for China to join such a system. China's policymakers did not believe that a free market financial system was inherently stable and self-regulating. They were fearful that the liberalized financial system in the high-income countries would eventually experience a deep crisis. The searing impact of the Asian financial crisis upon the countries around them strongly reinforced their fears. Moreover, China itself was far more deeply affected by the Asian financial crisis than most outsiders realized, mainly through the close economic links between Hong Kong and the mainland. In 2008 the global financial crisis erupted. It confirmed their worst fears about the inherent instability of freely functioning financial markets and reinforced their caution about financial sector reform and deep integration with the poorly regulated global financial system.

Part III examines China's wider position within the global political economy in the twenty-first century.

Chapter 5 ('China, Western Colonialism and the UN Convention on the Law of the Sea') analyses the impact of the United Nations Convention on the Law of the Sea.[1] In the Western media China is widely perceived to be engaged in a state-sponsored 'resource grab' in developing countries. It is also involved in a high-profile dispute with Japan over a group of tiny uninhabited islands, the Diaoyu (in Chinese) or Senkaku (in Japanese) Islands, which are on the edge of the South China Sea. The Western media are full of reports about China's claims to territory in the South China Sea and the fact that if the claims were successful this might bring China access to the natural resources that might be in or under the sea. The Western media routinely refer to China's alleged 'bullying behaviour' in the South China Sea. Some commentators have suggested that a new 'Peloponnesian War' might begin with the disputes in this sea. The territory in dispute is of great historical and strategic significance, and it may well possess substantial natural resources. However, the resources of the South China Sea are dwarfed in every sense by those involved in the UN's 'revolutionary' decision of 1982.

In 1982 the United Nations enacted a 'revolutionary' piece of legislation, the United Nations Convention on the Law of the Sea (UNCLOS), which allows countries to establish an 'exclusive economic zone' (EEZ) of 200 nautical miles from their coastline. China is a signatory to UNCLOS and the dispute over the South China Sea revolves primarily around the extent of the EEZ that is claimed by China compared with that of the countries with which it is in dispute. However, the area and the potential resources involved are dwarfed by the vast maritime territories that the former colonial powers have amassed as a consequence of UNCLOS. A large part of these territories are in and around the Pacific Ocean. Up until the late eighteenth century this was China's own 'backyard' with negligible Western presence. The colossal resource grab by the former colonial powers arises from the 'scattered remnants' of tiny territories that they still retain from their former empires. This process has almost entirely escaped international attention, while China's complex dispute with its neighbours over a vastly smaller EEZ, in an area with which it had a close relationship over a long span of history, has dominated international media discussion of the control over maritime resources in the Asia-Pacific region.

Chapter 6 ('A New Peloponnesian War? China, the West and the South China Sea') analyses the debate about the possibility of large-scale East–West conflict emerging from disputes in the South China Sea. There has been increasing discussion in the West about the possibility of a new 'Peloponnesian War' between the United States and China. The era of wild capitalist globalization has produced profound contradictions. Many of these involve potential conflict between the USA and China, including climate change, human rights, the struggle for access to natural resources, and regulation of the global financial system. Much international attention has focused on the possibility that the South China Sea will be a key channel through which a US–China conflict develops. From the point of view of the USA, and indeed the West as a whole, this would be a 'quarrel in a far-country between people about whom we know nothing'. However, the region is one about which a great deal is known in China. There are deep connections between the people of mainland China and the 30 million or so descendants of Chinese people who migrated and settled in Southeast Asia over the centuries. The United States is closely involved in the region. US secretary of state Hillary Clinton recently has warned China against the use of 'coercion, intimidation and threats' to resolve disputes over the South China Sea. In fact, in both the distant and the more recent past today's high-income countries have made extensive use not only of 'coercion, intimidation and threats' in the region around the South China Sea, but also extreme military violence, often directed against civilians. In 2011–12 it announced a comprehensive 're-balancing' of its military strategy towards the Western Pacific, with the self-evident goal of 'containing China'. This dangerously escalates the possibility of a new Peloponnesian War erupting.

Note

1 An abbreviated version of this chapter ('Imperial Archipelagos: China, Western Colonialism and the Law of the Sea') was published in *New Left Review* 82 (March–April 2013).

Part I

CHINA AND THE GLOBAL FINANCIAL CRISIS

Chapter 1

RE-BALANCING IN THE FACE OF THE GLOBAL FINANCIAL CRISIS (1): NOVEMBER 2008

Pile the sandbags to save the dyke and prevent it bursting:

Zhu lei sha dai,	筑垒沙袋
Jia gu di ba,	加固堤坝
Fang zhi jue kou,	防止决口

1. The Global Macro Economy

Act I. *The new age of boundless growth*

During the era of capitalist globalization since the 1970s, there has been a long, slowly developing global asset bubble, which gathered pace in the new millennium. The mechanism is exactly the one predicted by Keynes, Kindelberger, Minsky and Galbraith. They each warned that deregulated financial markets have an in-built tendency to create asset bubbles. A vicious circle develops naturally in which credit expansion based on increasing asset values stimulates further increases in asset values. The intensity of such asset bubbles is increased by the wide sense that a 'new age' has arrived in which the prospects for growth and profits are boundless due to new technologies and markets. The era of capitalist globalization has nurtured such sentiments on an unprecedented scale.[1]

The central mechanism of the financial crisis is the money-creation machine unleashed by financial market deregulation, led by Wall Street. Since the 1970s, under the leadership of the Washington Consensus institutions, driven by the interests of Wall Street banks, the United States promoted bank privatization and deregulation across the world. The period witnessed a growing 'financialization' of the economy, as credit expanded in all its various forms. Between 1980 and 2005, the ratio of financial assets to global GDP globally rose from 109 per cent to 316 per cent. By 2006–2007, the volume of global derivatives had risen to around ten times global GDP.

The IMF was confident that new forms of risk management and risk distribution had eliminated the possibility of a global financial crisis. In 2006, the IMF stated: 'Risk is now so widely distributed throughout the global economy, that the financial system is so "thick" as to be virtually indestructible.' The world had survived a series of financial crises, including the Mexican 'Tequila Crisis', the Russian crisis and the closely associated crisis at Long-Term Capital Management, the Asian financial crisis and the Argentinean crisis, and it had survived the shock of 9/11.

Act II. Financial crisis

Scene I. The first phase of the financial crisis began in August 2007 with the US 'subprime' crisis and the beginnings of the decline in US house prices. By the spring of 2008 it was apparent that the financial crisis was spreading beyond the subprime sector and into international financial markets. A process of debt deleveraging set in globally across the high-income countries. Interbank lending tightened. However, there was still a widespread belief that the crisis would be of relatively short duration, and no worse than other post-war crises. This belief was helped by the fact that 'emerging markets' in general, and China in particular, were thought to have 'decoupled' from the OECD countries. This helped to create a 'Severn Bore' of financial speculation, which entered global commodity markets, as the global 'money tsunami' was pushed into a narrower channel of speculation.[2]

Scene II. Confidence was shattered by the events of September and October 2008. These few weeks witnessed the collapse of a succession of leading financial institutions across the OECD countries, including giant financial firms such as Lehmann Brothers, AIG, Merrill Lynch, Washington Mutual, Wachovia, HBOS, Fortis and Dexia. Large swathes of the financial system were wholly or partially nationalized. Instead of being the 'lender of last resort', the state became the 'lender of first resort' in order to keep the financial systems of the OECD countries functioning. Across all countries, rich and poor, stock markets crashed and property prices began to fall seriously. Deleveraging accelerated. Interbank lending ground to a halt. Bank lending to commercial and individual customers slumped. The commodity price bubble disintegrated.

It was now no longer tenable to speak of the superiority of 'free, undistorted financial markets' over tightly regulated financial markets. The age of 'wild capitalism' had come to a shuddering halt. No one could now doubt that a new era of extensive regulation of financial markets was the only way forward, though no one could be certain of the way this might happen practically, and what the respective role for national and global regulation might be. It was no longer tenable to speak of the 'decoupling' of developing countries from the OECD countries in a closely integrated capitalist international economic system.

Following the Federal Reserve's rescue of Bear Stearns, Martin Wolf[3] commented: 'Remember Friday 14 March 2008: it was the day the dream of global free market capitalism died.' In the same week Joseph Ackerman, chief executive of Deutsche Bank, said: 'I no longer believe in the market's self-healing power.' In May 2008 the former head of the IMF, Horst Kohler, delivered a devastating verdict on liberalized global financial markets:

> The complexity of financial products and the possibility to carry out huge leveraged trades with little capital have allowed the monster to grow… The only good thing about this crisis is that it has made clear to any thinking, responsible person in the sector that international financial markets have developed into a monster that must be put back in its place… We need more severe and efficient regulation, higher capital requirements to underpin financial trades, more transparency and a global institution to independently oversee the stability of the international financial system.

Act III. From financial crisis to economic crisis

During the depth of the crisis in early autumn 2008 the global banking system had 'looked into the abyss'. The *Economist* magazine, the cheerleader of global deregulation, memorably had a cover picture in which a solitary person stared into a dark abyss. Only massive state intervention prevented a complete meltdown of the global banking system. This was a choice of no choice. US treasury secretary Hank Paulson said:

> I don't like the fact that we have to do this. I hate the fact that we have to do this. But it is better than the alternative… Government owning a stake in any private US company is objectionable to most Americans, me included. Yet the alternative of leaving businesses and consumers without access to financing is totally unacceptable.

Although the world pulled back from immediately falling into the abyss, the financial crises now began to enter the 'real economy'. Huge injections of government funds into the financial system and successive reductions in the official rate of interest were unable to stem the decline in asset prices and widespread deleveraging. It proved impossible to 'catch the falling knife'. By early November 2008, the main weapons available to OECD governments to avert a recession had already been used. The continuing decline in asset prices, including both property and the stock market, had a profound effect on the wealth of OECD citizens, causing a widespread effort to rebuild household balances by saving more and spending less on 'inessentials'. This effect was reinforced by greatly increased insecurity, including the prospect of reduced pensions, and by tightening bank lending. The severe economic downturn was likely to lead to a massive second wave of credit losses on consumer and corporate loans, which would cause further deep damage to the already eroded capital bases of banks and other financial institutions, causing further restrictions to bank credit. The market for a wide array of assets dried up as the leverage machine went into reverse and everyone tried to get to zero leverage.

From fears about inflation during the final phase of the asset bubble, global markets suddenly realized that the OECD countries faced the possibility of a long period of 'malign deflation', with a high risk that a negative spiral would be set in motion in which people postponed spending in the hope of further price falls. Moreover, during this process there was the prospect that the real value of debt would increase, thereby further damaging households' wealth position, and reducing their incentive to spend in a further vicious twist to the downward spiral. The spectre of looming deflation drove government bond yields to historically low levels as investors rushed to their relative safety away from equities and other asset classes: 'The mood is "give me Treasuries at the expense of all other asset classes" as spreads blow out and stocks slump… There is no place to hide but in US Treasuries. You cannot hide in corporate or mortgage bonds.' The shocking realization loomed that the world faced the prospect of enduring on a global scale the ills that had afflicted Japan on a national scale in the 1990s following the bursting of its asset bubble in the 1980s.

In the space of two months in autumn 2008 the *Financial Times'* reports on the crisis had moved from 'global financial crisis', to 'global economic slowdown', to 'world in recession'. The *Financial Times'* headline on 21 November read: 'Fear stalks the world economies.' Its headline on 22 November read: 'Dark days see warnings of far worse yet to come':

> Any lingering hopes that some parts of the world economy, particularly the fast-growing emerging markets such as China, would remain immune from the crisis were snuffed out. With remarkable speed in the past two months, a worrying but apparently manageable credit crunch has turned into a global financial crisis and a recession across much of the world's economy.

In early November the IMF forecast that in 2009 there would be negative GDP growth across the whole of the OECD, with a decline of −0.2 per cent in Japan, −0.5 per cent in the eurozone, −0.7 per cent in the USA and −1.3 per cent in the UK. By the third quarter of 2008, consumer demand was falling seriously across the whole of the OECD, including demand for automobiles, trucks, electrical appliances, furniture, toys, footwear and clothing. In the United States between July and September consumption fell at an annual rate of 3.1 per cent. US car sales fell from an annual rate of 16.1 million units in October 2007 to 10.7 million units in October 2008. In the eurozone, as early as August 2008, car sales fell by an annual rate of 16 per cent. The CEO of Renault, Carlos Ghosn, said: 'The issue is: how are we going to survive for the next three months? not; how are we going to compete for the next ten years?'

Conclusion

The prospect over the next 6–18 months of a serious recession in the OECD countries and a fall in the growth rate of imports, or even an absolute decline in imports, is hugely important for developing countries. The OECD countries account for 73 per cent of total world imports. These are the crucial motors for economic development in developing countries in the era of capitalist globalization. The impending recession will reduce the profitability of firms headquartered in the OECD countries. In addition, they will face much tighter conditions in credit markets. These factors combined will cause them to reduce their plans for capital investment globally. The collapse of world commodity prices will cause large difficulties for LMIEs (low- and middle-income economies) that rely heavily on primary commodity exports (Table 1.1), which will lead to a slow increase or even an absolute fall in demand for imports by primary commodity producers.

Table 1.1. Primary commodities as a share of total exports, 2006 (%)

Latin America/Caribbean	47
Middle East/North Africa	85
Russia	83

2. Implications for China in the Next 6–18 Months

China's unbalanced growth model

Deep integration with the international economy

Since the policies of 'reform and opening up' began in the late 1970s, China has become ever more deeply integrated into the international economy.

Foreign trade. China's growth strategy has been heavily oriented towards foreign trade. Since the 1980s, no other economy has achieved such rapid export growth as China. Between 1985 and 1995 its export volume grew by 15 per cent per annum, and between 1995 and 2006 the rate of growth accelerated to 20 per cent per annum. The share of foreign trade in China's GDP rose from 10 per cent in 1978, to 33 per cent in 1990, and reached 49 per cent in 2002 (Table 1.2). It continued to rise thereafter, reaching no less than 67 per cent in 2006. China's foreign trade ratio today is far above that of other large, continental-sized economies, such as the USA, Russia, Brazil, India and even Japan, and is comparable with that of small- and medium-sized open economies, such as Denmark, Finland, Korea, Israel, Mexico and Sweden. The foreign trade ratio of the eurozone is 65 per cent, which is a similar level to China's. However, a large fraction of the 'foreign trade' is carried on within the eurozone itself, and the 'foreign' trade ratio of the eurozone as a whole in terms of the region's trade with the countries outside the eurozone is much lower.

Table 1.2. China's foreign trade ratio compared with selected countries (exports plus imports as a percentage of GDP, 2006)

China	67	Denmark	65
USA	23	Finland	69
Brazil	22	Israel	69
India	32	Korea	72
Russian Federation	48	Mexico	62
Japan	28	Sweden	71

China's deep integration with the international economy has profoundly affected the country's development. It has brought large gains from comparative advantage, enabling China to export labour-intensive goods in huge quantities. It has also made China deeply vulnerable to fluctuations in the international economy.

Foreign investment. International firms investing in China have become central to the country's economic growth. Foreign-funded enterprises account for 57 per cent of export earnings and 90 per cent of China's exports of 'new and high-technology products'. Two-thirds of the patents granted in China are awarded to foreign enterprises and persons.

High rates of saving and investment and rapid growth of heavy industry compared with light industry

A central criticism of the so-called 'planned economy' before 1978 was the fact that it was locked into a development path which had a high investment rate and unbalanced growth of heavy and light industry. It was widely argued that the move towards a market economy deeply integrated with the global economy would change this growth pattern. In fact, this growth pattern has intensified as China integrates into the global economy.

Savings and investment. China's savings rate has risen from 43 per cent in 1990, already a very high rate in international comparative terms, to 54 per cent in 2006 (Table 1.3), almost twice the average for LMIEs. By contrast, the share of consumption in GDP has fallen from 42 per cent in 1990, already a low share in international comparison, to just 33 per cent in 2006, far below the average for all LMIEs. The economy has relied on a very high rate of investment to generate growth. In 2006, the share of gross capital formation in GDP stood at 45 per cent, compared with 27 per cent for all LMIEs. This suggests an inefficient pattern of resource use, with low technical progress over a large part of the economy and a high incremental capital–output ratio, with a large amount of additional investment needed to generate an additional unit of output.

Table 1.3. China's consumption, savings and capital formation rates in international comparison

	Household consumption (% GDP)		Gross capital formation (% GDP)		Gross savings (% GDP)	
	1990	2006	1990	2006	1990	2006
China	42	33	42	45	43	54
LMIEs (incl. China)	60	56	26	27	25	30

Note: LMIEs = low- and middle-income economies

Heavy industry. In 1990, the share of heavy industry in China's overall industrial output was already high, standing at over 50 per cent of the total gross value of industrial output. By 2006, the share of heavy industry had risen to 70 per cent (Table 1.4). This reflects the highly resource-intensive pattern of development over much of the economy, including low-technology manufacturing for the mass of the Chinese population, and a large role for infrastructure investment.

Table 1.4. Share of heavy and light industry in the gross value of industrial output in China (%)

	1990	2006
Heavy industry	51	70
Light industry	49	30
Total	100	100

Regional imbalance

The process of China's integration into the world economy has produced an 'enclave' economy, which is deeply integrated into the global capitalist economy, alongside a vast hinterland, in which most Chinese people live, and which is only slightly integrated with the global economy.

Foreign trade. A tiny number of provinces with a quarter of the country's population dominate China's foreign trade. Guangdong, Jiangsu and Shanghai alone account for almost three-fifths of China's total exports (Table 1.5). If the provinces of Zhejiang, Shandong and Fujian are included, the total share rises to 80 per cent.

Table 1.5. Share of total Chinese exports from selected areas, 2006 (% total Chinese exports)

Selected provinces	Share of total Chinese exports	Share of total population
Guangdong	31.1	7.2
Jiangsu	16.5	5.8
Shanghai	11.8	1.4
Subtotal	*59.4*	*14.4*
Zhejiang	10.4	3.8
Shandong	6.0	7.2
Fujian	4.2	2.7
Total for above areas	*80.0*	*28.1*

The ratio of foreign trade to provincial GDP varies enormously between the key coastal areas and the hinterland. In a small group of 'super-integrated' coastal areas, including Jiangsu, Shanghai, Beijing and Tianjin, the ratio of foreign trade to GDP stands at over 100 per cent, on a par with small open economies, such as Malaysia, the Netherlands and Estonia (Table 1.6). A group of 'moderately integrated' areas, such as Zhejiang, Fujian and Shandong provinces, have foreign trade ratios of between 40 and 80 per cent. However, for a wide array of provinces, the direct connection with global capitalist markets is weak. Their foreign trade ratios are less than 20 per cent, much below the average for LMIEs. For these provinces, domestic inter-provincial trade is much more important than international trade.

Table 1.6. Foreign trade ratio in selected Chinese provinces and in selected countries (exports plus imports as a proportion of GDP, 2006)

Selected Chinese areas		Selected countries	
Super-integrated areas		*Deeply integrated*	
Shanghai	183	Hungary	134
Guangdong	167	Malaysia	194
Jiangsu	109	Netherlands	133
Beijing	165	Belgium	184
Tianjin	122	Estonia	139
Moderately integrated areas		*Moderately integrated*	
Zhejiang	74	Denmark	65
Fujian	63	Mexico	62
Shandong	36	Korea	72
Negligibly integrated areas		*Low degree of integration*	
Hunan	8	Nepal	32
Hubei	13	Niger	41
Henan	7	Sierra Leone	42
Anhui	17	Sudan	37
Sichuan	11	*Low-income economies*	44
Chongqing	13		
China	*69*		

Foreign investment. Foreign direct investment (FDI) is highly concentrated geographically. Seventy per cent of the exports from foreign-invested enterprises come from Guangdong and Jiangsu/Shanghai alone (Table 1.7).

Table 1.7. Share of total export value from foreign-funded enterprises, 2006 (%)

China	*100*
Guangdong	34
Jiangsu	22
Shanghai	14

Unequal distribution of the gains from economic growth

The impact of 'economic growth with unlimited supplies of labour' has ensured that during the phase of 'reform and opening up' real wages for unskilled and low skilled labour have increased only slowly at best. In addition, the enclaves of international investment brought with them a relatively small proportion of the population employed at global wages. The investments from Hong Kong have brought with them a small group of fabulously wealthy Hong Kong business people. The explosion of property development provided opportunities for immense personal gains for political 'insiders'.

Overlaid on these processes were the distributional consequences of the partial privatization of large state-owned enterprises. In 2007 alone, the total value of IPOs by mainland Chinese companies in Hong Kong and the mainland was $62 billion. Typically, the share prices of China state enterprise IPOs have increased greatly during the early days of trading, even more so during the domestic stock market bubble of 2006–2007. In 2006 the average first day price rise for IPOs of Chinese mainland companies was 23 per cent in Hong Kong, and on the mainland between June 2006 and June 2007 the average first day rise was 97 per cent. This means that the IPOs of mainland Chinese firms 'left $25 billion on the table'. Unsurprisingly, both in Hong Kong and in the mainland, applications for share allocations typically vastly exceeded the number of shares available. This has provided large opportunities for 'spinning', by which well-connected entities and individuals obtain privileged access to the shares issued in IPOs. Well-connected insiders have made huge personal fortunes from this near risk-free chance to 'gamble on the stock market'.

The national Gini coefficient for China's income distribution rose from 0.28 in the early 1980s to 0.50 in 2005. In 2007, the World Bank estimated that the size of the Chinese 'middle class', defined by a global standard, totalled 56 million, which amounts to just 4 per cent of the total population. It is estimated unofficially that the top 1 per cent of the population account for 61 per cent of household wealth, and that the top 0.1 per cent of households account for 42 per cent of total household wealth. The World Bank estimated that in 2004 over 500 million Chinese people lived on less than $2 per day and around 100 million lived on less than $1 per day. In 2007, it dramatically re-estimated China's national product, reducing its estimate in terms of PPP dollars (purchasing power parity) by no less than 40 per cent. As a result it tripled its estimate of the number of people living on less than $1 per day (in PPP dollars) to 300 million.

The Chinese government is fully aware of the dramatic rise in inequality and injustice since the 1980s. It is working hard to devise policies that deal with the surging contradictions of the market economy. It emphasizes the need to use the market to achieve desirable ends. However, it recognizes the need to regulate the market in the overall social interest. At the core of its philosophy, which has taken shape in recent years, is the attempt to construct a 'harmonious society'. It regards the provision of 'positive freedom' for all members of society as the bedrock of a good society, with ethics at its foundation. In order to address the widening income disparity between town and countryside, between 2002 and 2007 the government rescinded the agricultural tax and introduced substantial subsidies for the main agricultural products, as well as for agricultural machinery and superior seeds. These measures had a large impact on rural incomes.

In 2007, the 17th Party Congress emphasized the importance of speeding up reforms to improve access to welfare services, especially in poor areas and among disadvantaged groups of the population. The government's overall philosophy is to 'guarantee people's basic needs': 'Only by appropriately spreading the fruits of economic development among the people can we win their support and maintain social stability' (Wen Jiabao 2008). The government has promised to improve the provision of medical services for the rural dwellers. China has begun to promote a new type of rural cooperative medical insurance, which covered 86 per cent of all counties by 2008. It is building a system of health clinics in every village, and creating a rural medicine supply network 'in order to ensure that rural residents have access to safe, effective, convenient, and reasonably priced medical and health care services'. The major communicable diseases, such as AIDS, tuberculosis and schistosomiasis, are now treated free of charge.

The government is working through several channels to improve the social safety net for urban residents, including improvements to the basic old-age pension system, unemployment and medical insurance. By 2007, there were 200 million urban residents participating in basic old-age insurance, 54 million more than in 2002. By 2007 also, 180 million urban residents participated in basic medical insurance, double the number in 2002. This scheme 'mainly covers major illnesses'. The government provides targeted assistance for the poor segments of the urban population. It has determined to set up a nationwide basic minimum cost of living allowance system for all residents, through a combination of contributions from both the local and the central government: 'Setting up a basic cost of living allowance system for all urban and rural residents has great and far-reaching significance for promoting social fairness and building a harmonious society' (Wen Jiabao 2007). The government is devising policies to address the housing difficulties of poor urban dwellers. It is giving priority in housing development to housing for low- and middle-income families. It is accelerating the construction of low-rent housing for poor families.

The government is paying close attention to resolving the disadvantages experienced by rural migrant workers and their families in the cities, attempting to overcome their position as second-class citizens. It has announced measures to ensure that children from poor families and children of rural migrant workers in cities enjoy the same access to compulsory education as other children of urban dwellers. It is developing an old-age insurance system and is working to upgrade the social safety net for rural migrants working in the cities, including medical insurance for major diseases.

The various measures taken by the government since 2002 to improve social welfare for poor people have had a large effect. However, the challenge to social stability posed by the global financial crisis is deep.

In the 1990s, there was a large-scale decline in employment in state-owned enterprises, with up to 50 million people losing their jobs. While there were many protests, overall social stability was not under threat. The protests were mainly economistic in nature, seeking financial redress within the context of the existing system. The laid-off workers were mostly able to acquire their apartments at below-market prices, which provided a cushion to their wealth and their sense of security. They mostly received some form of severance pay and a stream of income in the form of unemployment or retirement pay, from some combination of their employer and the local government. They mainly possessed a level of skill that enabled them to move into alternative employment, albeit of a less secure and less well-paid nature. They had a strong local network of relationships that facilitated their move into alternative employment, including the employment opportunities in the web of second and third tier non-core businesses of their former employer. Their enterprises were deeply embedded in the local political economy and worked hard with the local government to ensure that the restructuring process minimized social disturbance. The restructuring process took place over many years in the context of a fast-growing economy and was widely distributed across the country.

The present situation is different. Even under the worst scenarios imaginable, the number of migrant workers who may lose their jobs in the export sector in the next 1–2 years is unlikely to exceed the number who lost their jobs in the state-owned enterprises in the late 1990s. However, the number could well total several tens of millions, especially if the indirect impact is included. The migrants have only a minimal asset cushion. They have limited skills which might enable them to find alternative employment. They are highly geographically concentrated. The impact is likely to take place over a much shorter time period, and it will do so against the background of an economic crisis and severe decline in the overall rate of economic growth. The migrants are not 'citizens' of the local society, lacking a 'hukou' (household registration), which greatly reduces the incentive of the local authorities to find solutions to their unemployment difficulties. The fast-increasing protests are mostly oriented against the factory owners, who are mainly based outside China and have only limited roots within the local political economy. The protests have already assumed an intensity and a class nature that is quite different from those of the laid-off workers from state-owned enterprises.

Implications for China in the global recession

The impact of the global recession upon China over the next 6–18 months will be heavy due to China's decision to engage deeply with the international economy under the policy of 'reform and opening up'. Seventy per cent of China's total exports (direct plus net re-exports through Hong Kong) go to the OECD countries, which face a severe downturn in consumer expenditure. In addition, China's exports to the primary commodity-producing countries will also be affected negatively by the collapse of world commodity prices. It is likely that China's export growth in 2009 will fall to negligible levels and may even become negative. This is a tremendous macro-economic shock after the sustained explosive growth of exports over the last two decades. This is the first time during the era of 'reform and opening up' that the economy has received a shock of this magnitude. Few people in China's policymaking circles had anticipated such a situation.

The global recession significantly increases the possibility of socio-political instability. China's minister of public security issued a series of warnings in November 2008 about the threat posed by the deteriorating export situation to the employment of millions of migrant workers. On 24 November he warned that 'there were lots of social problems affecting stability under the current circumstances'. He urged local officials to be 'sober-minded and fully realize the importance and urgency of safeguarding social stability'. At the end of November China's minister of human resources and social security warned: 'The current situation is grim and the situation is still unfolding. Since October, our country's employment situation has been affected along with changes in international economic conditions.'

The possibility of socio-political instability is increased due to the geographically concentrated nature of the impact of the downturn in global demand for Chinese exports. The key export-oriented areas contain the workplace of a huge number of rural–urban migrants in low-skilled or unskilled occupations. Should such instability occur it would drastically change international perceptions of China, and thereby affect the flow of foreign investment into the country. It would also tend to increase the incentive for capital to flow out of China through the many channels by which this can take place, despite official controls on capital movements.

The impact of the fall in demand from the OECD countries is likely to be even more severe due to the high degree of integration with the global economy of a small number of key areas, notably the Yangtze River delta, which includes Shanghai, Southern Jiangsu and Northern Zhejiang provinces, and the Pearl River delta in Guangdong province. These areas have been the 'engine' for China's economic growth under the policies of 'reform and opening up'. Together they account for 28 per cent of China's GDP, 58 per cent of its FDI (41 per cent for the Yangtze River delta and 17 per cent for the Pearl River delta) and 66 per cent of its exports. They will receive the full force of the global recession.

The Yangtze River delta benefited greatly from export-led economic development, especially in the years after China joined the WTO. Foreign firms dominate the region's surging exports, which are 30 per cent greater than those of South Korea and twice those of Taiwan. With an almost limitless supply of bank loans enterprises expanded rapidly, relying on large-scale borrowing to fund their growth. But now the region faces profound challenges from the global financial crisis. The crisis has brought most of the delta's leading enterprises to the verge of bankruptcy. Shanghai sits at the heart of the Yangtze River delta. In September 2008 its industrial growth rate (year-on-year) slumped to just 6 per cent. In the first three-quarters of 2008 the year-on-year profits of large-scale enterprises in the delta's major exporting cities of Nanjing, Ningbo and Shanghai declined by 44 per cent, 31 per cent and 8 per cent respectively.

In Guangdong province since 1979 GDP has grown at an annual average rate of 14 per cent. In the first three-quarters of 2008 export growth slumped, during which time around 7,000 exporting firms disappeared from the province's customs records. In the toy industry alone, more than 3,600 toy factories in the province shut between January and July 2008. The massive export base in Dongguan, on the border with Hong Kong, reported that it expected 9,000 factories to close by the spring of 2009 with the loss of 2.9 million jobs. In early November Guangzhou railway station was thronging with an estimated 150,000 migrants each day going out of the region to look for work.

The impact may also be felt through a slowdown in the growth rate, or even an absolute decline of FDI inflows into China from global companies due to their reduced profits, reduced credit from global banks, and a slowdown in their export growth from China. The effect of this will also be highly concentrated spatially. Between January and September 2008 the volume of FDI in Shanghai fell by 20 per cent year-on-year. Zhejiang's provincial government revenue fell by 7 per cent in the first three-quarters of 2008. In the same period the value of contracted FDI fell precipitously in key areas at the heart of the Yangtze River delta, including a decline of 20 per cent in Jiaxing, Huzhou and Shaoxing, 63 per cent in Taizhou and 80 per cent in Zhoushan.

The collapse of the Chinese stock market, the sharp fall in Chinese property prices, the fear arising from the global financial crisis and the global recession, and the possibility of an economic crisis in China, make it likely that there will be a still further increase in the marginal propensity to save for ordinary Chinese people. The level of income of Chinese people is still very low. In 2006, at the official rate of exchange, the average per capita income of Chinese urban dwellers was $2.9 per day, while for rural dwellers, it was just $0.9 per day. Moreover, the distribution of income and wealth has become extremely uneven during the period of 'reform and opening up'. The efforts to build up a welfare safety net and re-balance growth towards poorer people, especially towards the countryside, are in the early stages. Chinese people still have a high incentive to save in order to ensure some degree of guarantee of household welfare, and the incentive to do so can only increase due to the global crisis. This will tend to slow down the growth of domestic demand.

The global recession is likely to affect seriously the balance sheet of Chinese financial institutions. It is even possible that a serious banking crisis might develop. The impact on the banking sector might occur through several channels.

Firstly, there are direct losses resulting from the international operation of China's big financial institutions. Hong Kong is a point of particular vulnerability due to the absence of supervision by mainland supervisory bodies and the difficulty that Hong Kong's regulators have in supervising the internal workings of mainland entities operating in the territory. During the Asian financial crisis it was revealed that mainland entities in Hong Kong had borrowed as much as $70 billion, a large fraction of which was invested in the Hong Kong property and stock market during the 1990's asset bubble, which collapsed during the crisis. Only through drastic action to allow Guangdong International Trust and Investment Corporation (GITIC) to go bankrupt were the demands of international creditors kept at bay, and severe consequences for the whole Chinese financial system avoided. This action was termed 'cutting the trees to save the forest' (kan shu jiu lin). In November 2008 it was reported that the China International Trust and Investment Corporation Pacific (CITIC Pacific) had lost around $2 billion on its investments in foreign exchange derivative markets. It was reported also that China Steel Construction and China Railway Construction Corporation, which are both listed in Hong Kong, had substantial losses arising from their foreign exchange investments. These large losses may be merely the tip of the iceberg.

The operation of Chinese financial institutions in international markets beyond Hong Kong also poses significant risks. As of September 2008, leading Chinese financial institutions had substantial holdings of US assets, the value of which has fallen heavily. Bank of China (BOC) held $3.274 billion of US subprime mortgage-backed securities, $1.379 billion in Alt-A mortgage-backed securities, and $4.337 billion of non-agency mortgage-backed securities, for a total of $8.99 billion. China Construction Bank (CCB) held $244 million of US subprime mortgage-backed securities, $191 million of Lehman Brothers–related debts, and $1.512 billion of securities connected to Freddie Mac and Fannie Mae. It was preparing to write down $673 million. The Industrial and

Commercial Bank of China (ICBC) held $1.207 billion of US subprime mortgage-backed securities, $605 million of Alt-A mortgage-backed securities, $55 million in structured securities, for a total of $1.867 billion. China Investment Corporation (CIC) is estimated to have lost between $40 million and $80 million from its investment in the Reserve Primary Fund, which was affected by Lehman Brothers' bankruptcy, and it also made losses from its investments in Blackstone and Morgan Stanley. The losses incurred by the State Administration of Foreign Exchange (SAFE) from its investment loss in Washington Mutual (WAMU) are unknown. In addition, Ping An Insurance Group is estimated to have lost $1.3 billion from its investment in Fortis Group holdings, and China Development Bank has made large losses on its investment in Barclays Bank.

Secondly, the possibility of a banking system crisis may be increased through the continued impact of political pressure on lending by financial institutions, especially, but not exclusively, at the local branch level. The effect of such decisions on bank balance sheets will be compounded by the effect of the domestic economic downturn. When the water level falls, the rocks will appear (*shui luo shi chu*), as was the case in the Asian financial crisis. As economic growth slows down, non-performing loans are likely to increase. The effect will be most pronounced in the areas that are most deeply integrated into the international economy. If economic growth declines substantially, then many investment decisions which were justified by high rates of growth and short payback periods will become loss making. In addition, if growth declines the likelihood of excess capacity will increase in both the export-oriented industries and also in the industries that supply them with capital goods and current inputs. This will also tend to increase losses at marginal enterprises in those sectors.

Thirdly, the collapse of the stock market and the decline in real estate prices will affect banking sector profits. This will arise due to the fact that as much as 25–30 per cent of bank loans in recent years have been made to property developers and construction companies. In addition, many large state-owned enterprises have been heavily involved in investment in the stock market and the property sector, the decline in which will damage their profitability, and reduce their ability to service their debts to the banking sector.

On 9 November 2008 the government announced a huge $586 billion package of spending over the next two years. Some of this will be on power plants, highways and other projects that were already in Beijing's 2006–2010 investment plans. However, it appears likely that the stimulus will result in a net addition of around $350 billion on top of previously planned spending over 2008–2010, or the equivalent of around 5 per cent of China's GDP. The government also announced an increase in export rebates for nearly 4,000 products and the Ministry of Finance announced a reform of the value added tax, which would enable enterprises to benefit from a tax deduction of around $8 billion.

The package identified ten sectors on which to focus: low-cost housing; rural infrastructure; national transportation infrastructure including railways, highways and airports; medical care and education; environmental protection and conservation; support for national innovation and industrial restructuring; rebuilding in earthquake-hit areas; income support, especially for the rural population and for urban low-income residents and pensioners. The central government will allocate around $150 billion and the rest will come from local governments and society, following the same 1:3 proportion as was the case with the massive investment applied during the 1998 Asian financial crisis. Ways to help local government finance the package are under discussion with one possibility being to allow the issuance of local government bonds.

The fiscal implications of the slowdown in the Chinese economy are serious. The share of government revenue in GDP fell from 31.1 per cent in 1978 to just 13.5 per cent in 2000, which placed China on a par with those former planned economies which experienced 'state desertion' after the collapse of communism. Through hard effort, the share crept up, reaching 18.6 per cent in 2006, which is still a low share compared to most developing countries. The impact of the global financial crisis will threaten these hard-won gains.

The spending package will have a large impact on demand. However, such a large investment in infrastructure cannot be put into effect instantly. Infrastructure projects are typically of long gestation, even in China. Only a part of the impact of this investment will be felt in the next 6–18 months. Moreover, it is questionable how much additional infrastructure China will need in the immediate months ahead if the country faces a large-scale economic slowdown. It is even possible that it may move quickly into a situation of short-term excess capacity in sectors such as ports and airports, and perhaps even in the power generation and highway sectors. In November 2008, it was reported that year-on-year power generation fell for the first time in a decade. Substantial excess capacity was reported in China's major airlines.

Conclusion

Since the 1970s the global economic system has become ever more deregulated, following an ever-widening application of the Washington Consensus approach to economic policy. Under the impact of the global financial crisis, the world stands poised to move into a new era of greatly increased economic regulation.

Over the past 30 years, China has become ever more deeply integrated into the global economy. The degree of integration has continued to increase in recent years, with the foreign trade ratio rising to 67 per cent in 2006, an extraordinarily high ratio for a country of China's size. This provided China with large benefits from comparative advantage and the export of labour-intensive manufactures. However, it also meant that the economy and society have become highly vulnerable to the impact of a downturn in demand from the OECD countries.

There is a high possibility of a 'hard landing' for the Chinese economy in the next 6–18 months as the Chinese unbalanced growth model comes under severe pressure due to the gathering force of the global recession. The year-on-year industrial growth rate plummeted from 19 per cent in October 2007 to 8 per cent in October 2008. The prospect is for stagnant exports in 2009, following two decades of high-speed growth. The full impact of the global financial crisis upon the real economy of the OECD countries has only just begun to come into play. The year-on-year growth rate of GDP may fall to under 6 per cent, which would present a severe policy challenge. The social instability caused by the large-scale job losses among migrant workers is likely to pose a much larger threat than that experienced in the late 1990s among the workers in state-owned enterprises.

In trying to deal with the coming impact of the global recession, in the short term the Chinese government will need to focus its policy work closely on the core parts of the country that are the most deeply integrated into the international economy, especially the Yangtze and Pearl River deltas. It is in these areas that the likely effects of the hard landing will be felt most sharply. The government will need to adopt a comprehensive package of ameliorative and preventive measures to deal with the coming difficulties in these areas. The Yangtze and Pearl River deltas are criss-crossed with complex water control facilities. If a dyke bursts at its most vulnerable point, in the face of the 'rising water level' of the global economic crisis, the central government will need to ensure that it 'piles the sandbags to save the dyke and prevent it bursting':

Zhu lei sha dai,	筑垒沙袋
Jia gu di ba,	加固堤坝
Fang zhi jue kou,	防止决口

The shocks that are being delivered to the Chinese system of political economy due to the global financial crisis are exceptionally severe. The key question is whether the 'umbrella' of increasing social welfare is sufficiently strong to withstand the shocks that will be delivered to China in the period immediately ahead.

The severity of the challenge was recognized fully by Premier Wen Jiabao in his article in *Qiu Shi* on 1 November 2008:

> 2008 is the most difficult year in recent years and maintaining high growth is the top priority. We must be crystal-clear that without a certain

pace of economic growth, there will be difficulties with employment, fiscal revenues, and social development...and factors damaging social stability will grow.

By the turn of the millennium, China's social welfare system had been substantially dismantled and most welfare spending came from individuals' personal payments. Since 2002 the Chinese government has worked hard to reverse the tide and construct a 'harmonious society'. Under this philosophy, it is intended that in the long run the model of China's political economy will be re-balanced away from the path followed since the early 1990s. The objective is to redistribute income towards the poorer segments of society, especially towards those in the rural areas and towards the lower strata of the income distribution in the urban areas, including the migrant workers, as well as moving towards a more energy efficient path of development. These policies have already had a powerful effect, but they are still in their early stages of implementation. The package of emergency measures announced by the Chinese government in November 2008 will accelerate the process. These improvements in social security measures reduce the country's vulnerability to economic shocks. Paradoxically, if the implementation of these measures is sped up by the global financial crisis, this may provide the opportunity to accelerate the re-balancing of China's growth model towards one that is more sustainable over the long term, through increased orientation towards social justice and domestic demand, and through increased energy efficiency.

Notes

1 It is widely thought that China's purchase of US government debt was a key factor in the US asset bubble, through its impact on US interest rates. In the crude populist version of this view, China's savings caused the global financial crisis. In fact, the holdings of the oil-exporting countries and other Eastern economies greatly exceed those held by China. Indeed, it was not until November 2008 that China's holdings of US government treasury bills, notes and bonds exceeded those of Japan. Even the UK's holdings of US government debt is no less than three-fifths of that held by China.

2 In the west of England the Bristol Channel narrows into the Severn Estuary. As the incoming high tide is confined within an ever-narrower channel the water level rises into a steep wave, forming the 'Severn Bore'. 'When the bore comes, the stream does not swell by degrees, as at other times, but rolls in with a head foaming and roaring as though it were enraged by the opposition which it encounters' (Thomas Harrel 1824).

3 Martin Wolf is deputy editor of the *Financial Times*, and author of the best-selling book *Why Globalization Works*.

Chapter 2

RE-BALANCING IN THE FACE OF
THE GLOBAL FINANCIAL CRISIS (2):
NOVEMBER 2011

1. China: From the Asian Financial Crisis to the Global Financial Crisis

Impact of the Asian financial crisis

It is widely thought that the Asian financial crisis of 1997–98 had no substantial impact on China, due to the fact that China did not have capital account convertibility. In fact, China was highly vulnerable to financial contagion, which entered the Chinese domestic system through Hong Kong, and made its impact upon neighbouring Guangdong province.

During the course of China's economic reforms the economies of the Pearl River delta and Hong Kong became more and more closely interconnected. In the mid-1990s, a speculative 'frenzy' developed over the prospects that the region offered for capital from both within and outside China. Behind the speculative boom lay the lure of explosive growth rates in Guangdong province, especially in the Pearl River delta. Foreign investors who bought into 'red chip' companies in Hong Kong, supported by mainland state 'parents', bought bonds of 'government-backed' mainland companies from Guangdong and provided them with commercial loans, as they considered that these investments offered a virtually risk-free method of achieving high returns. From within China also, capital poured into the region attracted by the 'concept' of local-government-backed investment vehicles in townships and cities in China's fastest-growing and most capitalistic province.

'Moral hazard' was involved in most aspects of the crisis.[1] There was moral hazard in relation to the deposits made by Chinese investors in the non-bank financial institutions in Guangdong, which were thought to be supported by the local government. There was moral hazard in relation to the loans from international financial institutions, which believed that the Chinese government would simply step in to support their 'own' institutions, no matter how poorly they made investment decisions. There was moral hazard in relation to the behaviour of the Chinese borrowing institutions, which believed that they were 'too big to fail' in relation to the Guangdong government (GITIC and GDE) or the local government (the local non-bank financial institutions). There was moral hazard in relation to those who borrowed from these institutions, as they believed that they would never be called upon to pay back 'dad's money' (*aye de qian*).

During the Asian financial crisis huge problems emerged in Guangdong's leading non-bank financial institutions (NBFIs), Guangdong International Trust and Investment Corporation (GITIC) and Guangdong Enterprises (GDE), both of which were owned by the Guangdong provincial government. The insolvency of these enterprises attracted great international attention, not least because they had total debts of around $11 billion. If the Chinese government stepped in to ensure that their debts were met in full, foreign investors would expect that the other Chinese international trust and investment companies and red chip companies also would, with the support of the Chinese government, repay their debts in full. In addition, a crisis emerged in the small-scale local NBFIs of Guangdong province, which was largely hidden to the outside world. A large number of the rural financial associations, the urban credit cooperatives and many of the rural credit cooperatives were revealed to be insolvent. This stimulated 'bank runs' across the whole province, and widespread social disorder as angry depositors were unable to withdraw their deposits.

Surviving the crisis involved an intense policy effort by both the Guangdong and the central governments. It was a day and night battle in the midst of immense pressure on all sides, both from within and from outside China. In January 1998 the Chinese central government appointed Wang Qishan as executive vice governor of the province. He had been governor of CCB since 1994. The central government coordinated closely with the Guangdong government in formulating the responses to the crisis.

Fine considerations of moral hazard needed to be weighed against immediate issues of system survival. It was often necessary to take decisions that had problematic consequences in terms of moral hazard in order to prevent the rapid spread of social and political instability. In the face of the Asian financial crisis, the Chinese government took a sequence of three inter-related policy measures ('the three steps', or *san bu zhou*) to solve the crisis in Guangdong's financial institutions and prevent the spread of contagion to the rest of the country. These were: first, the bankruptcy of GITIC, second, the restructuring of GDE, and third, the restructuring of over 800 local non-bank financial institutions. The Guangdong provincial government, supported by the central government, took two years to resolve the payment crisis across Guangdong.

In the midst of the raging fire the steps taken were the only way in which to ensure system survival and stop the contagion from the Asian financial crisis spreading deep into the Chinese financial, social and political system.

The Asian financial crisis was a shocking lesson of the destructive power of a badly regulated global financial system. The crisis caused deep discussion and profound reflection among Chinese policymakers. Writing in July 1998 Zheng Bijian considered that the Asian financial crisis 'serves indeed as a rare teacher for us without paying too much in tuition fees' (Zheng Bijian 2011). He noted that in 1991 Deng Xiaoping had pointed out that 'finance is the core of the present day economy'. The explosion of global financial markets had been facilitated by comprehensive liberalization of the operating environment for banks with headquarters in the developed economies and greatly stimulated by the tremendous advances in information technology.

The experience of Guangdong in the Asian financial crisis provided a profound lesson for China's policymakers as they planned the country's strategy for financial reform in the coming years. China was able to avoid disaster by highly astute and extremely difficult policy choices in the face of intense pressure from outside the country, as well as from different domestic interests at many different levels. The successful resolution of the crisis provided a breathing space for the leadership. It gave it time to undertake the necessary reforms in the country's financial system.

The Asian financial crisis, including its impact on Hong Kong and Guangdong province, shocked China's policymakers. The State Council held its first Financial Work Meeting in November 1997, and by the time China entered the WTO in 2001 significant steps had been taken to reform the state-owned banks. However, fundamental issues of corporate governance had not been resolved. The level of non-performing loans (NPLs) was still alarmingly high and the structures that produced new NPLs had not been changed fundamentally.

Following China's entry to the WTO, there raged a fierce argument about the path of reform for the SOE banks. Many domestic and international economists argued that the SOE banks were incapable of being turned into globally competitive financial firms without privatization and fully opening the sector to international competition. They argued that the giant domestic banks were being retained as state-owned entities mainly to serve the vested interests of the ruling bureaucracy and in order to keep alive the state-owned industrial enterprises. An intense struggle developed around the desirability of keeping the big four banks as single, unified entities. A substantial body of academic opinion both within and outside China argued for 'increasing competition' by splitting each of them into several smaller entities. The same voices typically argued also for the privatization and break-up of the state-owned enterprises in other sectors, and for the state to abandon an industrial policy dedicated to building a group of global champion firms.

In February 2002, the State Council held the second Financial Work Meeting. This took place in the immediate wake of China joining the WTO amid turbulent debate about the path of bank reform, and was accompanied by intense pressure from both internal and external lobby entities. The central government determined to continue along and deepen the reform path outlined five years previously. In the following few years a comprehensive set of measures was introduced to transform the main state-owned banks, including financial restructuring and establishing joint shareholding companies, constructing a robust corporate governance structure, introducing strategic investors, upgrading IT and risk control systems, flotation in capital markets and shareholding diversification.

Structural transformation

In the early 1990s few people outside China could imagine the extraordinary structural transformation that China would experience in the following two decades. Between 1990 and 2009 China's GDP growth rate was almost 11 per cent per annum compared with less than 3 per cent per annum in the high-income countries. In 1995 China's GDP (at market prices) was the eighth largest in the world, but less than one-tenth of that of the USA. By 2009 it was the third largest, and 35 per cent of that of the USA. In terms of PPP dollars, by 2009 China was the world's second largest economy, 65 per cent of that of the USA (WB 2011). In just a decade, between 1998 and 2009 China's share of world manufacturing output tripled from 5.9 per cent to 18.6 per cent.

Population is at the heart of development. It has been calculated that spending on family planning is five times more effective at cutting carbon dioxide emissions than conventional low-carbon technologies. China's 'one-child' policy has radically slowed the growth of the country's enormous population and hugely affected the population's age structure. Between 1980 and 2015 China's population will have expanded by 42 per cent, increasing from 977 million to 1.38 billion. In the same period, India's population will grow from 673 million to a predicted 1.23 billion, an increase of 83 per cent. India's efforts to control population growth have failed. China's one-child policy has been a striking success in controlling the country's population growth. If China had followed India's path, it would have an extra 405 million people by 2015 compared with the predicted population. These 'missing millions' are an enormous, if unintended, contribution to controlling global warming.

The structure of residence and employment has shifted radically since the early 1990s. Between 1990 and 2009 China's official urban population rose by 321 million people and the share of total population rose from 26 per cent to

47 per cent (SSB 2010). The numbers employed in the urban areas increased from 170 million to 311 million, rising from 26 per cent of total employment to 40 per cent of the total. If the unofficial rural–urban migrants are included the transformation in the structure of residence and employment would be even more dramatic.

The living standard of both the urban and rural population was transformed between 1990 and 2009 (Table 2.1). Life expectancy rose from 68 years to 73 years, a remarkably high level for a developing country. The improvement was made possible by major developments in health provision, such as the attendance of skilled staff at births. Infant mortality and maternal mortality rates fell sharply between 1990 and 2009. There was a remarkable advance in education at all levels. China's high educational attainment from primary through to tertiary level provides a robust foundation for all aspects of China's modernization in the twenty-first century, including engagement in public debate about China's development pattern, which has been greatly facilitated by the revolution in information technology.

Table 2.1. Transformation of the livelihood of Chinese urban and rural population

	1990	2009
Whole population		
Life expectancy at birth (years)	68	73
Births attended by skilled staff (%)	50	99
Infant mortality rate (no./1,000)	37	17
Maternal mortality rate (no./1,000 live births)	110	38
Access to improved water (%)	67	89
Access to improved sanitation (%)	41	55
Promotion rates (%):		
primary to junior secondary	75	99
junior secondary to senior secondary	41	86
senior secondary to higher education	27	78
Population living on less than $1.25 per day (million) (a)	683	208 (2005)
Population living on less than $2.0 per day (million) (a)	961	474 (2005)
Urban population		
Engel coefficient	54.2	36.5
Average per capita housing space (sq. metres)	13.7	31.3
Average per capita food consumption (kgs):		
grain	131	81
fresh vegetables	139	120
edible oil	6.4	9.7

(*Continued*)

Table 2.1. Continued

	1990	2009
meat and aquatic products	32.9	47.3
fresh eggs	7.3	10.6
milk	4.6	14.9
fruit	41.1	56.6
Ownership of consumer durables:		
washing machines	78	96
refrigerators	42	95
colour TVs	59	136
air conditioners	negl.	107
water heaters	30	83
microwaves	negl.	66
computers	negl.	57
mobile phones	0	181
Rural population		
Engel coefficient	58.8	41.0
Average per capita housing space (sq. metres)	17.8	33.6
Average per capita food consumption (kgs):		
grain (unprocessed)	262	189
fresh vegetables	134	98
edible oil	5.2	6.3
meat and aquatic products	14.7	26.9
milk and milk products	1.1	3.6
eggs and egg products	2.4	5.3
fruit	5.9	20.5
Ownership of consumer durables:		
washing machines	9.1	53.1
refrigerators	1.2	37.1
air conditioners	negl.	12.2
motor cycles	1.0	57
mobile phones	negl.	115
colour TVs	5	109
computers	0	7

Source: SSB (2010), except for (a) which is from WB (2011).

A major contribution to people's welfare was also made by improvements in nutrition, with substantial increases in per capita consumption of eggs, aquatic products, milk and fresh fruit (SSB 2010). Although China's level of meat consumption per person also increased substantially, it is still far below that of the high-income countries. The spread of domestic and commercial refrigeration as well as other improvements to the food distribution and processing system meant that there was less wastage of food on its journey from the farm to the final customer. Between 1990 and 2009 the share of food consumption in household expenditure declined from 54 per cent to 37 per cent in the cities and from 59 per cent to 41 per cent in the countryside, reflecting the large rise in average living standards.

Between 1990 and 2009 in the cities the average housing space per person rose from 14 sq. metres to 31 sq. metres, and in the countryside the amount increased from 18 sq. metres to 34 sq. metres. Tremendous progress occurred in the ownership of consumer durables in both urban and rural areas. The widespread diffusion of washing machines, refrigerators, air conditioners, water heaters, microwave ovens and colour TVs made an enormous impact upon the quality of daily life for the vast majority of the urban population and a large fraction of the rural population. The revolution in information technology had a profound impact on the whole population. By 2009 there was near universal use of mobile phones and ownership of computers was spreading very rapidly. By 2009, 30 per cent of the population were internet users (WB 2011). These advances represented a tremendous increase in the quality of life for most people.

Integration with the global political economy

Since the early 1990s China has become ever more deeply integrated into the international economy. In 1995 China was only the world's tenth largest exporter, with smaller exports even than Belgium. By 2009 China had become the world's largest exporter, with exports that were more than double those of Japan. The share of foreign trade in China's GDP rose from 10 per cent in 1978 to 49 per cent in 2002 and by 2006 it had reached 67 per cent, which is an exceptionally high ratio for a continental-sized economy (WB 2008). A huge number of the country's workers are reliant on exports. Energy imports have become critically important for China's modernization. China's reserves of oil and gas are far smaller than were once hoped. China has just 1.5 per cent of the world's natural gas reserves and a mere 1.1 per cent of its oil reserves. The growth of China's oil and gas consumption has increasingly outpaced the growth of domestic production (BP 2011). By 2010 net oil imports amounted to 59 per cent of China's total consumption, and the prospect is for this to keep rising. Energy security has become ever more important in China's international relations.

Since the early 1990s the global business system has gone through comprehensive restructuring. In almost every sector a small group of giant companies with leading technologies and brands has emerged, which between them command 50 per cent or more of the global market in that sector. Pressure from the cascade effect has stimulated comprehensive restructuring of the value chain surrounding core companies and intense industrial concentration has occurred far down in the supply chain. The companies that have established themselves at the core of the global business system almost all have their headquarters in the high-income countries. Global brands and global technical progress are concentrated in a small number of firms from high-income countries that stand at the apex of the global business system. One hundred giant firms, all from the high-income countries, account for over three-fifths of the total R&D expenditure among the world's top 1,400 companies (BERR 2008). They are the foundation of the world's technical progress in the era of capitalist globalization. The leading firms with their headquarters in the high-income countries have 'gone out' into the rest of the world to establish global business systems. The outward stock of foreign direct investment (FDI) rose from $2.1 trillion in 1990 to $19.0 trillion in 2009 (UNCTAD 2010).

Among late-industrializing countries China has been uniquely open to FDI. The Chinese operations of multinational firms constitute a key part of their global business system. According to UNCTAD (2011) the inward stock of FDI in China in 2010 stood at around $579 billion. However, the Chinese Ministry of Commerce estimates that the total stock of inward FDI in 2011 was $1,048 billion (SSB 2011, 240). Multinational firms account for around 28 per cent of the country's overall industrial value added and for two-thirds of the overall value added in high-technology industries. They account for 55 per cent of China's total exports and for 90 per cent of exports of high-technology products (Nolan 2012). The numbers of people working in China within the value chain of foreign firms is extremely large and beyond easy calculation. Global firms in a wide range of sectors, including automobiles, IT hardware and software, consumer electronics, beverages, quick-service restaurants, media and marketing, branded footwear and clothing, exert a deep influence on the pattern of Chinese development, including both the direction of technical progress and the patterns of consumption.

The level and nature of China's energy consumption has become a major aspect of its international relations. The share of coal in China's electricity generation rose from 71 per cent in 1990 to 79 per cent in 2009, while the share of the main renewable source of energy, hydro power, fell from 20 per cent to 17 per cent in the same period (SSB 2010). China's total energy consumption rose from 863 million metric tons (oil equivalent) in 1990 to 2.1 billion tons in 2008. China's CO_2 emissions rose from 2.6 billion metric tons in 1990 to 6.5 billion in 2007, making China the world's largest CO_2 producer.

However, in 2007 China's CO_2 output per person was still only 40 per cent of that of the high-income countries as whole, and just 26 per cent of that of the USA (WB 2011).

The population in the high-income countries is deeply alarmed at the potential impact upon the global ecology of the large increases in energy consumption and CO_2 production in prospect for developing countries, especially China and India: 'A level of per capita income in China and India comparable with that of industrialized countries would, on today's model, require a level of energy use beyond the world's energy resource endowment and the absorptive capacity of the planet's ecosystem' (IEA 2007). The International Energy Agency expresses the hope that 'all countries – China, India, the industrialized countries and the rest of the global community – cooperate on moving quickly towards a genuinely sustainable lifestyle' (IEA 2007). However, it is hard to imagine that technical progress will be sufficiently rapid or that the pattern of consumer demand will alter sufficiently to enable China to follow a completely new development path of 'clean and sustainable' economic development. It is hard to imagine that it would agree to bind itself to a target for CO_2 emissions that prevents its population from enjoying the advances in income that the already developed countries have achieved.

Pattern of development

China's pattern of development has relied on a high and rising rate of investment. Between 1995 and 2009 the rate of gross capital formation rose from 42 per cent of GDP to 48 per cent while the share of household consumption fell from 43 per cent to 35 per cent. China's rate of capital formation is now far above that of almost every other country. Heavy industrial output is the foundation of the capital goods sector. This is itself intensive in the use of other heavy industrial products, including transport and electricity. It has proved extremely difficult to shift the Chinese economy away from this 'unbalanced growth path'. China has 20 per cent of the world's population. However, in 2010 its share of total world consumption reached 53 per cent for cement, 48 per cent for iron ore, 47 per cent for coal, 45 per cent for steel and lead, 41 per cent for zinc and aluminium, 39 per cent for copper and 35 per cent for nickel. China is now the world's largest importer of a wide range of non-renewable commodities.

No country in history has experienced such explosive growth of the urban population as China since the 1980s. The total floor space completed for all types of building across the whole country rose from 196 million sq. metres in 1990 to 2.2 billion sq. metres in 2008 (SSB 2009). Building construction projects on the scale undertaken in China require vast amounts of steel, cement and glass, all of which are highly energy intensive. The energy efficiency standards of China's urban buildings are still 'low and varied' and it is anticipated that China's urban building codes will not reach the level of today's OECD countries until 2030 (IEA 2007). Few of China's residential tower blocks are being built with centrally provided heating and cooling systems. Instead, most residential blocks use air conditioners attached to the outside of the building, which is a far more energy-intensive way to control the temperature in buildings. The huge increase in the stock of air conditioners and appliances has led to a large rise in demand for electricity. The energy efficiency of Chinese household appliances is still considerably less than the average in the OECD.

China has moved inexorably down the path of truck-based freight, which has been followed in the high-income countries. Between 1990 and 2009 the length of railways increased by 38 per cent while the length of highways increased almost fourfold (SSB 2010). In the same period the number of trucks increased from 3.7 million to 13.7 million. In 1990 China's railways carried more than three times the amount of freight as China's highways (in terms of ton-kilometres), but by 2008 China's highways carried one-third more freight than the railways (SSB 2010). Between 1990 and 2009 the number of public transport vehicles per 1,000 urban residents rose from 2.2 to 11.1, and China's metro network has grown at high speed over this period. However, in the same period the stock of passenger vehicles increased from 1.6 million to over 48 million (SSB 2010). Trucks and cars do not only require fuel in order to function. Their manufacture requires steel, aluminium and plastics, and they require roads to run on, which require cement, tarmac, steel and aggregates.

Behind all of the above developments lies demand for electricity. China's electricity output has grown at around 10 per cent per annum since 1990 (SSB 2009). China has been extraordinarily successful at eliminating 'energy poverty'. Electricity output per person rose from 157 kwh in 1990 to 2,790 kwh in 2009 (SSB 2010). By 2005, 99 per cent of the population had access to electricity (IEA 2007). However, in 2005, China's electricity output per person was just 26 per cent of that of the high-income economies and a mere 18 per cent of that of the USA (WB 2008).

Conclusion

China's rapid growth since the early 1990s has been based heavily on bank lending, which has re-channelled savings towards investment mainly through state-owned enterprises and state infrastructure projects. The growth model has been 'unbalanced', relying on a high and rising investment rate and rapid growth of heavy industrial output. It has relied heavily on FDI to achieve technical progress. It has involved deepening interaction with the global political economy, leading China's economy to be increasingly dependent on the international economy and increasingly engaged with the international political system. Despite the low share of consumption in GDP the high rate of growth has permitted a comprehensive improvement in the well-being of the mass of the Chinese population. The rapid growth in infrastructure has contributed to the improvement in public welfare through advances in housing, electricity supply, information technology, sewage and water supply, public transport, hospitals and schools. The overall development achievement in China since the early 1990s represents an extraordinary success for the country's public policy.

China's success in public policy can be seen most vividly in relation to the USSR and India, each of which provides a relevant comparison for China. China's approach to the 'transition' from a Stalinist political economy to a market economy consisted of 'groping for stones' to cross the river under Communist Party leadership in the sharpest contrast to the USSR's approach of a 'Big Bang' in both political system reform and economic reform. In the late 1980s and early 1990s almost all Western analysts believed that the Russian approach under Gorbachev and Yeltsin was greatly superior to that of China under Deng Xiaoping. Between 1990 and 2000 Russia's GDP fell by 4.7 per cent per annum while China's grew by 10.6 per cent per annum. Today, the adult mortality rate in Russia is 396/1000 for males and 147/1000 for females.[2] In China the comparable figures are 147/1000 and 88/1000 respectively (WB 2011).

China's authoritarian political system, with 80 Communist Party members at its core, has proved far superior to India's open, corrupt and noisy democracy in terms of devising policies to stimulate growth and improve the well-being of the mass of its citizens. Between 1990 and 2009 the average annual growth rate of China's GDP reached 10.7 per cent compared with 6.8 per cent in India. China was able to control population growth much more effectively than India and it achieved a far more effective expansion of its infrastructure, including transport, housing, information technology and energy supply (WB 2011). In 2008 China's electricity supply per person was 2,455 kwh compared with just 566 kwh in India, and China has 29 internet users per 100 people compared with 5.3 in India (WB 2011). In 2009 the container traffic in China's ports totalled 106 million 20-foot equivalent units (TEUs) compared with 7.9 million in India. In China between 1980 and 2009 the number of people living on less than $1.25 per day (in 2005 PPP $) fell from 835 million to 208 million, while in India the number rose from 420 million to 456 million (WB 2011). Life expectancy in China stands at 73 years compared with 64 years in India.

The contrast between the public policy success in China and the public policy failure in both the USSR and India is one of the most important issues of the age, and the contrast is fully appreciated by the mass of the Chinese population. The contrasting performance of public policy underpins any evaluation of China's political economy and the prospects for China in the teeth of the storm in the international financial system.

2. The Crisis in the OECD Countries

Origins of the crisis

The era of capitalist globalization witnessed a revolutionary transformation of financial firms (see Chapter 3). An explosive round of mergers and acquisitions resulted in the creation of a small group of super-large global financial firms, such as HSBC, Citigroup, JPMorgan Chase, Bank of America, Deutsche Bank, UBS and BNP Paribas. These giant firms benefit from large economies of scale in procurement of information technology systems, from risk spreading across a wide range of economies, from their attractiveness to high quality human resources in the sector, and from high standards of corporate governance imposed by regulators in high-income countries. Across large swathes of Latin America and Eastern Europe, international banks undertook extensive acquisitions, and dominated the financial sector.

Since the 1970s advances in mathematical modelling of financial markets contributed to greatly improved capabilities for risk evaluation in financial institutions. A wide range of new financial products were devised, notably the vast array of derivative products that distributed risk far more deeply in the financial system. The IMF believed that as a result of these developments the global financial system had become so 'thick' as to be nearly indestructible. The global financial system survived a succession of financial crises in this period, including the Mexican, East Asian, Russian, Long-Term Capital Management and Argentinean crises, as well as the shock of 9/11, which appeared to be a vivid testimony to its greatly improved robustness.

Financial markets have an inherent propensity towards speculation and asset price bubbles. Keynes famously warned of the dangers of financial speculation:

> Speculators may do no harm as bubbles on a steady stream of enterprise. But the position is serious when enterprise becomes the bubble on a whirlpool of speculation. When the capital development of a country becomes a by-product of the activities of a casino, the job is likely to be ill-done. (Keynes 1936, 159)

The initiating factor in speculative bubbles is typically the optimism generated by a feeling that the economy has entered a 'new era'. No period has created a greater sense of a new era than the recent era of capitalist globalization.

Once the speculation process gets under way, powerful positive feedback loops drive markets ever higher. Monetary expansion is endogenous to the economic system. In spite of the efforts of monetary authorities to control the supply of money, it has tended to expand in periods of asset price inflation to finance speculation. Credit is extended on the basis of increased asset prices, which supports a still further increase in asset prices, and still further credit expansion.

The period of capitalist globalization witnessed an unprecedented global asset bubble, fuelled by the huge increase in money in its myriad forms. The asset bubble was self-reinforcing, with speculation driving up asset prices in a self-reinforcing cycle around the world. In the high-income economies the asset price bubble, especially that in property, formed the foundation for an explosive growth of credit to fund both speculation and current consumption. The index of real house prices in the high-income countries rose strongly from the early 1970s until around 1990 (Table 2.2). After slumping in the early 1990s, the real house price index rose steeply from the late 1990s (McKinsey 2009, 11). By 2007 the index of real house prices (1970=100) had risen more than fourfold in the UK, more than threefold in Spain, Belgium, the Netherlands, Ireland and Australia, and had more than doubled in Norway, Canada, France, the USA and Italy. Among the high-income countries Germany was alone in experiencing a fall in real house prices between 1970 and 2007.

Table 2.2. Real house price index, 2007 (1970=100)

UK	420	Canada	240
Spain	390	France	240
Belgium	370	USA	215
Netherlands	320	Italy	215
Ireland	300	Sweden	150
Australia	300	Japan	105
Norway	270	Germany	80

Source: McKinsey (2009, 11).

During the era of capitalist globalization, the economic system became increasingly 'financialized'. Between 1980 and 2007 financial assets in North America, Europe and Japan tripled from around $53 trillion to $158 trillion (McKinsey 2009). The ratio of global financial assets (including equities, private debt securities, government debt securities and bank deposits) to global GDP rose from 109 per cent in 1980 to 343 per cent in 2007. In the United States financial assets rose from 194 per cent of GDP in 1980 to 442 per cent in 2007.

The volume of new 'money' that was created through speculation in newly developed financial instruments dwarfed the 'real' economy. At the end of 2006 central bank 'power money' amounted to around 10 per cent of global GDP, but amounted to just 1 per cent of total global liquidity. So-called 'broad money' amounted to around 122 per cent of global GDP, but still accounted for only around 11 per cent of total global liquidity. Securitized debt amounted to around 142 per cent of global GDP, but still accounted for just 13 per cent of total global liquidity. Derivatives, which didn't exist 20 years ago, now amounted to no less than 802 per cent of total global GDP, and fully 75 per cent of total global liquidity. In other words, 'cyber money' now amounted to more than eight times the total global output of goods and services.

As financial markets were progressively deregulated after the 1970s, so the extent of debt increased. Total global borrowing, comprising all loans, forms of credit and debt securities, rose by 70 per cent from 2000 to 2008, when it reached $131 trillion (McKinsey 2009). In the United States, the share of non-government debt (including non-financial corporates, households and the financial sector) in GDP rose from 130 per cent in 1980 to 220 per cent in 2000, reaching 290 per cent in 2007 on the eve of the financial crisis. In the UK non-government sector debt increased from 60 per cent of GDP in 1987 to 220 per cent in 2000, before climbing to 450 per cent in 2007. In the eurozone, non-government debt rose from 159 per cent of GDP in 2000 to 230 per cent in 2008.

The long-developing debt and asset bubble profoundly affected the behaviour of both households and firms. In the USA, household borrowing rose from around 50 per cent of personal disposable income in the late 1970s to 90 per cent in 2000, before reaching 130 per cent on the eve of the financial crisis. Based on the enormous increase in asset prices and 'wealth', increased household debt provided a source of social stability and a stimulus to aggregate demand.[3]

The global financial system was now deeply integrated across national boundaries, far more deeply even than the integration of production systems. The massive extent of repackaging and sale of debt meant that debt was far more deeply distributed throughout the economy. This provided a source of stability and enhanced the ability of the financial system to ride out relatively small-scale crises, but it meant that the whole global financial system was far more susceptible to a giant financial crisis should it erupt.

The transition from primarily national to global markets was not accompanied by a strengthening of international regulatory governance.

The IMF, the institution that was supposed to guide the global financial system, was described as a 'rudderless ship in a sea of liquidity'. The problem for regulators was exacerbated by the fact that the global financial system developed instruments of such great complexity and at such a high speed, that no one understood how to regulate the whole system, even assuming that the political will existed to do so.

In 2008 the global financial crisis erupted. At the core of the Washington Consensus was the confidence that unregulated financial markets based on privately owned banks were self-correcting. The financial crisis demolished this 'market fundamentalist' view. In May 2008 the former managing director of the IMF, Horst Kohler, delivered a devastating verdict on liberalized global financial markets, likening it to Mary Shelley's Frankenstein monster:

> The complexity of financial products and the possibility to carry out huge leveraged trades with little capital have allowed the monster to grow… The only good thing about this crisis is that has made clear to any thinking, responsible person in the sector that international financial markets have developed into a monster that must be put back in its place.

In October 2009, Jean-Claude Trichet, president of the European Central Bank, told banks that they should return to 'their traditional role of providing a service to the real economy': 'looking back on the crisis we can see that there was a dramatic shift in focus in large parts of the financial sector – away from facilitating business, trade and real investment towards unfettered speculation and financial gambling.' Monsieur Trichet said that this change 'above all requires a change in the mentality within the financial industry itself'.

OECD in the financial crisis

Private sector deleveraging

Without the existence of the welfare state and massive countermeasures taken by the governments of the G20 countries in 2008–2009 the global economy would have suffered a catastrophic collapse, possibly even exceeding that of the Great Depression. However, the asset price inflation of the preceding decades had enabled a large fraction of households in the high-income countries to enjoy increases in consumption far beyond the increase in their earnings, achieved through the mechanism of greatly increased debt. It will take many years for the impact of deleveraging to work its way through the economies of the high-income countries. House prices in the US are 30 per cent below the peak and it is estimated that losses on owner-occupied housing have reduced household wealth by more than $7 trillion over the past five years (Larry Summers, in the *FT*, 24 October 2011). There is no sign of house price recovery in other high-income countries. Even though interest rates for borrowers are low, the continuing decline in house prices means that in 'real' terms, deflated by house prices, they are strongly negative. After decades of unlimited optimism about the increase in household wealth, the shock on household psychology is profound and is still far from reaching its conclusion in terms of the long-run pattern of household savings and investment.

Unemployment

The wealth effect upon consumer demand arising from the fall in house prices has been compounded by high levels of unemployment. Across the high-income countries unemployment rates have risen alarmingly, and even more so if involuntary short-time working is included. Across the whole OECD the unemployment rate rose from a 25-year low of 5.6 per cent in 2007 to a 25-year high of 8.5 per cent in July 2009. In this period, 15 million people lost their jobs. A further 10 million people had lost their jobs by the end of 2010.

Within the EU-27 area by the third quarter of 2011 there were over 23 million people unemployed, amounting to 9.7 per cent of the workforce (Directorate-General 2011). In countries that had already enacted fiscal consolidation, with large cuts in government spending, levels of unemployment were especially high. In September 2011 the rate of unemployment reached 23 per cent in Spain, 14 per cent in Ireland, 13 per cent in Portugal, and over 8 per cent in the UK.

The governments of the high-income countries have comprehensively failed in one of their central duties, to provide employment and hope for their young people. Across the EU the level of unemployment among young people (aged 16–24) rose from around 15 per cent in 2007 to over 21 per cent in the third quarter of 2011 (Directorate-General 2011). By the second quarter of 2011 the level of youth unemployment had reached 45 per cent in Spain, 43 per cent in Greece, 30 per cent in Ireland, 29 per cent in Portugal, 23 per cent in France, and 21 per cent in the UK.

In the USA, the official number unemployed rose from 6.8 million (4.4 per cent) in late 2006 to 14.9 million (9.7 per cent) in August 2009, an increase of over 8 million people. The level of unemployment has hovered at around this level since then. In the third quarter of 2011, 9.6 per cent of US full-time workers were unemployed. However, in addition to those officially unemployed, more than 9 million Americans are working part-time for economic reasons, making a total of around 15 per cent of the working population who are wholly unemployed or involuntarily working part-time.

The numbers of long-term unemployed in the US (defined as those who are jobless for more than 26 weeks) rose from around one million in 2007 to nearly 7 million in 2011, rising from 5 per cent of those unemployed to nearly 45 per cent (*FT*, 14 October 2011).

Consumption and investment

Across the high-income countries households have reduced consumption. Household consumption in 2011 had barely recovered to the pre-crisis level. In countries that had enacted severe reductions in government spending, such as the UK, Spain, Portugal and Ireland, the fall in private consumption was especially severe. Sustained stagnation, or even falling personal consumption, has profound effects on consumer psychology and patterns of saving.

During the global financial crisis transnational corporations (TNCs) have sustained their revenues and profits by increasing their investment in developing countries, which have continued to grow robustly. However, both large and small businesses have greatly reduced their investment in the high-income countries. During the depth of the crisis in 2008 and 2009 investment collapsed across the high-income countries (Table 2.3). However, in the aftermath of the crisis, investment growth remains extremely weak, far below the pre-crisis levels.

Table 2.3. Annual changes in consumption and investment (%): EU forecast, November 2011

	2002/6 (a)	2007	2008	2009	2010	2011 (b)	2012 (b)
Private consumption volume							
Euro area	1.5	1.7	0.4	−1.2	0.9	0.5	0.4
UK	2.9	2.7	−1.5	−3.5	1.1	−1.1	−0.5
USA	3.0	2.3	−0.6	−0.9	2.0	2.1	1.3
Japan	1.2	1.6	−0.7	−1.9	1.8	−0.6	0.6
Total investment volume							
Euro area	2.1	4.7	−1.1	−12.2	−0.5	2.0	0.5
UK	3.7	8.1	−4.8	−13.4	2.6	−1.6	1.1
USA	2.8	−1.6	−5.8	−16.0	1.8	3.3	4.0
Japan	−0.1	−1.2	−3.6	−11.7	−0.2	0.2	4.0

Source: Directorate-General (2011).
Notes: (a) annual average
         (b) forecast

Financial markets

'Markets' are treated in the press and in economics textbooks as though they are an abstract force like water or air. In fact, 'markets' are composed of real flesh-and-blood institutions, whose *raison d'être* is to make a profit by using money to make money. From the ancient world through to the present day the power, lure and destructive power of usury has been feared by philosophers in all cultures.

The 'markets' today consist of multiple overlapping entities that determine activity in commodity, equity, foreign exchange and fixed income markets. These institutions include commercial banks, insurance companies, hedge funds, asset management firms, pension funds and investment banks. There is a host of diverse institutions that compose the loosely regulated 'shadow banking sector'. The Financial Stability Board (FSB) estimates that the assets of non-bank credit intermediaries in Australia, Canada, Japan, Korea, the UK, the eurozone and the US, grew from $27 trillion in 2002 to $60 trillion in 2008. After falling to $56 trillion in 2008, they once again increased to $60 trillion in 2010. The US has by far the largest shadow banking sector with $24 trillion of assets. The FSB estimates that the shadow banking sector accounts for 25–30 per cent of the total financial system (*FT*, 23 November 2011). Towers Watson (2010) estimates that the world's largest asset managers, almost all from the high-income countries, have around $62 trillion of assets under management. The world's hedge funds are now larger than ever, with a total of over $2 trillion of funds under management (*FT*, 20 April 2011), which can be leveraged to produce a much greater impact upon 'markets'.

As we will see in more detail in Chapter 3, each of the key sectors has a small number of players who dominate the market and set the pattern for the much greater number of smaller firms in the sector. Around 5 per cent of hedge funds control two-thirds of the sectors' total assets. Twenty-five giant global banks account for 45 per cent of the assets of the top 1,000 global banks (*The Banker*, Global 1000, July 2010). The top ten banks account for 77 per cent of the London Foreign Exchange (*FT*, 1 September 2010). The top 50 firms, all from high-income countries, account for 61 per cent of the total funds managed by the world's top 500 asset managers (Towers Watson 2010).

Financial sector deregulation was the core of the Washington Consensus. Under this philosophy, which increasingly dominated policymaking in the high-income countries from the 1970s onwards, global financial institutions were allowed ever-greater freedom of operation. These same forces from within the high-income countries are now killing the real economic system from which they sprung, in a form of economic system suicide in which the Frankenstein monster devours its creator.

Government debt

The social welfare safety nets in the high-income countries prevented levels of real income falling as they did during the Great Depression. However, they required greatly increased outlays from government budgets. In addition, the various emergency measures taken by the high-income countries helped to produce a level of government debt that is unprecedented in peacetime. Government expenditure has risen to an unprecedented level, and the severe economic downturn has had a widespread damaging effect on government revenues.

One option is for the high-income economies to reduce government debt through large increases in personal progressive taxation. These could be used to fund spending on infrastructure, including transport, green energy, health and education. In other words, the response to the crisis would be analogous to wartime, reinforcing the society's collective identity and mutual support systems in order to face the crisis together. Such a path requires visionary political leadership to present the hard choices clearly to the electorate, to lead the electorate to understand better the long-term nature of the challenges they face, and to lead them towards a collective response to these challenges. Such a path requires visionary political leadership that can see beyond short-term sound bites, internet 'blogs' and 'twitter' comments, which lead to risk-averse political behaviour at the top of the main political parties in the West. It requires the kind of political leadership demonstrated by Churchill or Stalin in the face of national catastrophe during World War II.

However, the political leadership in the West has failed to show such leadership. There are severe political constraints on increases in taxation using progressive taxation. In the face of these constraints, during the financial crisis the ratio of government debt to GDP rose rapidly. Between 2007 and 2010 gross government debt in the eurozone increased from 66 per cent of GDP to 86 per cent and in the UK it increased from 44 per cent to 80 per cent (Directorate-General 2011). Governments that failed to implement policies to achieve balanced budgets were targeted one by one by the 'markets', forcing up the cost of borrowing and threatening national governments with bankruptcy. Sovereign debt ceased to be risk free. A succession of national governments felt that they had no choice other than to achieve 'fiscal consolidation' through greatly reduced government spending. High-income countries that failed to establish credible plans for reducing government debt were punished by the 'markets', and forced to pay a large premium on their debt. It was widely thought that bond yields of above 7 per cent for 10-year government debt were unsustainable.

Major government spending cuts have been introduced in Ireland, Portugal, Spain, Greece and the UK. At the time of writing (November 2011) France and Italy have both just announced similar measures. In the summer of 2011 the US Congress was locked in a prolonged battle over government spending. The Republicans successfully resisted President Obama's proposals to substantially raise government spending in order to stimulate demand. The widespread measures to reduce government spending have had a direct effect on final demand as well as a strong indirect effect through continued high levels of unemployment and the impact on consumer confidence.

Growth prospects

During the golden era of capitalist globalization from the 1980s until the global financial crisis, the average annual growth rate of GDP in the high-income countries was around 2.5 per cent per annum. On the eve of the global financial crisis, almost all experts and government officials looked forward to a continuation of the Great Globalization Boom.

In 2009 output fell sharply across the high-income countries (Table 2.4). The combination of social welfare measures and increased government spending after the G8 meeting in April 2009 arrested the decline and in 2009–2010 output recovered strongly in the high-income countries. Most economists and official forecasters believed that the crisis was over and that the high-income countries would return to the growth trajectory of pre-2008. Instead, the combination of continued private sector deleveraging, continued high levels of unemployment and the effect of fiscal consolidation depressed growth. In 2011 it is likely that GDP growth in the high-income countries will be only around one-half of that in 2010, and the IMF forecasts that it will grow at around the same 'anaemic' rate in 2012. Output in the high-income countries in 2011 is only fractionally higher than in 2008, and, in Italy, Spain, Japan and the UK, GDP in 2011 is still substantially below that level (IMF 2011a). In its World Economic Outlook of September 2011, the IMF warned:

> In the systemically important advanced economies, activity and confidence are still fragile, and a sudden increase in household savings rates remains a distinct possibility. If fiscal consolidation were suddenly stepped up further at the expense of the disposable income of people with a high marginal propensity to consume, these economies could be thrown back into stagnation… By the same token, if sound medium-term consolidation plans are not implemented, households and businesses may take an increasingly dim view of future prospects and drastically raise their savings rates. *The result would be a lost decade of growth.* (IMF 2011a, 13–14)

Table 2.4. Growth in the advanced economies (% change, year-on-year)

	2009	2010	2011	2012
Advanced economies	−3.7	3.1	1.6	1.9
USA	−3.5	3.0	1.5	1.8
Euro area	−4.3	1.8	1.6	1.1
Germany	−5.1	3.6	2.7	1.3
France	−2.6	1.4	1.7	1.4
Italy	−5.2	1.3	0.6	0.3
Spain	−3.7	−0.1	0.8	1.1
Japan	−6.3	4.0	−0.5	2.3
UK	−4.9	1.4	1.1	1.6
World trade volume	−10.7	12.8	7.5	5.8
Imports				
advanced economies	−12.4	11.7	5.9	4.0
developing economies	−8.0	14.9	11.1	8.1
Exports				
advanced economies	−11.9	12.3	6.2	5.2
developing economies	−7.7	13.6	9.4	7.8

Source: IMF (2011a).

World trade collapsed in 2008, with total volumes falling by almost 11 per cent. In 2010 world trade bounced back robustly, rising by 13 per cent. However, in 2011 the volume of world trade has grown by just 8 per cent and is forecast to grow by a mere 6 per cent in 2012. High-income countries' imports grew by only 6 per cent in 2011 and are forecast to grow by just 4 per cent in 2012. Although the share of developing countries' exports to high-income countries has declined, more than two-thirds of developing countries' exports are to high-income countries. In the case of the Asia-Pacific region (excluding Japan) 74 per cent of exports are to the high-income countries (WB 2011). Exports from developing countries fell by 7.7 per cent in 2009 but grew by 14 per cent in 2010. However, their growth fell to 9.4 per cent in 2011 and they are predicted to grow by just 8 per cent in 2012.

Instead of achieving renewed growth which would allow government debt to fall in relation to GDP, the stagnation of GDP due to the combined impact of debt deleveraging and the sharp reduction in government spending led to a further increase in government debt relative to GDP, with little prospect in sight for a decline.

The outlook for the world economy contained in the IMF's September 2011 World Economic Outlook was bleak. However, within two months of its publication, the prospects for the global economy had darkened. In November 2011, the EU drastically cut its growth forecasts from those it had issued in spring 2011. Its forecast for real GDP growth in the euro area in 2012 was reduced from 1.8 per cent in the spring of 2011 to just 0.5 per cent in the autumn forecast (Table 2.5). The decline in predicted GDP was especially severe in those economies that had followed the IMF's advice by sharply reducing government spending. The EU's forecast of growth in the UK in 2012 was reduced from 2.1 per cent to 0.6 per cent, in Portugal from −1.8 per cent to −3.0 per cent, and in Spain from 1.5 per cent to 0.7 per cent. The EU report of November 2011 warned:

> If left unchecked, negative interactions between debt concerns, weak banks and slowing growth are likely to lead to a relapse of the EU economy into recession... The weakening real economy, fragile public finances and the vulnerable financial sector appear to be affecting each other in a vicious circle.

It concluded:

> We do not expect a recession in our baseline scenario. But the probability of a more protracted period of stagnation is high... A deep and prolonged recession complemented by continued market turmoil cannot be excluded.

Table 2.5. Real GDP growth (% per annum)

	2010	2011	2012 spring 2011 forecast	2012 autumn 2011 forecast
Euro area	1.9	1.5	1.8	0.5
Germany	3.7	2.9	1.9	0.8
France	1.5	1.6	2.0	0.6
Spain	−0.1	0.7	1.5	0.7
Italy	1.5	0.5	1.3	0.1
Portugal	1.4	−1.9	−1.8	−3.0
UK	1.8	0.7	2.1	0.6
USA	3.0	1.6	2.7	1.5
World	5.0	3.7	4.1	3.5

Source: Directorate-General (2011).

In the short period after the publication of the EU report the picture darkened still further. The crisis in Greece and Italy's sovereign debt raised the serious possibility of both Greece and Italy leaving the euro. This would have enormous consequences for the whole global economy, which would dwarf the impact of the collapse of Lehman Brothers. By mid-November yields on both Spanish and Italian 10-year government bonds were in the critical danger zone of 6.5 per cent to 7 per cent. In the week of 14–18 November the crisis spread from Italy and Spain to France and Austria (Table 2.6). The whole of the eurozone apart from Germany was now viewed as 'contaminated' for bond investors. These markets were widely viewed as 'broken and possibly beyond repair'. There were even small signs that the contamination was spreading to Germany (*FT*, 19 November 2011). The only hope for the resolution of the eurozone crisis was for the imposition of tight controls by Brussels over member states in order to enforce 'fiscal consolidation' enacted by technocratic governments such as that of Mario Monti in Italy. However, it is uncertain if this is politically feasible. Moreover, if it does turn out to be feasible, it will contribute to still more deflation of final demand within the eurozone. In the unlikely event that the eurozone is able to achieve a fiscal union along the lines advocated by Angela Merkel (*FT*, 25 November 2011), the result would be even tougher Brussels-imposed budget cuts across the eurozone, which would still further depress growth prospects in the region.

Table 2.6. Gross government debt relative to GDP (%)

	2007	2010	2011	2012
Euro area	66.3	85.6	88.0	90.4
Germany	65.2	83.2	81.7	81.2
France	64.2	83.2	85.4	89.2
Italy	103.1	118.4	120.5	120.5
Ireland	24.9	94.9	108.1	117.5
Portugal	68.3	93.3	101.6	111.0
UK	44.4	79.9	84.0	88.8

Source: Directorate-General (2011).

Gilt yields in the 'safe havens' of Japan, the UK and even the USA all reached historic low levels. However, these countries all had levels of government debt never seen before in peacetime as well as a massive overhang of private sector debt. It would not take much to trigger a panic over sovereign debt in these 'safe havens'. Increasingly, in the autumn of 2011, analysts' attention was turned towards the shocking possibility that the UK and the USA might not ultimately be 'decoupled' from the eurozone crisis. In late November 2011 the US congressional committee responsible for striking a deal on deficit reduction failed to reach agreement, which diminished the prospect for a fresh stimulus package (*FT*, 22 November 2011). In the UK the prime minister, David Cameron, admitted that the UK economy was stuck in a vicious downward spiral: 'High levels of public and private debt are proving to be a drag on growth, which in turn makes it more difficult to deal with those debts' (quoted in the *FT*, 22 November 2011).

The world economy is now in a far less robust state than in 2008. The leaders of the high-income countries have failed to achieve a cooperative solution to the crisis, which was itself the consequence of policies pursued by the high-income countries over the preceding three decades of the Washington Consensus. These problems were not those of a 'black swan' swimming unexpectedly into sight. They were fundamental to the nature of the liberalized free market system established during these preceding three decades, in which the domination of finance capital over the real economy grew ever greater. This fact was widely recognized by China's political leaders.

Conclusion

The bursting of the bubble of the golden age of globalization has had profound effects on the way in which the citizens of high-income countries view their governments and their political-economic system. The enormous power of giant banks and global businesses headquartered in the high-income countries combined to underpin the philosophy of the era of the Washington Consensus. The fundamental ideology was a belief in the superiority of free market capitalism in terms both of economic efficiency and the morality of freedom of choice. Behind these views was a belief in the practical and ethical superiority of the Western political system based on regular competitive elections contested by multiple political parties. This system delivered three decades of economic growth, but it contained deep systemic contradictions, including environmental damage, growing inequality of income and wealth, growing concentration of business power, and a financial system that dominated the rest of the economy. Politicians were held in increasing contempt. A generation of populist, media-friendly political leaders are now viewed as having sacrificed the long-term interests of citizens to short-term electoral gain.

3. China's Response to the Crisis

At the time of writing (November 2011) it seems highly likely that the high-income countries face, at best, the prospect of prolonged stagnation of output, high unemployment, static or falling real incomes, and great social and political dislocation. At worst, it is possible that they may enter a deep recession. The illusions of the 'green shoots of recovery' that permeated discussion in 2010 have disappeared, just as they did in Japan in the early phase of its 'debt depression'. If this is the case it will pose a considerable challenge for China. It is possible to construct both a pessimistic and an optimistic scenario for China's response in the months ahead.

Pessimistic prospect

Leadership

The evolving global system crisis is taking place at a time of leadership transition in China. When the global financial crisis erupted in 2008, the Chinese leadership team under President Hu Jintao and Premier Wen Jiabao was already well into its period in office. The severe intensification of the global financial crisis in the autumn of 2011 coincides with an exceptionally challenging period in China's political development. The handover of power to the 'fifth generation' of Chinese leaders is a protracted process. Indeed, the final outcome in terms of leadership positions may itself be affected by the way in which the global crisis affects China.

End of the Lewis phase of development

The prolonged global financial crisis has coincided with the fact that China may already have reached the end of the 'Lewis' phase of development. The 'Lewis' model has been centrally important in the analysis of the political economy of development. The model distinguishes between an early phase of development in which the supply of labour is 'unlimited' due to the existence of rural surplus labour, and a later phase in which urbanization and industrialization have absorbed the rural labour surplus. In the early phase the non-farm economy can expand using unlimited supplies of unskilled rural labour at a constant real wage. In the later phase, urban real wage rates and the share of wages in national income rise due to labour market shortage. The political economy of the developing country changes radically at the end of the first phase of development. China appears already to have entered the second phase of development. It has done so at an unusually early stage in its development, while average per capita incomes are still at the lower middle-income level. There is an abundance of evidence of increases in real wages for unskilled and low-skilled employment in the areas that are most deeply integrated into the global economy. The competitive position of these parts of China has declined in relation to other parts of the world, which are still

firmly stuck in the 'Lewis' phase of development, such as Bangladesh, India,
Indonesia and Vietnam.

Over-investment

Since the policies of 'reform and opening up' were introduced, China's
investment rate has risen ceaselessly. In 1990 China's gross capital formation
rate stood at 35 per cent, already a high level. Since then the rate has risen
to 48 per cent (WB 2011). This is far above the average level for developing
countries as a whole. In upper middle-income countries today the rate of gross
capital formation stands at 20 per cent, less than one-half of that of China.
China's capital productivity has fallen significantly. Increasing amounts of
capital have been needed to generate an incremental output. The incremental
capital–output ratio rose from 1.02 in 1990–2000 to 1.28 in 2000–2009
(Table 2.7). It is widely thought that the global financial crisis is coinciding
with a crisis in China's growth pattern. It is argued that China has come to
the end of 'extensive growth' based on the mobilization of huge amounts of
capital and that it must now turn towards 'intensive growth'. However, shifting
away from the previous pattern of growth is extremely challenging even in
propitious external circumstances. To achieve this transition in the growth
model in the midst of the global crisis may be even more difficult.

Table 2.7. Growth of investment and consumption in China and other developing
countries/regions

	GDP growth rate (% p.a.) (a)		Gross capital formation growth rate (% p.a.) (b)		ICOR (b)/(a)		Average per capita household consumption growth rate (at 2000 $) (% p.a.)	
	1990–2000	2000–2009	1990–2000	2000–2009	1990–2000	2000–2009	1990–2000	2000–2009
China	10.6	10.9	10.8	13.9	1.02	1.28	7.7	7.1
LIEs	3.1	5.4	5.5	8.7	1.77	1.61	0.5	2.2
MIEs	3.9	6.4	2.6	9.9	0.69	1.55	2.6	4.5
LA/C	3.2	3.8	5.4	5.0	1.69	1.32	2.0	2.9
S. Asia	5.5	7.3	6.5	12.4	1.18	1.70	2.6	4.8
SSA	2.5	5.1	4.6	8.5	1.84	1.67	0.6	2.4

Source: WB (2011, Tables 4.1 and 4.9).
Notes: ICOR: incremental capital–output ratio
          LIEs: low-income economies
          MIEs: middle-income economies
          LA/C: Latin America/Caribbean
          SSA: Sub-Saharan Africa

Impact of the crisis on demand for China's exports

In addition to the underlying supply-side difficulties that China faces, the demand-side of the equation has been altered radically by the global financial crisis. Under the IMF scenario of September 2011, import growth in the high-income countries was forecast to weaken sharply, slumping from 12.3 per cent in 2010 to 6 per cent in 2011 and falling to just 4 per cent in 2012 (see Table 2.3). However, the growth prospects for the high-income economies have worsened considerably in the subsequent two months. The possibility of a full-blown system crisis in the global financial system has increased. During the global crisis of 2008–2009 imports into the advanced economies collapsed, falling by over 12 per cent in 2009. This had an enormous impact on developing countries, especially China, due to its deep integration in the global economy. The areas that were the most deeply integrated, especially the Pearl River delta and the Yangtze River delta, were severely affected by the downturn in demand from the high-income countries, with heavy unemployment among migrant workers.

On the eve of the global financial crisis, China's foreign trade ratio was exceptionally high. In 2006, China's merchandise trade had reached 67 per cent of GDP, compared with 34 per cent in South Asia, 43 per cent in Latin America and the Caribbean and 23 per cent in the USA (WB 2008). Although the share of foreign trade in GDP has declined, in 2010 it still stood at over 50 per cent of GDP (SSB 2011), an exceptionally high ratio for a continental-sized economy. The share of China's exports that go to the high-income countries is exceptionally high. In 2008, 75 per cent of its exports went to high-income countries, compared with 65 per cent of exports from Latin America and the Caribbean, and 66 per cent of those from South Asia (WB 2010). If demand from the high-income countries slows down seriously, or, even worse, if it declines substantially, as it did in 2008–2009, the consequences for output, employment and social stability would be very serious in the areas of China that are most deeply integrated into the global economy.

Financial crisis

China's financial system faces a set of interconnected difficulties that many analysts believe will end in a full-blown financial crisis. This would not only affect China, but also the whole global economy, since China's position has become extremely important in the structure of the global economic system. Positive views of China have been centrally important in sustaining confidence in the international economic system.

IMF evaluation. In November 2011 the IMF published its Financial System Stability Assessment of China (IMF 2011b).[4] The assessment added to international pessimism about the prospects for the Chinese financial system. The IMF warned of the possibility of a sequence of 'medium-to-high' risks that faced the Chinese banking system in the next three years (IMF 2011b).

The *Financial Times* commented: 'Years of gradual reform and the government-led transition towards a more commercially oriented system saw improvements in the structure, transparency and oversight of financial institutions. But the risk is that, in a global sector changing at lightning speed, reform is not moving fast enough' (*FT*, 18 November 2011). The IMF highlighted a 'steady build-up of vulnerabilities' in Chinese banking, which stem from 'the government's iron grip on its banking sector'. The report draws attention to the growth of the shadow banking sector and 'distortions in capital allocation created by the government's dominant role in dictating bank lending policies'. In the view of the *Financial Times* 'Beijing must loosen its grip, not just on how banks lend, but also on interest rate and exchange rates': 'only this will make banks robust enough to face shocks similar to those that have convulsed the global financial system'.

The IMF warned that due to China's continuing high degree of integration with the global economy, stagnation or recession in the high-income countries would have a serious impact on the Chinese economy, causing growth slowdown and rising unemployment. This would be likely to adversely affect the balance sheets of China's banks, increasing the NPL ratio. The IMF also warned that if the international environment turned sharply for the worse, it would be extremely difficult to introduce another stimulus package of the size of that of 2008–2009. It warned that there was an inverse relationship between the speed of credit growth and the quality of bank assets. Chinese banks 'have limited ability to apply prudent risk management practices', which 'suggests potential credit risks'.

Local government investment platforms. Loans to local government investment platforms were a key vehicle through which the Chinese government channelled the greatly increased flow of credit during the financial crisis. It is estimated that by mid-2010 bank loans to the local government platforms amounted to 16 per cent of all loans and were equivalent to 23 per cent of GDP (IMF 2011b).

The corporate structure of the local government platforms is opaque and there is no serious academic study of their modus operandi. There is a widespread perception that the enormous increase in loans supplied to the platforms during the financial crisis helped to deepen the extent of corruption in China's local political economy. The IMF warns that the very rapid expansion of bank loans to the local government investment platforms 'creates sizeable risks of NPL build-up, as some projects may not generate sufficient returns to make loan payments' (IMF 2011b).

The terms of the loans to the platforms vary, with some of them not repayable until 2020. However, around two-fifths of the loans are repayable in the second half of 2011 and in 2012. If China's growth in 2012 is seriously affected by the global financial crisis, it will be much harder for the local government platforms to repay their debts to the main commercial banks, which may sharply increase the ratio of their NPLs.

The IMF warns that a sharper-than-anticipated correction in real estate prices would spill over into local infrastructure projects undertaken by the local government platforms. This would 'test banking system resilience, given high dependence on land collateral in local government finance platform funding' (IMF 2011b).

Shadow banking. China's shadow banking system has grown rapidly in recent years. The Chinese financial system is highly 'repressed' with strict control over the interest rate paid on deposits by the commercial banks. However, there are only limited alternative opportunities legally to invest savings, so the bulk of savings are deposited in the safety of the commercial banks. There are strict limits also on the interest rate charged on loans, which means that there is a high incentive to find other investment channels which can produce higher returns in the 'shadow' banking system, which includes trust companies, as well as 'min jian' (people to people) and SOE lending.

China's 'trust' companies have expanded rapidly in recent years. By the end of the 1990s there were several hundred trust companies. Following the massive restructuring in the early 2000s, trust companies were re-licensed from 2007 onwards. By 2010 there were 65 registered trust companies in China. Their terms of operation are wide. They bring together private banking, asset management and private equity operations, and 'include everything from lending to hedging and equity deals'. Demand for 'trust products' has soared because many have delivered returns of as much as 15 per cent, which is far above the official rate of interest on bank deposits. Real estate constitutes the largest single set of trust products, and typically yields a return of 12 per cent or more to investors (KPMG 2011). Most provinces and several large cities have their own trust company. There is close cooperation between the commercial banks and the trust companies. Moreover, several trust companies have been established by commercial banks themselves. The underlying assets of the trust companies are typically loans originated by the banks themselves which are packaged as securitized bank loan wealth products. The main driving force behind the growth of trust products has been the banks' desire to retain high net worth customers by offering them high yield products. There were around

RMB 7 trillion ($1,083 billion) in outstanding wealth management products, more than triple the level at the end of 2010, amounting to around 9 per cent of total Chinese bank deposits (*FT*, 30 June 2011). The rapid development of the trust sector and the banks' close involvement with it has aroused fears that it may involve risks for banks' balance sheets if the wealth products perform badly, for example, due to a decline in property prices.

The Chinese bank regulators are concerned that significant amounts of loans from commercial banks to individuals and corporate entities have found their way into the illegal credit system, attracted by the high rates of return. In parts of China where the private economy is more highly developed, the extent of '*min jian*' credit at high rates of interest has expanded greatly in recent years. If the economy encounters serious difficulties, repayment rates are likely to fall. It is hard to enforce repayment of illegal debt, and ultimately the balance sheet of the main commercial banks will be affected. In Wenzhou in 2011 a crisis erupted in the informal financial sector due to the fact that, faced with the economic downturn, borrowers often simply ran away from their debts to other parts of China or went abroad in order to escape.

SOE lending. It is widely known that non-financial SOEs systematically re-channel loans from the commercial banks through numerous channels into other sectors, especially real estate. Many SOEs in the non-financial sector have turned themselves into quasi-financial entities. This is another form of the Chinese domestic 'carry trade' borrowing at low interest from state banks and lending to other sectors or investing in non-core business, especially real estate, for much higher rates of return. The IMF pointed out that de facto financial holding companies are developing rapidly, with some of them 'investing in banks, securities firms and insurance companies' (IMF 2011b). It believes that this could increase risks both to the industrial and the financial sector due to 'lack of effective oversight'.

Housing bubble. Increased bank lending is the main channel through which the Chinese government has stimulated the economy during the global financial crisis. Between 2007 and 2010 lending from financial institutions rose by 83 per cent, from RMB 26.2 trillion to RMB 47.9 trillion while China's GDP rose by 51 per cent (SSB 2009 and 2011). The ratio of bank assets to GDP rose from 194 per cent in 2007 to 234 per cent in 2010 (IMF 2011b).

Direct lending by the banks for property development is tightly controlled by China's bank regulators, and loans to real estate companies typically amount to less than 8 per cent of the loans made by China's commercial banks. However, bank loans for mortgages are now an important part of bank assets. The IMF warned of the dangers of 'extraordinarily high bank lending to the real estate sector' (IMF 2011b). By December 2010, loans for real estate development and mortgages accounted for around 20 per cent of total bank loans. However, there is a high level of indirect exposure. In the five largest banks, 30–45 per cent of loans are backed by collateral, the majority of which is real estate (IMF 2011b).

Faced with financial system repression due to tight control of interest rates, a significant fraction of the stimulus package found its way into the property sector. It is widely thought that this fuelled a speculative bubble in the property market. Between 2007 and 2010 the total floor space of real estate under construction grew by 72 per cent, roughly in step with the increase in lending by financial institutions. The IMF estimates that from 2000 to 2010 the average price of housing per square metre more than doubled from around RMB 2,000 to almost RMB 5,000 in 2010 (IMF 2011b). Official data on property selling prices indicate that between 2008 and 2010 they rose by 32 per cent and the total value of real estate projects completed increased by 91 per cent between 2007 and 2010 (SSB 2011). Unofficial data suggest much higher increases in residential property prices in key cities, with prices per square metre more than doubling between 2005 and 2011 (January–August) in Beijing, Tianjin, Shanghai, Guangzhou and Shenzhen.

The speculative aspect of much of the property development can be seen by the fact that the annual completion rate of real estate construction fell from 38.1 per cent in 2000 to 32.2 per cent in 2007, before plummeting to 19.4 per cent in 2010 (SSB 2011, 195). By the middle of 2011 it is estimated that there were 65 million vacant properties (*FT*, 23 May 2011). In the view of many analysts 'China has the classic symptoms of a typical investment bust'. China's construction boom has coincided with 'the greatest level of bank lending in history'. In this view, although China has arrived at its property bubble by a different route, the end result will be the same as in the West.

In late November 2011 it was reported that in October property transactions had fallen by 39 per cent year-on-year in China's 15 largest cities (*FT*, 22 November 2011). It was reported that banks were 'often unaware that loans to state-owned enterprises had been funnelled into real estate subsidiaries'. It was also reported that China's bank regulators acknowledged that they had not taken into account the full impact of a large fall in property prices upon collateral, 'yet most collateral in the banking system is land or property, so a slump could force write-downs across the board' (*FT*, 22 November 2011). It was reported that these knock-on effects had been 'barely tested' in the stress test exercises conducted by the China Banking Regulatory Commission (CBRC).

If the pessimists are correct about the Chinese property bubble the consequences for the economic system would be extremely severe, since housing investment accounts for around 25 per cent of fixed asset investment, with a much greater eventual impact upon the related industries, such as steel and cement. It accounts for around 25 per cent of the country's steel output. Therefore, the impact of a property price collapse on bank balance sheets would be enormous, affecting them not only through their direct lending to the property sector but also through their lending to the local government platforms, to industrial and commercial enterprises, to the trust companies and through '*min jian*' lending. The IMF warns: 'Given the importance of the real estate sector for economic growth, an economic slowdown as a result of real estate correction could adversely affect the banking system's asset quality.' Moreover, local governments' ability to support the local government investment platforms via land sales and subsidies depends heavily on the real estate market. Fears about the Chinese banking sector have helped to depress Chinese bank shares. By July 2011 the Industrial and Commercial Bank of China (ICBC)'s share price on the Shanghai stock exchange had fallen by almost 20 per cent compared with the end of 2010, and Bank of China (BOC) had fallen by 26 per cent.

Optimistic prospect

Leadership

Although the intensifying global crisis is coinciding with the complex process of leadership transition in China, the transition process is being conducted smoothly, with a widely agreed set of procedures, and a clear indication of who will fill key positions in the new government. Moreover, the crisis is occurring after three decades of extraordinary policy success, and after a long and deep process of training and professional upgrading of China's government and party officials. In most key respects the capability of China's bureaucracy is much above that in the West and the internal debate and diversity of opinion is far beyond the imaginings of lurid Western accounts of the Chinese political system. Moreover, China's party and government officials are able to think in a long-term fashion that is impossible for Western politicians, who are driven by short-term electoral considerations.

End of the Lewis phase of development

The fact that the phase of economic development with unlimited supplies of labour may be coming to an end has been interpreted by most analysts in a negative fashion. However, shortage of labour has helped to stimulate a rapid growth of wages. In the period 2005–2010 real wages rose by an average of almost 12 per cent per annum, with the growth rate unaffected by the global financial crisis (SSB 2011, 124). This was a powerful form of 're-balancing' without the need for active government policy and without pressure from trade unions.

In the UK in the nineteenth century, real wages for manual workers began to rise from the 1840s onwards. Mass trade unions did not develop until the end of the century, long after real wages started to rise. The main influence was the exhaustion of the reserve army of rural surplus labour. In East Asian newly industrializing countries, exhaustion of the reserve of rural surplus labour in the 1970s radically changed the nature of the whole development process, shifting labour market power towards workers. It is likely that the same process is already under way in China. The speed with which this process has affected China has been exacerbated by the one-child policy, which has greatly reduced the size of the workforce today compared with what it would have been in the absence of this policy.

The relative early exhaustion of rural surplus labour will tend to intensify pressure on employers to move up the ladder of value added and employ more productive, capital-intensive methods of production. This pressure may help rather than hinder China's move towards becoming an upper middle-income country by 2030. The possibility for China to move up the value-added ladder is enhanced by the country's high level of educational attainment and by the high level of physical infrastructure, both of which have continued to advance rapidly during the financial crisis.

Human capital

The raw facts of China's educational progress are self-evident. By 2009, 78 per cent of the relevant age group were enrolled in secondary education in China, compared with 52 per cent in South Asia and 34 per cent in Sub-Saharan Africa. Twenty-five per cent of the relevant age group were enrolled in higher education in China compared with 11 per cent in South Asia and 6 per cent in Sub-Saharan Africa (WB 2011). China's educational system continued to make strong progress during the global financial crisis. The number of students enrolled in higher education increased by 19 per cent between 2007 and 2010, and the number enrolled in post-graduate education rose by 28 per cent in the same period (SSB 2011). In the same short period, the number of students studying abroad rose from 144,000 to 285,000 and the number of returned students increased from 44,000 to 135,000 (SSB. 2011).

Investment performance

As we have seen, China has generated an extraordinarily high growth of investment and the increments to capital formation have generated declining returns in terms of GDP growth. However, low- and middle-income countries as a whole have accelerated their rate of growth of capital formation, and have experienced more severe deterioration in their ICOR ratio than China has. Although China's growth of capital formation was sustained at a high rate, so too was the growth of household income per person. China's real household income per person almost quadrupled between 1990 and 2009. In middle-income countries household income per person roughly doubled in the same period and in low-income countries increased by around 50 per cent. As we have seen, from 1990 to 2009, real incomes in China increased enormously in almost every respect, far outpacing achievements in other developing countries.

Infrastructure expansion

The surge in infrastructure construction in China during the global financial crisis is widely regarded as delaying the re-balancing of the Chinese economy towards consumption. However, 'infrastructure' investment can have powerful positive effects on mass welfare. Expanding China's conventional and high-speed rail system, including greatly improved railway stations, has been an important component of the stimulus package. These have made a significant contribution to public welfare. Increased investment in telecommunications infrastructure, mass transit railway (MTR) systems, public bus systems, airports, roads, schools, hospitals and sports stadiums, all contribute to improved public welfare. During the financial crisis local government financing platforms channelled a large fraction of the loans they received from the banks into infrastructure projects that benefited the general public. The pace of completion of infrastructure projects in China is extremely rapid compared with other developing countries, let alone high-income countries, so that these investments have tended to have short gestation lags and quickly contribute to public welfare.

The advances in transport were remarkable during the global financial crisis. Between 2007 and 2010 the length of railways increased by 17 per cent and the length of highways increased by 12 per cent (SSB 2011, 616). Between 2007 and 2009 the stock of automobiles increased from 32 million to 61 million, almost doubling in just three years during the global financial crisis (SSB 2011, 634). Between 2007 and 2010 passenger traffic increased by 21 per cent on China's railways and 30 per cent on the highways (SSB 2011, 616).

The advances in information technology infrastructure were even more remarkable. Between 2007 and 2010 the number of mobile phone subscribers rose from 547 million to 859 million, while the number of internet users increased from 210 million to 457 million (SSB 2011, 646).

Housing

Between 2007 and 2010 the amount of real estate under construction surged from 2,363 million to 4,054 million sq. metres, an increase of over 71 per cent (SSB 2011, 195). Although completion rates declined, China's real estate boom during the global financial crisis provided a powerful stimulus to output and employment in the construction industry as well as in the closely related network of industries. The number of people employed in the construction industry increased from 31 million in 2007 to 42 million in 2010 (SSB 2011, 565). Despite house price inflation, the amount of residential floor space sold increased by one-third between 2007 and 2010 (SSB 2011, 198). In both the rural and the urban areas the amount of residential floor space per person continued its long-run increase, which directly improved welfare.

China's house prices have increased substantially in the past decade. Property development has been the most important single driver behind the large increase in wealth inequality. Given the limited range of other investment opportunities, a large proportion of investment funds has been attracted to the property sector. However, the rate of house price increase in most parts of China has been relatively muted compared with most Western countries in the years before the global financial crisis. The Chinese government closely monitored the housing market and introduced a wide range of regulations to contain the increase in house prices after 2007.

China has experienced a massive influx of population into the urban areas, and there is an extremely high income elasticity of demand for housing, both for first-time buyers and for those wishing to move up the property ladder. The rate of default on mortgage payments has been consistently low. Despite its many negative observations about the Chinese financial system, the IMF's evaluation of November 2011 is that the housing sector does not pose a major risk to the balance sheets of China's commercial banks.

Welfare and social stability

The intensity of the global financial crisis and the alarm it created over social stability provided the opportunity for the central government to increase spending that targeted the poorest and most vulnerable social groups. The increased public spending ensured that the compulsory nine years of schooling is free for both urban and rural children, with special measures to ensure educational provision for children of migrants. Rural students in compulsory education are now provided with free textbooks. The government guaranteed that by 2012 it would set up systems to guarantee basic medical services to all urban and rural dwellers. During the crisis it greatly expanded and improved the new rural cooperative medical care system. It set up a new national system to provide patients with access to safe and affordable drugs. It raised the monthly per capita cost of living allowance for urban and rural residents, and raised the basic pension benefits for retirees from state-owned enterprises. The proportion of the labour force covered by pensions increased from 33 per cent in 2007 to 46 per cent in 2010 (IMF 2011b). The near-universal availability of some form of secure, modern housing with access to piped water and sanitation makes an important contribution to social stability in China's cities compared with other developing countries, most notably India, in which a large fraction of urban dwellers live in subhuman conditions in shanty towns.

Global crisis and FDI

In the immediate wake of the global financial crisis, inflows of FDI into the developing countries slumped, falling by over one-fifth in 2008–2009 (UNCTAD 2011). In view of the fact that the developed economies face the prospect of a prolonged period of stagnation, developing economies offer the main avenue for multinational firms to increase their revenue and profits. In 2010 inflows of FDI into developing economies recovered to their level of 2007.

We have seen that FDI plays a vital role in China's modernization. China is the most dynamic market for global corporations. Although FDI inflows into China declined somewhat in 2008–2009, in 2010 they recovered to reach a level close to their previous peak in 2008, and 26 per cent above the level of 2007 (UNCTAD 2011). Although China's real wages are increasing significantly, China is now even better provided with infrastructure, which is vital for attracting FDI to China compared with other developing economies. For example, India lags far behind China in the provision of infrastructure. There seems little prospect of a shortage of FDI inflows hindering China's growth in the medium term.

Banking regulation

As we have seen, the deep impact of the Asian financial crisis powerfully stimulated China's financial sector reform. The crisis demonstrated the extreme dangers of financial globalization, in which the world economy had, in Zheng Bijian's words, 'almost turned into a casino', and the vastly increased volume of financial transactions was 'creating the conditions for a financial crash across the world'. Zheng Bijian observed soberly:

With modern Western financial theory guiding the international financial system, the leading developed countries in the West are working hard to promote financial liberalization free from control and urge developing countries to open their financial markets, while they themselves refuse to do something in order to prevent financial risks and curb excessive speculation.

In the face of intense pressure from international banks and institutions to progress rapidly with liberalization, China persisted with its own experimental, cautious approach to financial sector reform. The leading banks were reformed as a single entity (*zheng ti gai ge*). The state maintained majority ownership of the main banks with control over the appointment of the banks' leaders and direct control over the banks' lending policies. CBRC has exercised tight control over the banking sector, preventing the banking system from entering markets for more complicated and poorly understood financial products. The degree of regulatory control over the banking system is much greater than that exercised by Western bank regulators. The system produced financial repression and all the associated difficulties. However, it provided the Chinese government with the capability to control directly the supply of credit and provide a huge stimulus package through the banks in order that the Chinese economy could continue to grow robustly during the global financial crisis.

Throughout the global financial crisis, China's leaders have emphasized China's contribution to helping stabilize the global economy, while simultaneously stressing that the crisis was created by the Wall Street–driven policies of the Washington Consensus, not China's export surplus. They have always been aware that the crisis was likely to be long lasting and that it potentially constituted a critical turning point in the evolution of the global system of political economy. In November 2011 Wang Qishan, China's vice premier with responsibility for finance, warned: 'Now the global economic situation is extremely serious and, in a time of uncertainty, the only thing we can be certain of is that the world economic recession caused by the international crisis will last a long time' (reported in the *FT*, 21 November 2011).

The pressure arising from the global financial crisis is likely to intensify the efforts to reform the Chinese financial system in order to protect it from the damaging effects of the global financial and economic crisis. However, it is unlikely that the fundamental relationship of the Chinese state to China's commercial banks will alter. It is likely that China's commercial banks will remain tightly controlled by the Communist Party. The global financial crisis will greatly reinforce the political voice of those who realize the dangers of China's excessively deep integration with the global financial system for as long as the global system remains in its current chaotic state.

Shadow banking

There is no doubt that financial repression has contributed to the rapid growth of the shadow banking sector in recent years. However, the problem is less of a threat to the overall banking system than some lurid analyses suggest. The problem of debtors 'running away from their debts' is highly localized. It is especially prominent in areas in which private SME firms dominate the economy, with Wenzhou the outstanding example. These areas rely mainly on low-technology, labour-intensive industries. They have found it extremely difficult to make the transition to high-productivity, high-technology production. Areas that are more heavily reliant on large state-owned enterprises have not encountered this problem to anything like the same degree.

China's banking regulatory authorities closely monitor the shadow banking sector. For example, since the trust sector was permitted to return to life in 2007, CBRC has continually and closely monitored its behaviour. Newly established trust companies are all approved and regulated by CBRC, which has published a stream of regulatory requirements to guide the sector towards a more sustainable, lower risk business model. It bears little relationship with the much greater and poorly supervised trust sector that sprang into life in the 1990s, when there were as many as 1,000 such entities operating in a supervisory vacuum similar to that of Western shadow banking today.

Banking crisis

In June–December 2010 the IMF undertook its Chinese Financial Sector Assessment Programme (FSAP). Although the final report contained numerous critical observations about the Chinese financial system its overall evaluation was extremely positive. It observed that NPL levels had shrunk to a very low level, and the ratio had continued to decline between 2008 and 2010. The IMF's stress test concluded that even if NPL levels were to increase fourfold in two years, no bank would have a capital adequacy ratio of below the minimum requirements (i.e., 8 per cent). During the crisis the banks were forced by regulators to achieve enhanced capital positions, so that even under the most severe assumptions they would be able to meet the regulatory minimum capital adequacy ratio (IMF 2011b, 31).

Although real estate prices have increased considerably in recent years, the rise in house prices is not on the same scale as that in Europe and the USA. The IMF conducted stress tests which assumed not only a 30 per cent decline in property prices, but also simulated insolvencies in the 'vertically integrated' industries closely connected to the real estate sector. These included steel, cement, other building materials, construction, furniture and household electrical appliances. The stress test concluded that a 30 per cent decline in house prices and the associated impact on closely related industries would have 'only a minimal impact', lowering the capital adequacy ratio by less than one-quarter of a percentage point (IMF 2011b, 32).

Growth prospects

China's exceptional long-run growth performance was based on a number of factors that were not altered by the global crisis. China has a huge, increasingly well-integrated domestic market, with 1.3 billion people, compared with around 1 billion people in the whole of the OECD, which is far from a unified political economy. Its physical infrastructure and human capital has expanded rapidly during the past three decades, which has enabled it to pull steadily ahead of other developing countries in these critical areas. It has a vibrant quasi-private economy, with a huge number of SME entrepreneurs. The country's giant SOEs have made steady progress in absorbing foreign technology and upgrading their management and technical level. China enjoys the 'advantages of the latecomer', able to make use of cutting edge global technology, in order to leapfrog many aspects of the development process in the high-income countries. High-income countries have large sunk costs in an infrastructure that is rapidly becoming obsolescent. FDI continues to flood into China, contributing powerfully to the country's modernization and technical progress. Above all, China's government has a long proven track record of competence in policymaking.

China's performance during the global financial crisis has been remarkable. In 2011 GDP in the high-income countries is no higher than in 2007, but in China GDP in 2011 is more than one-third greater than in 2007.

The initial impact of the global crisis was extremely severe. At the core of China's ability to sustain a high rate of growth throughout the crisis has been the state-controlled banking system, which was the foundation of the enormous increase in public spending during the crisis. The financial system is under great strain due to the repressed financial markets. However, the benefits of the system have been made clear during the crisis. Long-term stagnation or even recession in the West will have a serious impact on the Chinese economy. However, the Chinese economy and its banking system is in a sufficiently robust condition to withstand a further substantial injection of bank lending into the economy.

The welfare of ordinary Chinese people was not sacrificed during the crisis. On the contrary, the crisis was taken as an opportunity to repair many of the deficiencies in the social welfare system. Moreover, the continued high rate of economic growth and the rapid expansion of labour-intensive infrastructure building and house construction ensured that levels of unemployment were contained. Average real wages continued to grow at around 12 per cent per annum during the crisis. The high rate of investment in infrastructure provided tangible welfare benefits for a large fraction of the population. The continued high rate of growth of real estate construction helped to meet intense demand for more and better housing. Both the explosive growth of local government investment platforms and the rapid growth of real estate construction fuelled ever-greater wealth disparities, but at the same time they contributed to the satisfaction of real welfare needs. Despite continuous strains on China's social structure, the advances in welfare for most Chinese during the global financial crisis helped to cement the underlying socio-economic stability, especially through the provision of confidence among Chinese people in the policymaking capabilities of the Chinese state bureaucracy.

4. Conclusion

Pessimistic scenario

It is possible to construct a deeply pessimistic perspective for the Chinese economy. The intensifying global crisis coincides with the complex process of generation change in the Chinese leadership. China has reached the end of the Lewis phase of development. It has reached the end of the 'extensive' phase of economic growth and the switch to 'intensive' growth will be long and complicated. The intensifying global financial crisis may lead to a severe decline in demand for China's exports. The Chinese financial system may face severe difficulties due to the impact on economic growth of the decline in Chinese exports, itself due to the collapse of the housing bubble, the rise of insolvency among the local government investment platforms and the inability of the regulatory authorities to control lending in the shadow banking sector. In this view, a second stimulus package would be beyond the capabilities of the Chinese government. There is a deep paradox that through a different route the Chinese economy may end up in the same place as Europe and the USA: 'The fear is that the impact of a bursting of the property bubble could yield a crisis just as dramatic as the one unfolding in Europe' (*FT*, 22 November 2011). The intensification of the global economic crisis will lead to deep economic system difficulties for China. In a more extreme version, it may even be the trigger for the system collapse that has been regularly predicted by Western commentators since the 1980s.

Optimistic scenario

In the optimistic scenario for the Chinese economy China's policymakers are able to build on the foundation of extraordinarily successful policymaking in the past three decades and make use of the greatly enhanced talents of the bureaucracy. China's policymakers have seen China through the turbulence of *Tian An Men*, the Soviet collapse, profound hostility from the West in the early 1990s, the Asian financial crisis, the collapse of the dotcom bubble and the impact of the global financial crisis in 2008–2009. The leadership transition has been handled with great care. Even though there are intense struggles for position in the new leadership team, the overall line taken by the leadership is unlikely to be affected radically by the final disposition of personnel. The end of the Lewis phase of development may stimulate re-balancing through the impact of market forces. China's high rate of investment and the tremendous increase in infrastructure and housing construction since 2007 have contributed to continued major improvements in the welfare of ordinary Chinese people. Policies to address the deficiencies in China's welfare system were accelerated during the financial crisis. The flow of FDI continued at a high rate during the crisis, stimulated by the continued growth of markets within China and supported by an outstanding infrastructure, high level of human capability and the high quality of public policymaking compared with other developing countries. China's banking regulators have retained far tighter control over the banking system than is the case in the high-income countries. This has enabled the banking system to remain essentially a 'public utility' system, which lacks the sophistication and range of operations of global banks, but is much better able to support government policy objectives and is better able to control risk. Where dangers have arisen, such as in shadow banking, the regulators have acted promptly to devise a wide array of policies to contain risk. The experience of the Asian financial crisis made the Chinese government extremely cautious and risk averse in its approach to bank regulation. This places the Chinese government in a position to be able to enact further stimulus packages if necessary. It means that the growth prospects for the Chinese economy are far better than those for the high-income countries and for most developing countries.

Implications

If the West continues to stagnate, or even enters a phase of recession while China's bureaucratic system is able at the same time to continue to generate substantial growth, the implications for the global political economy are enormous. We may be at a major turning point in international relations. If China is able to resolve its difficulties successfully it will be due to intelligent government policy choice. The deep systemic difficulties that the West confronts are because of bad policy choices made due to the regulatory capture of policymaking combined with populist democratic politics. During the golden age of capitalist globalization the mass of Western electors were extremely satisfied with the continuous increase in their 'wealth' and the matching increase in debt to finance their consumption. They were the willing partners in the construction of policies that have caused profound long-term damage to the Western economies. The fate of Western economies is in the hands of the 'market', to which Western policymakers have ceded power. The 'markets' that we have created and let loose from our control are destroying our own political economy. The 'monster' turned against its maker – us. Far from being irrelevant, Karl Marx's analysis of the contradictory nature of free market capitalism has never seemed more apposite. Many of the cheerleaders of free market fundamentalism over the past 30 years have proudly proclaimed 'We were always Marxists.'

The pre-Qin (221–207 BC) Chinese philosophers had many differences among themselves. However, they were in agreement that the selection and motivation of government officials was the most important pre-condition for the successful government of a state (Yan Xuetong 2011). Only a state in which the rulers have found the Way and can demonstrate their moral quality in meeting the interests of the mass of the population can hope to survive in the long run. Only a state with such qualities can hope to unify 'all under heaven':

Appointing the worthy is the root of governance. (Mozi, quoted in Yan Xuetong 2011, 54)

When you honor the worthy and employ the capable, then outstanding people will be at their posts, and then all exemplary persons under heaven will be happy and will want to serve in your court. (Mencius, quoted in Yan Xuetong 2011, 60)

One who contends for all under heaven must first contend for men. (Guanzi, quoted in Yan Xuetong 2011, 60)

Let morality be whole and attain its highest peak; cultivate civilized principles and unify all under heaven. (Xunzi, quoted in Yan Xuetong 2011, 40)

The working of the great Way is for all under heaven to be owned by all. (Confucius, quoted in Yan Xuetong 2011, 45)

China today is trying hard to devise policies to deal with immense development challenges and faces tremendous turbulence in the global economy. China has charted its own reform path, using the combined intelligence of a huge policymaking apparatus. China's leaders have emphasized that no matter what the world thinks of us 'we must focus on doing our own things well' (*zuo hao women de shiqing*). At the core has been an effort to guide the market to serve the interests of the whole society rather than allow economic development to be controlled by the abstract forces of the 'market'. Against the vast body of Western advice to let loose the 'monster' of market forces, China's policymakers have, following the country's long tradition, attempted to plot a path with makes use of the strength of the market while keeping it under control.

If China is successful in sustaining growth and welfare for the mass of its people, following its own approach to regulating the market, the rest of the world will think very deeply. China will not need to boast about its achievements. It will not need to conquer territories through 'hard power' or plot and scheme through 'soft power' in order to gain 'all under heaven'. It will then have achieved the goal set out by Lao Tse:

> I have seen that is not possible to acquire all under heaven by striving. All under heaven is a spiritual vessel and cannot be run or grasped. To try and run it ends in failure; to try and grasp it leads to losing it. (Lao Tse 2009, 29)

Notes

1 The term 'moral hazard' came to refer to 'any situation in which one person makes the decision about how much risk to take, while someone else bears the cost if things go badly' (Krugman 2000, 66).

2 Adult mortality is the probability of dying between the age of 15 and 60, that is the probability of a 15-year-old dying before the age of 60.

3 Between the late 1970s and 2008 the official US median household income (at 2008 prices) remained stagnant at around $50,000. However, real median household consumption received a substantial stimulus due to the decline in the real price of goods and services, especially through imports from developing countries and through technical progress in information technology.

4 The report was completed in June 2011, but was not released publicly until November 2011.

Part II

INDUSTRIAL POLICY AND THE GLOBAL BUSINESS REVOLUTION

Chapter 3

CHINA'S INDUSTRIAL POLICY
AT THE CROSSROADS

Chinese companies should expand their overseas presence at a faster rate, enhance their co-operation in an international environment, and develop a number of world-class multinational corporations.
—President Hu Jintao, Report to the 18th Party Congress,
8 November 2012

Introduction

Throughout China's economic reforms since the 1980s the central plank of the country's industrial policy has been the attempt to transform its giant state-owned enterprises into globally competitive firms. A large fraction of the world's leading firms were supported in one way or another by their national governments at some stage in their development (see, e.g., Ruigrok and Van Tulder 1995, table 9A, 239–68). The avenues of state support included full or partial state ownership, protection from international competition through tariffs and import quotas, government procurement policy, government support for research and development, and preferential loans from state-owned banks. China's planners studied the experience of other countries and adapted their policies to its own situation. The structure and operational mechanism of the country's state-owned enterprises have been comprehensively transformed since the 1980s. The results have been remarkable. China's state-owned enterprises have grown at high speed and are highly profitable. China now has a large group of state-owned enterprises in the *FT* 500 and *Fortune* 500 global rankings.

However, behind this apparent success, there are deep problems that are widely acknowledged within the Chinese government. The success of China's SOEs has been based heavily on their privileged position within the fast-growing domestic market. The country's banks lend primarily to the SOEs. Small- and medium-sized firms operate outside the 'glass wall' of the formal banking sector, which greatly handicaps their expansion. Insofar as the country's SOEs have built international businesses, these are mainly in developing countries, selling low-technology and low-value-added products. China's SOEs have made a negligible impact within the markets of the high-income countries, either in terms of sales or in foreign direct investment (FDI). At the same time, in a wide range of high-technology and heavily branded industrial sectors, global firms have rapidly built their production base within China, both for the domestic market and for export.

Thus, after 30 years of industrial policy the blunt reality is that China's giant SOEs have failed to build globally competitive firms. Their high market capitalization masks their fundamental weakness in global competition. It is widely acknowledged that China's SOEs will enter a new round of system reform under the incoming leadership. However, the direction and content of that reform is an open question.

1. China's Industrial Policy Success

From the earliest days of China's economic reforms in the 1980s, the country's leadership has been committed to developing a group of globally competitive giant firms to match those from the high-income countries. As early as 1987 central policymakers pointed out that 'the development of business groups is of profound long-term importance to the development of production capabilities and deepening the reform of the economic system'. These policies have been remarkably successful. By 2012 China had 70 firms in the *Fortune* 500 and 22 firms in the *FT* 500. The aggregate market capitalization of Chinese firms in the *FT* 500 was third, behind only the US and the UK. In the *Fortune* 500 list the number of Chinese firms, which are mainly SOEs, is second only to the United States.

Constructing an industrial policy in China presented special challenges compared to other latecomer countries such as Japan and South Korea after 1950. China was attempting to reform a closed centrally planned economy with a negligible private sector. Japan and Korea both were bastions of the West's struggle against communism, with a massive US military presence. The West was prepared to accept a robust nationalist industrial policy in its East Asian partners who were in the frontline in the struggle against communism. Communist China was viewed by the West as a profound ideological and military threat. Moreover, China's attempt to construct an industrial policy has occurred in the midst of the era of capitalist globalization, which has produced unprecedented global industrial concentration of business power far beyond that which faced Japan or Korea at a similar phase in their development. The industrial policies pursued by Japan and Korea could not easily be transferred to China and they cannot easily be transferred to developing countries today.

From the outset in the late 1970s China's economic reforms were cautious and experimental, 'groping for stones to cross the river'. They have been viewed as part of a much wider process of 'system reform', with cautious experimentation, analysis and feedback into the ongoing reform process.

The essence of China's enterprise reform policy was crystallized in the slogan 'grasp the large, let go of the small'. By the late 1990s most of the small- and medium-sized enterprise sector had been removed from state ownership, and a wide array of institutional structures emerged from the process. Although widely referred to as 'privatization', this term does not fully capture the complexity of this process or its outcome. The non-state sector, which consists mainly of small- and medium-sized enterprises, has made a vital contribution to China's growth. Removing the constraints over this sector unleashed the force of China's vibrant tradition of entrepreneurship, which had been smothered since the mid-1950s under the administratively directed economy.[1]

Alongside the rapid growth of the non-state sector, the commanding heights of the economy remained firmly under state ownership. A long series of experimental reforms attempted to create a group of globally competitive large enterprises. The leadership regarded this as a central focus of the country's development strategy. In 1998 Vice Premier Wu Bangguo summarized the government's policy as follows:

> International economic comparisons show that if a country has several large companies or groups it will be assured of maintaining a certain market share and a position in the international economic order. America, for example, relies on General Motors, Boeing, Du Pont and a batch of other multinational companies. Japan relies on six large enterprise groups and Korea relies on ten large commercial groupings. In the same way now and in the next century our nation's position in the international economic order will be to a large extent determined by the position of our nation's large enterprises and groups.

Initial cautious experiments in the 1980s increased enterprise autonomy, enhancing the right to retain profits and engage directly with the market. From the early 1990s onwards the reforms deepened. Large enterprises were transformed into corporate entities with diversified ownership. Minority equity shares were floated on domestic and international stock markets. In this process large state-owned firms were subjected to public scrutiny, including meticulous examination of the floated companies by international accounting firms and investment banks. Joint ventures were established with leading international companies. A new generation of highly trained professional managers moved into senior positions. Extensive corporate restructuring took place through merger and acquisition. The number of 'national champion' firms was gradually reduced to around eighty super-large firms. Increasingly the corporate structure of China's giant enterprises resembled that of their international competitors. This was a remarkable achievement in terms of institutional transformation.

The main body of the national champion firms was in 'strategic industries'. These were broadly the same industries in which many high-income countries had established their own state-owned 'national champion' firms after World War II. Although the Western state-owned enterprises were mostly privatized after the 1970s, prior to this many of them had achieved significant scale and technical progress, which laid the foundation for their international success after privatization. China has constructed a large group of giant companies in key sectors, including telecoms (China Mobile, China Unicom and China Telecom); oil and chemicals (Sinopec, China National Petroleum Corporation [CNPC], China National Offshore Oil Corporation [CNOOC] and Sinochem); aerospace (Aviation Industry of China [AVIC], Commercial Aircraft Company of China [COMAC] and China Aerospace Science and Technology Corporation [CASC]); military and related equipment (China North and China South); automobiles and trucks (Shanghai Auto, Yiqi and Dongfeng); power equipment (Shanghai Electric, Harbin Electric and Dongfang Electric); metals and mining (Baosteel, Wugang (Wisco), Shenhua, China Minmetals and Aluminium Corporation of China); electricity generation and distribution (China Southern Power Grid, National Grid (Guodian), Huaneng, Huadian and Datang); construction (China State Construction, China Rail Construction and China Construction); airlines (Air China, China Southern and China Eastern); and banking (Industrial and Commercial Bank of China, China Construction Bank, Bank of China, Agricultural Bank of China and Bank of Communications).

In these sectors, the state's majority equity share makes it difficult for international firms to expand within China through merger and acquisition and the national champion firms benefit from their access to procurement contracts from government projects. Since these firms are all state owned they are able to think in a long-term fashion. They can work together as a single team, sharing knowledge, supporting each other and buying each other's products. They can cooperate in the development of new technologies to meet China's needs for sustainable development in transport, buildings, electricity generation and transmission, and oilfield services. Each of these sectors has witnessed significant technical progress among domestic companies. China's booming economy has been based on an extremely high investment rate, which has created intense demand for output from the main body of the country's strategic industries, mainly in the capital goods sector.

This has meant that revenues and profits at China's national champion firms have grown rapidly.

In key strategic industries, including electricity generation and distribution, railways, oil and gas, aircraft and banks, China's largest state-owned enterprises have made substantial technical and management advances, supported by the surging growth in domestic demand.

Electricity generation and distribution. In the 1990s the international market for power stations manufacture was dominated by a handful of giant companies from the high-income countries, including Alstom, Mitsubishi, GE and Siemens. However, the growth of electricity production and distribution in China has far outpaced that in other parts of the world. Between 1990 and 2007 China accounted for one-third of the total global increase in electricity production. The Chinese government has ensured that the main body of China's power equipment has been bought from domestic companies. Over four-fifths of China's electricity generation uses coal as the primary energy, with a secondary role for hydro power and a fast-increasing role for nuclear power. The Chinese government has gradually tightened environmental regulations so that an increasing share of the market has been supplied with less polluting larger power generation units. The main domestic equipment companies (Harbin, Shanghai and Dongfang) have made steady technical progress. Harbin is the leading domestic company with around one-third of the domestic coal-fired market and two-thirds of the hydro-market. In the 1980s Harbin was only able to manufacture units of 30–200 MW. In 1990 it installed its first sub-critical units of 300 MW and 600 MW, and in 2004 it installed its first super-critical unit of 600 MW. It has supplied more than 250 units of 300 MW to the domestic market and more than 200 units of 600 MW. It has recently supplied 13 super-critical units of 1000 MW. In addition to numerous small hydro power units it has supplied more than 40 units of 700 MW or above to different Chinese hydro-projects including 14 units to the giant Three Gorges project. Working closely with other elements in the Chinese engineering industry it has steadily increased its capability in the nuclear power sector, including the supply of 16 units of third generation AP-1000 steam generators for China's nuclear power plants. It has exported power stations to Pakistan, Vietnam, Indonesia and Sudan. These have almost all been small units of less than 200 MW. However, it has begun to export large units to Pakistan, and in 2010 it was announced that China's power equipment companies would be given massive orders to export power plants to Indian power generating companies.[2]

High-speed trains. China has been at the forefront of the global expansion of high-speed rail travel. By 2010 it already had the world's largest high-speed rail network with plans to triple the high-speed rail capacity to 16,000 km by 2020. The high-speed train industry outside China is an oligopoly shared mainly between Siemens, Alstom, Bombardier and Kawasaki Heavy Industries, and these companies dominated the early phase of high-speed train development in China. However, in order to gain access to the Chinese market, foreign firms were required to transfer technology to the indigenous Chinese companies, which rapidly upgraded their technology. Around 70 per cent of the new high-speed rolling stock and ancillary equipment is now purchased from domestic companies, principally the state-owned firms China North (CNR) and China South (CSR). Many commentators viewed the rapid technical progress of Chinese large state-owned companies in this sector as the beginning of a wider process of 'catch-up' in high-technology industries. China appeared to be poised to begin exporting high-speed trains on a large scale. In July 2011 the first export deal was announced, with the sale of a batch of high-speed trains to Malaysia. However, in the same month the Beijing–Shanghai high-speed train crashed, killing over forty people and injuring many more. It was widely suggested that this would greatly harm the possibility not only for China's export of high-speed trains but also other high-technology products. In fact, the long-term impact may be less severe than many analysts fear.[3] The rapid absorption and adaptation of advanced technologies in the high-speed train sector is a remarkable achievement for a developing country.

Oil and gas. In the 1990s it seemed that China's oil companies might be split into smaller units, with great opportunities for global companies to penetrate the domestic market through joint ventures and acquisitions. Instead, in the late 1990s China's oil industry went through a massive restructuring which resulted in two giant vertically integrated companies, CNPC and Sinopec, and one smaller company focusing on offshore oil and gas, CNOOC. So remarkable has the transformation been that by 2010 PetroChina, the listed subsidiary of CNPC, became the world's largest listed oil company by market capitalization, surpassing even the US giant ExxonMobil. Unlike the oil majors, which have outsourced a large share of their activities to specialist oilfield service companies, CNPC and Sinopec remain highly vertically integrated, including large research departments. In 2010 CNPC's R&D investment surpassed that of Shell, which had the largest R&D expenditure among the oil majors. Faced with stagnant domestic oil reserves, CNPC has made important technical progress in many areas, especially those connected with extracting oil from mature oilfields and developing unconventional sources of oil and gas, such as coalbed methane. Due to the rapid rise in domestic oil demand and the stagnation of domestic output, China's oil companies have pushed hard to expand their international operations and in the process they have developed technical skills in the operation of oil and gas fields across a wide range of conditions. Between 2003 and 2010 the share of international production in CNPC's total oil output rose from 11 per cent to 26 per cent.

Aircraft. In 1970 the Chinese government announced a project to build a large commercial airliner of the same size as the Boeing 707. The first Y-10 aircraft was completed in Shanghai in 1978 and made 130 test flights between 1980 and 1983. Just two aircraft were built, one of which was tested to destruction in ground tests. It was a remarkable achievement for a developing country to produce such a technologically advanced product. The remaining Y-10 can still be visited at COMAC's headquarters in Shanghai. In front of it is a sculpture with the characters 'never give up' (*yong bu fang qi*). However, the aircraft was not a commercial success and the programme was halted in 1985.

Between 1986 and 1993 McDonnell Douglas assembled 34 MD 82/83 aircraft in Shanghai. In 1992 it was agreed that McDonnell and AVIC would jointly produce in Shanghai 150 MD-90 commercial airliners, with a substantial share of domestically produced components. In 1997, shortly after it had acquired McDonnell Douglas, Boeing announced that it was terminating the project. At this point just two of the MD-90s had been assembled in Shanghai. In 1996 AVIC and Airbus agreed a plan to jointly design and produce a new commercial airliner, the AE100. Just two years later, Airbus decided that the proposal was not commercially viable and terminated the project without any planes having been produced. The termination of the joint ventures with Airbus and Boeing set the Chinese commercial aircraft industry back by around ten years. Since then China's fleet of large commercial aircraft has grown at great speed, consisting entirely of planes bought from Boeing and Airbus.

However, China has consistently expressed its intention to build its own indigenous large commercial aircraft industry. In 2002 the Chinese government initiated a plan to build its own domestically assembled regional jet, the ARJ21. The State Council's Long-Term Programme for National Science and Technological Development (2006–20) identified the development of large commercial aircraft as one of 16 key areas for the country's industrial development. The programme also identified enhancing indigenous innovation capability in the aircraft sector as an important part of the country's science and technology development objectives. The 12th Five Year Plan (2011–15) emphasizes the development of high-end manufacturing industries. Large commercial aircraft embody a large bundle of the world's most advanced technologies, including new materials, propulsion systems and information technology.

In 2008 the two segments of AVIC were merged into a single company and a new enterprise was established, the Commercial Aircraft Corporation of China (COMAC),[4] with the specific purpose of developing a large commercial aircraft, the C919. The consortium responsible for producing the ARJ21 was merged with COMAC in 2009.[5] The ARJ21, which is assembled by COMAC in Shanghai, made its maiden flight in November 2008. By late 2010 there were over 200 orders for the ARJ21, around three-quarters of which were from China's domestic airlines. The C919 will be a 160–70 seat plane that competes directly with Boeing's B737 and Airbus's A320 in both domestic and international markets. It is planned that the maiden flight will take place in 2014 and the plane will enter service in 2016. In late 2010 COMAC announced it had received 100 orders for the plane. Both Boeing and Airbus stated that they welcomed the arrival of a third competitor in the large commercial aircraft industry, which would help to stimulate innovation in this critically important high-technology industry.

Banks. A decade ago China's banking industry was mired in massive bad debts, with a chorus of expert opinion calling for the break-up of the country's big banks. Within ten years China's leading state-owned banks had accomplished a comprehensive transformation. They absorbed investment from foreign strategic partners, who contributed their expertise to upgrading management systems. The management has undergone a wide-ranging process of skill upgrading, including personnel exchange with giant global banking partners and intensive international training programmes. Flotation of part of the banks' equity on domestic and international stock markets has intensified media pressure on senior management. Corporate governance has been upgraded steadily, with increasing international representation on the banks' board of directors, including their key committees such as audit and risk management. Annual general meetings have become open and noisy affairs, with close questioning of the banks' senior managers. They have completely transformed their information technology systems, which has improved customer service and permitted greatly increased central control of risk. By 2012 China had the world's two largest banks by market capitalization, Industrial and Commercial Bank of China (ICBC) and China Construction Bank (CCB), and four of the world's top ten banks by market capitalization. China has a total of ten banks in the *FT* 500. Its closest rival, the United States, has just seven banks in the *FT* 500. Few people predicted such a remarkable transformation in the global banking industry.

Conclusion

Throughout the period of 'transition' from the centrally planned economies, the Washington Consensus institutions, with the World Bank at the forefront, have argued unceasingly that state-owned enterprises are inherently inefficient. The classic text was the World Bank's publication *Bureaucrats in Business* (1995), which echoes in modern form Adam Smith's strictures against state intervention in business. A wide array of reports was produced by the World Bank and other international institutions which argued that state-owned enterprises were incapable of competing on the global level playing field of international business. The 'Big Bang' of institutional reform in the former Soviet Union and Eastern Europe was widely heralded as the model that China ought to follow, privatizing and breaking up its state-owned monopolies. Innumerable publications by international institutions argued that China's industrial policy should be abandoned in favour of comprehensive privatization.

The collapse of the Russian economy discredited the Washington Consensus approach. However, China's entry to the WTO coincided with intensified international pressure for widespread Chinese privatization. It was widely felt both inside and outside China that the country's entry to the WTO would stimulate a fundamental re-thinking of its industrial policy and that widespread privatization would allow greatly increased space for global firms within China's strategic industries. Instead, despite intense ideological pressure, China's leaders persisted in the effort to build globally competitive large firms that are majority owned by the state. Foreign companies have negligible assets and market share in key strategic industries.

The heads of the national champion companies are selected by the Central Organization Department of the Chinese Communist Party. They frequently move on to positions within the party and government system. The party secretary remains the most powerful person in the state-owned companies. The party retains tight control over personnel issues from the top to bottom of state-owned enterprises. The State-owned Assets Supervision and Administration Commission (SASAC) retains tight control over all key aspects of the leading state-owned enterprises, including mergers and acquisitions, human resources policy, remuneration, flotation and international expansion. Between 2002 and 2011 the value of assets managed by SASAC rose from RMB 7.1 trillion to RMB 28.0 trillion, and their revenues rose from RMB 3.4 trillion to RMB 20.2 trillion (*FT*, 12 November 2012).

After 30 years of reform, China's industrial policy appears to have succeeded, with a large batch of giant state-owned companies in the *Fortune* 500 and the *FT* 500. Their remarkable success suggests that the mainstream view of the Washington Consensus institutions was fundamentally flawed. Non-mainstream economists have seized on the evidence of China's apparent industrial policy success to argue that state-led industrial policy can build a group of globally competitive companies which are state-owned firms to match those built by the United States in the nineteenth century, by Western Europe after World War II, and by Japan and Korea in the 1960s and 1970s.

The leaders of global companies that have substantial business in China frequently praise the success of China's industrial policy in public. The international media have widely reported the rise of a new form of state capitalism in China. Its giant state-owned firms are widely thought to be 'buying the world', greatly reinforcing Western fears about 'China's rise'.

2. The Challenge of the Global Business Revolution

After the 1970s the world economy entered a new phase of capitalist globalization. This involved revolutionary changes in information technology, widespread privatization, liberalization of international trade and investment flows, opening up of the former communist 'planned' economies, and comprehensive policy change in the formerly 'inward-looking' non-communist developing countries. The liberalization promoted across the world by the policies of the Washington Consensus led to profound changes in the nature of the large corporation. Large firms with their headquarters in the high-income countries built global production systems, through both organic growth and explosive merger and acquisition. Their suppliers, also typically with their headquarters in the high-income countries, frequently followed them by themselves building global production systems. This period witnessed explosive industrial concentration among both giant 'systems integrator' firms and their supply chains.

Systems integrator firms

The period of the global business revolution witnessed massive asset restructuring, with firms extensively selling off 'non-core businesses' in order to develop their 'core businesses' and upgrade their asset portfolio. The goal for most large firms became the maintenance or establishment of their position as one of the handful of top companies in the global marketplace. An unprecedented degree of industrial concentration was established among leading firms in sector after sector. By the 1980s there was already a high degree of industrial concentration within many sectors of the individual high-income countries. However, the global business revolution saw for the first time the emergence of widespread industrial concentration across all high-income countries, which also extended deeply into large parts of the developing world.

During the three decades of capitalist globalization, industrial concentration occurred in almost every sector. Alongside a huge increase in global output, the number of leading firms in most industrial sectors shrank and the degree of global industrial concentration increased greatly. The most visible part consists of the well-known firms with superior technologies and powerful brands. These constitute the 'systems integrators' or 'organizing brains' at the apex of extended value chains. Their main customers are the global middle class. By the early 2000s, within the high-value-added, high-technology and strongly branded segments of global markets, which serve mainly the middle and upper income earners who control the bulk of the world's purchasing power, a veritable 'law' had come into play: A handful of giant firms, the 'systems integrators', occupied upwards of 50 per cent of the whole global market (Table 3.1).

Table 3.1. Industrial concentration among systems integrator firms, 2006–2010

Industrial sector	Number of firms	Global market share
Large commercial aircraft	2	100
20–90 seat commercial aircraft	2	75
Automobiles	10	77
Heavy duty trucks	4	89 (a)
Heavy and medium duty trucks	5	100 (b)
Fixed-line telecoms infrastructure	5	83
Mobile telecoms infrastructure	3	77
PCs	4	55
Mobile handsets	3	65
Smartphones	3	75
Plasma TVs	5	80
LCD TVs	5	56
Digital cameras	6	80
Pharmaceuticals	10	69
Construction equipment	4	44
Agricultural equipment	3	69
Elevators	4	65
Soft drinks	5	>50
Carbonated soft drinks	2	70
Beer	4	59
Cigarettes	4	75 (c)
Athletic footwear	2	55

Sources: *Financial Times*, various issues, and company annual reports.
Notes: All estimates of global market share are rough approximations only.
    (a) North American Free Trade Agreement (NAFTA) only
    (b) Europe only
    (c) Excluding China

The cascade effect

As they consolidated their leading positions, the systems integrator firms, with enormous procurement expenditure, exerted intense pressure upon the supply chain in order to minimize costs and stimulate technical progress. As firms struggled to meet the strict requirements that are the condition of their participation in the systems integrators' supply chains, industrial concentration increased rapidly. In sector after sector, a small number of firms account for a major share of the market within each segment of the supply chain (Table 3.2).

Table 3.2. Industrial consolidation among selected firms within global value chains, 2006–2010

Industrial sector	Number of firms	Combined global market share
Large commercial aircraft		
Engines	3 (a)	100
Braking systems	2	75
Tyres	3	100
Seats	2	>50
Lavatory systems	1	>50
Wiring systems	1	>40
Titanium lockbolts	1	>50
Windows	1	>50
Automobiles		
Auto glass	3	75
Auto instrumentation displays	4	57
Constant velocity joints	3	75
Tyres	3	55
Seats	2	>50
ABS/ESC braking systems	2	>50
Telematics	2	57
Automotive steel	5	55
Information technology		
Micro-processors for PCs	2	100
Integrated circuits for wireless telecommunication	10	65

(Continued)

Table 3.2. Continued

Industrial sector	Number of firms	Combined global market share
Database software	3	87
Enterprise resource planning programmes (ERP)	2	68
PC operating systems	1	90
DRAMS	5	82
Silicon wafers	4	89
Glass for LCD screens	2	78
Servers	2	63
Equipment to manufacture semiconductors	1	65
Beverages		
Beverage cans	3	57
Glass containers	2	68
Industrial gases	3	80
High-speed bottling lines	2	85
Forklift trucks	2	50
PET bottle blowing equipment	1	75
Miscellaneous		
Cash-dispensing machines	2	72
Thermostats on electric kettles	1	66
Specialist steel plate	5	62
Aluminium	10	57
Goal gasification technology	3	89
Media and marketing advertising revenue	4	55
Search engine advertising revenue	1	70
Financial information publishing	2	77
Container shipping	10	58
Sheet glass	4	65

Sources: *Financial Times*, various issues, and company annual reports.
Notes: All estimates of global market share are rough approximations only
      (a) including GE's joint venture with Safran

This 'cascade effect' has profound implications for the nature of competition and technical progress. It means that the challenge facing new entrant firms is far deeper than at first sight appears to be the case. Not only do they face immense difficulties in catching up with the leading systems integrators, who constitute the visible part of the 'iceberg' of industrial structure; they also face great difficulties in catching up with the powerful firms that now occupy the commanding heights in almost every segment of the global supply chains, in the invisible part of the 'iceberg' that lies hidden from view beneath the water. Firms from developing countries are joining the 'global level playing field' at a point at which the concentration of business power has never been greater. In developing countries that liberalized their business systems in line with the Washington Consensus policies oligopolies were established not only by the world's leading systems integrators but also in the upper reaches of the supply chain. Few people can imagine that just two firms produce 75 per cent of the global supply of braking systems for large commercial aircraft, that three firms produce 75 per cent of the global supply of constant velocity joints for automobiles, or that three firms produce 80 per cent of the global supply of industrial gases (Table 3.2).

Planning and coordination: The external firm

If we define the firm not by the entity which is the legal owner, but rather by the sphere over which conscious coordination of resource allocation takes place, then far from becoming 'hollowed out' and much smaller in scope, the large firm can be seen to have enormously increased in size during the global business revolution. Alongside the disintegration of the large firm the extent of conscious coordination over the surrounding value chain increased. In a wide range of business activities the organization of the value chain has developed into a comprehensively planned and coordinated activity. At its centre is the core systems integrator. This firm typically possesses some combination of a number of key attributes. These include the capability of raising finance for large new projects and the resources necessary to fund a high level of R&D spending to sustain technological leadership, to develop a global brand, to invest in state-of-the-art information technology and to attract the best human resources. Across a wide range of business types, from aircraft manufacture to fast-moving consumer goods, the core systems integrator interacts in the deepest, most intimate fashion with the major segments of the value chain, both upstream and downstream. This constitutes a new form of 'separation of ownership and control', in which the boundaries of the firm have become blurred. The numbers employed in the 'external firm' that is coordinated by the core firm, which possesses leading technologies and brands, typically far exceeds the numbers employed in the core systems integrator firm.

Technical progress

In its 2007 survey the UK government's Department of Trade and Industry (DTI)[6] compiled a survey of the R&D spending of the top 1,250 companies globally (the 'Global 1250') (DTI 2007). In 2006, these firms invested around $430 billion in R&D. The list is 'strongly concentrated by company, sector and country'. The Global 1250 revealed a picture in which global technical progress in each sector is dominated by a small number of powerful firms. In 2008, the analysis was extended to include the world's top 1,400 firms (the G1400). They invested a total of $545 billion in R&D (BERR 2008). This constitutes the main body of global investment in technical progress. The top 100 firms account for 60 per cent of the total R&D spending of the G1400. The bottom 100 firms account for less than 1 per cent of the total. In other words, around 100 or so firms in a small number of high-technology industries sit at the centre of technical progress in the era of globalization. Within each sector there was a high degree of industrial concentration of R&D expenditure (Table 3.3). Within the G1400, the top ten firms accounted for 46 per cent of investment in the technology hardware and equipment sector, 61 per cent in healthcare equipment and services, 65 per cent in autos and components, 65 per cent in chemicals, 68 per cent in software and computer services, and 80 per cent of investment in aerospace.

Far from witnessing a reduction in the level of competition, the recent period has seen a drastic increase in the intensity of competition, and investment in technical progress is a key source of competitive advantage. The DTI study concluded:

> Large companies are pouring money into research and development at an unprecedented rate, in response to growing competition… In many sectors profits are growing strongly and companies can afford to spend more on R&D… Where profits are weak, such as in the automobile industry, the competition is so fierce that companies dare not cut their investment. (DTI 2007)

Between 2001–2002 and 2005–2006 total R&D expenditure by the top 1,250 companies rose by 23 per cent (DTI 2007), and between 2005–2006 and 2009–2010 total R&D spending by the top 1,000 companies increased by a further 30 per cent (BIS 2010). In other words, between 2001–2002 and 2009–2010, R&D spending by the world's top 1,000 or so companies increased by around three-fifths.

Table 3.3. Industrial concentration and the global business revolution: Global 1400 R&D investment, 2007

Sector	Share of total G1400 R&D investment (%)	Number of firms	Share of sectoral investment in R&D (%)	
			Top five firms	Top ten firms
Aerospace and military	4.1	41	62	80
Autos and auto components	16.9	84	41	65
Chemicals	4.4	95	39	56
Electronics and electrical equipment	7.0	117	48	61
Healthcare equipment and services	1.8	59	42	57
Pharmaceuticals and biotechnology	19.2	178	35	57
Software and computer services	7.2	122	54	68
Technology hardware and equipment	18.3	224	28	46
Others	21.3	480	–	–
Total	100.0	1,400		

Source: BERR (2008).

Evidence from the automobile industry

The auto industry is the most important and visible of all global industrial sectors. The global stock of automobiles grew from 150 million in 1950 to 800 million in 2000, and is predicted to rise to around 1,600 million in 2030. In 1960 there were 42 independent automobile assemblers in North America, Western Europe and Japan. Through an intensive process of merger and acquisition that number has shrunk to just 15 firms. Among these are five giant auto assemblers with revenues in 2010 ranging from $108 billion to $221 billion. They account for over one-half of global passenger vehicle output. The top ten auto assemblers, which are all from high-income countries, account for almost 80 per cent of total global output. Even the leading automobile firms face threats to their survival due to the intense oligopolistic competition. It is difficult for an auto assembler to survive with an output of less than around five million vehicles per year.[7]

In order to survive in this ferocious competition, the leading assemblers must spend large amounts on R&D, in order to make vehicles lighter in weight, reduce CO_2 emissions and improve fuel efficiency, safety, durability and reliability. The world's top auto assembler, Toyota, spends almost $10 billion on R&D, and the top five firms each spend over $6 billion (BIS 2009). They also each spend several billion dollars each year on building their global brands.

The leading auto assemblers each spend several tens of billions of dollars annually on procurement of materials and components. GM, for example, has an annual procurement spend of around $80 billion. As the leading automobile assemblers have grown in terms of the scope and size of their markets since the 1970s, so also has the intensity of pressure they have imposed upon their supply chains. The pressure upon suppliers is felt most visibly in terms of price. However, the relationship is far from arm's length. The assemblers have selected a group of powerful sub-systems integrator firms that are able to partner them in their global expansion: 'We're looking for the top suppliers to help us grow in the market place. As we grow, they will grow with us' (from the GM website). The leading auto assemblers work together to plan the supplier firm's investment in new production locations close to the assemblers. Leading components suppliers such as Bosch, Delphi, Valeo, Denso, Johnson Controls, ZF, Bridgestone and Michelin each have more than 100 production plants across the world, close at hand to the assembly plants in order to minimize transport costs and inventories through 'just-in-time' supply.

There is a deep interaction between the direction of the core strategic suppliers' R&D and the needs of the assemblers. The leading auto assemblers have put intense pressure on leading components suppliers to invest large amounts in R&D to meet the assemblers' needs. In 2010 the leading components supplier, Robert Bosch, spent $5.1 billion on R&D, and the seven leading components suppliers, all from the high-income countries, each spent around $1 billion or more on R&D (BIS 2010).

The key suppliers themselves spend large amounts on their own procurement. Robert Bosch spends over $25 billion annually on purchasing inputs. Sub-systems integrators are deepening their relationship with their own suppliers beyond a simple price relationship. For example, Delphi is developing a group of its own 70–80 key 'strategic suppliers': 'These are the suppliers we'd like to grow with, they understand our cost models, where we are going, and being increasingly willing to put more of their research and development and engineering money behind projects for us.'

Due to the intense pressure from the cascade effect the auto components industry has been through a dramatic transition since the 1970s. The enormous rise in car volumes at the top assemblers has triggered a 'Darwinian struggle for survival' among the components suppliers. The number of components makers supplying the auto assemblers expanded from an estimated 20,000 in 1950 to over 40,000 in 1970. However, by 1990 the number had fallen to under 30,000. During the epoch of revolutionary growth and consolidation of the vehicle assemblers, the number of components makers shrank to less than 5,000 in 2000, and is predicted to fall still further, to less than 3,000 by 2015.

A handful of components makers has emerged, mainly through merger and acquisition, to dominate the upper reaches of the auto components supply chain. In each segment of the vehicle, a handful of sub-systems integrators, each with their own supply chains, dominate the global market. For example, four firms (Continental, Denso, Nippon Seiki and JCI) account for 57 per cent of global auto instrumentation displays; just three firms account for 55 per cent of total world production of auto tyres (Michelin, Bridgestone and Goodyear), 75 per cent of the world output of auto glass (Asahi, Saint-Gobain and NSG), and 75 per cent of the global market for constant velocity joints (GKN, NTN and Delphi); just two firms account for around three-quarters of the world's production of diesel fuel injection pumps (Bosch and Delphi), over one-half of all the automobile seat systems supplied to auto assemblers in Europe and North America (Johnson Controls and Lear), around 50 per cent of the global total of anti-locking brake systems and electronic stability control systems (Bosch and Continental), and 57 per cent of telematics equipment (Continental and LG). In each segment of the vehicle there is intense oligopolistic competition among the sub-systems integrators.

3. China's Industrial Policy Failure

Multinational companies 'going in' to China

It would be a serious misunderstanding of the strategy of multinational companies to exaggerate the significance of China compared with other parts of the developing world. For example, the growth of inward FDI into Latin America and the Caribbean, mainly from the leading international firms, has outpaced that into China by a wide margin. The stock of inward FDI in China is less than one-third of that in Latin America and the Caribbean (Table 3.4). China's large firms have only just begun their process of 'going out'. Outside China they must confront global giant firms with well-established production systems across the world, in both high-income and developing countries.

Table 3.4. Stock of inward FDI in developing countries, 2000 and 2009 ($ billion)

	2000	2009	Increase, 2000–2009	
			($ billion)	(% total increase)
Developing countries	*1,728*	*4,893*	*3,165*	*100.0*
Africa	154	515	361	11.4
Latin America/Caribbean	502	1,473	971	30.7
South Asia	30	218	188	5.9
Southeast Asia	267	690	423	13.4
East Asia	710	1,561	851	26.9
of which:				
China	193	473	280	8.8
Oceania	4	12	8	0.3
West Asia	60	425	365	11.5
Southeast Europe and the CIS	*61*	*497*	*436*	–

Source: UNCTAD (2010, annex, Table 3).

Leading businesses from the high-income countries have been 'going out' for the whole era of modern capitalist globalization. For example, US-based Caterpillar (CAT) is the world's leader in construction and earth-moving equipment.[8] In 2009 CAT's North American revenue amounted to $16.7 billion, compared with $4.5 billion from Latin America, $14.3 billion from Europe, Africa and the Middle East, and $6.4 billion from the Asia-Pacific region. The combined employment of CAT and its dealer network totalled 104,000 in North America, 31,400 in Latin America, 55,000 in Europe, Africa and the Middle East, and 32,800 in Asia-Pacific. Praxair is a company that few people have heard of, but it is representative of leading firms within the global value chain. It is a US-based firm that occupies a key position within the supply chain of many different sectors, supplying industrial gases around the world. In 2009 its assets were distributed as follows: $7.2 billion in North America, $3.2 billion in Latin America, $2.4 billion in Europe and $1.9 billion in Asia. It employed 10,183 people in the USA and 16,078 people in other parts of the world.

At the same time that Chinese firms are trying to 'go out', they must also face global companies who carry the competitive struggle deep into the Chinese economy, with their international production systems as the foundation. In terms of military strategy, the leading multinational companies are taking the 'war' into the enemy's camp, 'going in' to China in order to weaken the fighting capability of indigenous firms before they can build their capability outside the country. The 'war' is made more complex by the weakening relationship of the multinational companies with the political economy of their home country.

The Chinese government has kept around one-third of the economy substantially protected from penetration by global companies, by maintaining ownership in the hands of indigenous state-owned firms, which prevents them from making substantial mergers and acquisitions in these sectors. These sectors include metals and mining, electricity generation and distribution, railways, telecommunications services, airlines, oil and gas, ports and banking. Although this has greatly frustrated multinational firms in these sectors, it leaves a large fraction of the economy open for international firms to operate relatively freely.

Despite the attenuation of the relationship of global firms with their home country they urge their governments to lobby China to further open up its economy to investment by international firms. They argue passionately that China must establish a 'level playing field' for international firms operating in China. They complain bitterly about the 'unfairness' of China's industrial policy to nurture its national champion firms. In fact, in the view of some Western CEOs, China is a more friendly environment for business expansion even than the USA: 'It's like a well-managed company, China. You have a one-stop shop in terms of the Chinese foreign investment agency and local governments are fighting for investments with each other' (Muhtar Kent, chief executive of The Coca-Cola Company, quoted in the *FT*, 27 September 2011).

China is a key part of the growth strategy of most multinational companies. It has been consistently the largest recipient of inward FDI among developing countries. Although the role of foreign firms is tightly constrained in strategic industries, over large parts of the Chinese business system international companies have rapidly expanded their investments, employment and sales, occupying important positions within these sectors. They view expansion in China as critical to their long-term prospects. The rapid growth of the Chinese economy since the eruption of the global financial crisis has helped greatly to sustain the prospects for global companies based in high-income countries.

I will now look at the examples of the expansion in China of the business system of selected American, German and Japanese firms.

US firms. The United States has much the largest stock of global outward FDI, amounting to 27 per cent of the total for all developed countries in 2009. The United States has a total of nearly 60,000 investment projects in China. In 2008 the sales volume of these enterprises in China totalled $147 billion, their export volume was $72 billion and their profits were nearly $8 billion.

The US–China Business Council estimates that US companies have around $100 billion in FDI in China. China forms a key part of the global business system of a large fraction of America's top international companies across a wide array of sectors from iPads to fried chicken. Leading American global companies are deep 'inside' China (Table 3.5).

German firms. Germany's stock of FDI in China is much less than that of the USA. However, German firms have rapidly increased their investment in China and the total FDI of German firms in China stands at around $33 billion (*FT*, 29 August 2012). A group of giant German firms with global operations occupy a central position in several sectors of the Chinese system:

- ***Volkswagen.*** VW stands at the forefront of the German penetration of the Chinese market. It has two giant subsidiaries, in Shanghai and Changchun respectively.[9] They employ 53,000 people between them. In 2010 VW's operations in China had revenues of $42.4 billion, comparable to a global giant company such as Renault, Dow Chemical or PepsiCo. Profits from its business in China reached 2.63 billion euros, more than one-third of VW's total profits of 6.84 billion euros. VW and GM are the most powerful firms in the Chinese auto industry. China is VW's largest and fastest-growing market. In 2010 it sold 1.9 million cars in China and occupied around 17 per cent of the Chinese market. It plans to invest $13.9 billion in China in 2011–15 'in order to expand and consolidate its leading position'.
- ***Bosch.*** Bosch is by far the world's most powerful firm in the auto components sector. It is rapidly building its business system in China alongside the expansion of global systems integrators to which it is a key sub-systems supplier. It employs over 26,000 people in China and in 2010 its revenues reached $5.8 billion. It is investing heavily in China and plans that employment there will rise to 50,000 by 2015.
- ***Siemens.*** Siemens' portfolio of businesses in China includes power, medical and transport equipment, in each of which it has a leading global position. China also constitutes an increasingly important base for sourcing key components and sub-systems. Its Chinese operations employ 33,600 people, with revenues of $8.1 billion in 2010.
- ***BASF.*** BASF has played an important role in expanding the supply of chemicals in China. Since 1990 it has invested $5.3 billion in 26 wholly owned subsidiaries and 14 joint ventures, amounting to around one-fifth of total German FDI in China. Some of these are enormous investments, such as the $2.9 billion joint venture (50:50) with Sinopec in Nanjing. BASF

Table 3.5. China operations of selected US firms

Firm	Revenue ($ billion, 2011)		Total R&D spend ($ million, 2009)	Employment in China ('000s)	Comments
	Total	of which: China			
GM	150	30.5	6,068	35	GM sold 2.5 million vehicles in China in 2011. GM is investing $5–7 b. in China in 2010–15. GM has around 14% of the Chinese auto market
GE	147	6	3,324	–	GE is investing over $2 b. in China in 2010–12.
Apple	108	12 (a)	1,403	500	Apple's largest assembler, Foxconn, employs 1.3 million people in China. Apple accounts for around 40% of Foxconn's revenue.
Procter & Gamble	83	5.0	2,045	7	
Johnson & Johnson	65	1.5	6,985	5	Data are for 2007. J&J have 9 manufacturing plants in China. They have around one-half of the Chinese babycare product market.
United Technologies	58	3	1,558	17	UTC's Otis subsidiary has around 25% of the Chinese elevator market. Its Carrier subsidiary has around 20% of the Chinese market for commercial air conditioning systems. UTC is a key supplier to the Chinese aerospace industry.
Caterpillar	60	4	1,421	8.5	Caterpillar has 13 manufacturing sites in China excluding Caterpillar dealers. There are 70,000 employees in Caterpillar's supply chain in China.
Dow Chemical	60	3.7	1,492	4	Dow has 20 manufacturing sites in China.
Intel	54	–	5,625	–	Intel has invested $4.7 b. in China. Its micro-processors power over 75% of the PCs made in China. The Asia-Pacific region (excluding Japan) accounts for 57% of Intel's revenue.

Johnson Controls	41	3	336	18	Johnston Controls has around 45% of the Chinese automobile seat market. It has 47 manufacturing sites in China.
Honeywell	37	1.4	1,331	11	
3M	30	2.2	838	8	
Emerson Electric	24	3	—		Emerson Electric has 48,000 employees in the Asia-Pacific region.
Nike	21		—	176	Employment data is for Nike's subcontracted factories in China.
Coca-Cola	47		—	48	Over 400,000 employees work in Coca-Cola's supply chain in China. Coca-Cola has invested over $5 b. in China and plans to invest a further $4 b. in 2012–14.
PepsiCo	67		—	20	PepsiCo has 27 plants in China. Over 150,000 employees work in PepsiCo's supply chain in China.
Yum!	12	4.1	—	230	Yum! has 4,000 restaurants in China. They have around 40% of the Chinese QSR market
McDonald's	27		—	80	McDonald's has over 1,300 restaurants in China. The number of employees is planned to rise to 130,000 by 2013.
FedEx	39		—	8	
UPS	61		—	5	
Disney	41		—		Disney is investing $4.4 billion to build its Shanghai Disneyland
Walmart	447		—	95	China accounts for a large share of Walmart's global procurement. The number of people employed in Walmart's supply chain in China is likely to greatly exceed that of any other US company.

Source: Company websites.
Notes: (a) Greater China

employs 7,000 people in China. In 2010 the revenues from its Chinese operations reached $8.1 billion. It plans to invest more than $3 billion in China in the next few years, including an investment of $1.7 billion in the world's biggest MDI[10] plant in Chongqing and a further $1 billion in the Nanjing joint venture.

- **ThyssenKrupp.** ThyssenKrupp is a world leader in stainless steel for autos and domestic appliances, elevators and auto components. It has 11,000 employees in China, with revenues of $2.8 billion in 2010.

- **Adidas.** Adidas and Nike compete intensely. Between them they account for over one-half of the global market for athletic footwear, sports apparel and related products. In 2010 Adidas's global revenues reached $16.5 billion. Subcontracted suppliers, mainly in Asia, produced almost all of its products. In 2010 subcontractors in China supplied Adidas with 85 million pairs of sports shoes and 108 million pieces of apparel. At least 100,000 people are employed in China making Adidas sports goods.

Japanese firms. In terms of technological capability, Japanese companies are far ahead of any other country, with the exception of the USA. In 2010, among the world's top 1,000 companies ranked by R&D expenditure, the USA had 339 firms, with a total of $189 billion in R&D investment, and Japan had 199 firms, with a total R&D investment of $124 billion (BIS 2010). Germany was third ranked, with 75 firms and a total R&D investment of $60 billion, less than one-half of that of Japan. There are around thirty giant Japanese high-technology companies with an annual R&D investment of over $1 billion. Within these is a group of 11 super-giant Japanese high-technology companies each of which has an annual R&D investment of over $3 billion: Denso, Canon, NEC, Toshiba, Hitachi, Takeda Pharmaceutical, Nissan Motor, Sony, Panasonic, Honda Motor and Toyota Motor.

Japan has been at the forefront of investment in China. In 2004–2010 its average annual FDI inflows into China totalled $7.6 billion and in 2011 they increased to $12.6 billion. In 2011 China's outflow of FDI into Japan was $109 million, less than 1 per cent of Japan's flow of FDI into China. Over one-half of Japan's FDI in China is in different types of machinery. The machinery is mostly energy efficient and high technology, with transport and electrical machinery the most important. There are over 22,000 Japanese companies in China, employing around 3 million people, with a far larger number employed in the supply chain of these firms (Hong Kong Research 2012). Unlike European and American firms, Japanese companies are reluctant to provide detailed breakdowns of assets, sales and employment in China. The following are selected examples of Japanese firms' investments in China.

- **Toyota.** Toyota entered the Chinese market relatively late, but rapidly increased its investments and production there. By 2011 it had two main production bases, with over 28,000 employees, and a far greater number employed in its supply chain. Toyota's production in China increased from 445,000 vehicles in 2007 to 815,000 in 2011.
- **Hitachi.** Hitachi is a world leader in several interconnected high-technology areas. Its operations in China include ATMs, thermal power systems, railway systems, elevators and escalators, construction materials and medical equipment. Its China operations employ 60,000 people, with revenues of $16 billion in 2011, around 13 per cent of its total global revenues. It plans to increase its China revenues to $25 billion in 2015.
- **Nissan.** Nissan's operations in China produced 1.25 million vehicles in 2011 and its sales in China accounted for 26 per cent of its total global sales, making it Nissan's largest market. Nissan employs 71,000 people in China.
- **Honda.** In terms of its China strategy Honda is the weakest of the major Japanese auto assembly companies. However, it has a production capacity of 770,000 vehicles in China, and plans to increase this to 1.1 million by 2015. There are at least 30,000 employees in Honda's plants in China.
- **Toshiba.** Toshiba spans a similar range of high-technology products as GE and Siemens, including electricity generation and distribution, medical equipment and home appliances. Its international revenues in Asia in 2011 amounted to $15.4 billion, with 53,000 people employed. China has over fifty Toshiba subsidiaries, by far the greatest number in Asia, compared with just four each in India and Indonesia. Toshiba's activities in China include the construction of four PWR nuclear reactors.
- **Mitsubishi Electric.** Mitsubishi Electric is a world leader in industrial automation systems, electrical systems and home appliances. In 2011 its international sales revenue in Asia was $7.1 billion. It has several major production facilities in China. Among its milestones in China is the installation of 106 elevators in Shanghai Tower, China's tallest building, of which three elevators will be the world's fastest, travelling at 18 metres per second.
- **Mitsubishi Heavy Industries (MHI).** MHI is a world leader in several areas of heavy industry, including power and steel plants, high-technology ships, such as LPG and LNG carriers, aerospace (including the Mitsubishi Regional Jet), air conditioners and refrigerators, printing machinery and automobile turbochargers. MHI has a global market share of 21 per cent in auto turbochargers and a 30 per cent market share for hot-rolling steel machinery. Its revenues in 2011 were $35.7 billion, of which 43 per cent was from international sales, one-third of which was from Asia. Mitsubishi has a large production network in China, including plants making air conditioners

for businesses, households and automobiles; parts for gas turbines; forklift trucks; turbochargers; printing presses; rubber and tyre machines; and steel-making machines.

- **Suzuki.** Suzuki specializes in the manufacture of small automobiles and motorcycles. In 2011 it produced 2.8 million automobiles and 2.57 million motorcycles, and had revenues of $31.8 billion. Two-thirds of its automobiles are produced outside Japan. It is the largest automobile manufacturer in India through its 54 per cent equity ownership of Maruti. It sold over 1 million automobiles in India in 2011. Its position in China has not matched that in India. Nevertheless, in 2011 it sold almost 300,000 automobiles and 908,000 motorcycles in China, produced at its five manufacturing plants in the country.
- **Denso.** Denso is the world's second largest auto components manufacturer, with revenues of $32.9 billion in 2010. Its main overseas operations in Asia had revenues of $7.8 billion in 2001. The core production facilities are in China and Thailand, focusing on air conditioners and radiators supplied both to Japanese and other global auto assemblers.
- **Aisin Seiki.** Aisin Seiki is the world's fifth largest auto components supplier, with revenues of $24.6 billion in 2010. Its main products are brake systems and transmissions systems. Its revenues from overseas operations in Asia amounted to $2.8 billion in 2010.
- **Panasonic.** Panasonic is one of the world's leading producers of household electrical appliances as well as a wide range of related products. It faces intense competition from LG and Samsung in high-value-added products and from Chinese manufacturers in low-technology appliances. China accounts for 14 per cent of Panasonic's global sales, with revenues of $13.5 billion in 2011.
- **Sharp.** Sharp has been a world leader in consumer electronics, but it faces a severe challenge from the rapid technological transformation of the industry in recent years. It has large assembly facilities in China, with revenues of $6.0 billion in 2011.
- **Sony.** Like other leading producers of consumer electronic products, Sony faces intense challenges due to the pace of technical change and consumer preferences. Apple and Samsung have overtaken it in many key high-value-added products. However, it remains a huge company with a powerful brand. Its revenues in 2011 were $82 billion and it employs 42,000 people in Greater China and Korea.
- **Fujitsu.** Fujitsu has a strong global position in a wide range of information technology products. Its revenues in China in 2011 were $1.3 billion.
- **Ricoh.** Ricoh is one of the world's leading producers of printers and copiers. Its revenues in 2011 were $24.1 billion. China is important for production, sales and service, and it has 12,000 employees in the country.

- **Canon.** Japanese firms dominate the global market for high-technology photographic equipment. Canon has around 27 per cent of the Chinese market for cameras, with another 33 per cent for Sony and Nikon together. The three companies together have over three-fifths of the total Chinese market.

Multinational firms have made a critically important contribution to China's growth and modernization. They have been central to its ability to benefit from the 'advantages of the latecomer', especially through the application of the world's leading edge technologies in almost every sector from aircraft to soft drinks. Foreign-invested firms account for around 28 per cent of the country's overall industrial value added (Table 3.6). Their share of output is one-fifth or less in non-ferrous metals, metal products, ferrous metals, non-metallic mineral products and textiles (Table 3.7). However, their share of output rises to between one-quarter and a third in a wide range of industries, including food processing (23 per cent), raw chemicals (24 per cent), electrical machinery (24 per cent), plastics (25 per cent), medicines (26 per cent), clothing and footwear (31 per cent) and leather and fur-related products (34 per cent). In transport equipment their share is 44 per cent and in communications equipment it reaches 57 per cent.

Table 3.6. Foreign-invested enterprises (including firms from Taiwan, Hong Kong and Macao) in the Chinese economy, 2007–2009

Sector	Share of foreign-invested enterprises (%)
Industrial value added (2009)	*28*
of which:	
output from high technology industries (a)	66
of which:	
medical, precision and optical instruments (a)	43
electronic and telecoms equipment (a)	71
computers and office equipment (a)	91
Total exports (b)	*55*
of which:	
new and high technology products	90

Sources: Gao Yuning (2011), Steinfeld (2010), SSB (2010).
Notes: (a) 2009
     (b) 2007

Table 3.7. Market share of foreign-invested enterprises (including firms from Taiwan, Hong Kong and Macao) in the Chinese economy, 2010

	Market share (%)
Communications equipment (computers and other electronics)	57.1
Transport equipment	44.1
Leather, fur and related products	33.9
Clothing and footwear	31.0
Medicines	26.1
Plastics	25.3
Electrical machinery and equipment	24.3
Raw chemical materials and chemical products	24.1
Food processing	22.8
Special purpose machinery	20.8
Metal products	20.1
General purpose machinery	19.5
Textiles	16.4
Non-ferrous metals	13.6
Ferrous metals	13.4
Non-metallic metal products	12.9

Source: OECD (2012, 86).

The contribution of foreign firms is especially important in high-technology sectors. Foreign-invested enterprises account for around two-thirds of the overall value added in high-technology industries. They account for 71 per cent of total value added in the electronic and telecommunications equipment sector and 91 per cent in the computer and office equipment sector. It is estimated that foreign-invested enterprises employ 37 per cent of China's total high-technology workforce and 41 per cent of China's scientists and engineers (Steinfeld 2010, 161).

China's large commercial aircraft are entirely purchased from Boeing and Airbus. China faces an enormous challenge in its efforts to build a globally successful large commercial aircraft industry. China's aircraft components industry has only a small role within the supply chain of the global industry. China's indigenously assembled commercial aircraft is based on the ARJ21 regional jet and the C919 large commercial aircraft, neither of which is yet in commercial service. They consist mainly of sub-systems supplied by leading global aerospace companies, mainly from the United States, including GE,

United Technologies, Honeywell, Rockwell Collins, Parker Hannifin and Eaton.

Despite 30 years of industrial policy aimed at building globally successful automobile companies through the mechanism of joint ventures, the Chinese automobile market is dominated by global companies, which have over three-quarters of the national market in terms of units sold, and close to 90 per cent in terms of sales revenue. The auto sales of the three Chinese firms in the *Fortune* 500 (Shanghai Automobile Industry Corporation (SAIC), China FAW Group, Dongfeng Motor Group) rely almost entirely on joint ventures controlled by global giant auto companies. Two giant global auto assemblers, GM and VW, together account for over 30 per cent of the Chinese automobile market. Domestic auto firms are confined to low-value-added, low-technology vehicles.

The IT hardware and software systems from global firms are at the core of China's modernization in a wide array of sectors. For example, leading international firms, mainly those from the United States, have been at the heart of the high-speed modernization of the IT systems of China's main banks. The mainframes in China's largest banks are from IBM, the servers from IBM and HP, the software packages from Oracle and SAP, and the ATMs from Diebold, NCR and Wincor-Nixdorf.

The Chinese market for high-value-added consumer information technology products is dominated by global giants. In 2012 in the Chinese market for 'tablet' PC devices, Apple's iPad had a market share of 73 per cent. In the 'smartphone' market, Android (Google) devices account for around 80 per cent and Apple for around 12 per cent (*Guardian*, 14 August 2012).[11] The indigenous Chinese PC assembler, Lenovo, relies on Intel for its core micro-processor technology and Microsoft for its main software platform.

There are a large number of indigenous pharmaceutical companies in China, mainly manufacturing generic, low-margin pharmaceuticals. Most patented pharmaceuticals are supplied by global firms, such as Pfizer, Novartis, Bayer, Johnson & Johnson, GlaxoSmithKline and Astra-Zeneca.

In high-technology sectors that are less visible, the world's leading firms also occupy a large fraction of the market. The Chinese auto components industry is mostly controlled by the global giants, such as Bosch, Denso, Valeo, Visteon, Delphi, Continental and Johnston Controls, which have large investments in production facilities within China in order to meet the needs of their global customers. The key installations in heating, ventilation and cooling systems for buildings are mostly supplied by global firms including Carrier (United Technologies), Mitsubishi Electric, GE and Siemens. Most elevators and escalators are supplied by global firms. Otis, Mitsubishi and Hitachi have an estimated 70 per cent of the Chinese elevator market (*China Daily*, 8 July 2011).

Global firms dominate the Chinese market for branded goods, including beverages, confectionary, cosmetics, luggage, watches, jewellery and clothing (Bain 2010). When asked to name their 'most desired luxury brands', the top ten positions are entirely occupied by global brands. In branded consumer goods indigenous firms are mainly confined to low-value-added sectors.

Multinational firms in China account for 55 per cent of China's total exports, and for 90 per cent of exports of high-technology products, including 99 per cent of its exports of computers and office equipment (Gao Yuning 2011).

The number of people working in China within the value chain of foreign firms is extremely large and beyond easy calculation.

China is unique among large latecomer countries in the degree of importance of foreign firms in its modernization and national economic catch-up. It is remarkable that such an exceptionally high degree of openness has occurred under Communist Party rule, which contradicts the predictions of almost all international experts on the 'transition' from central planning.

Chinese firms 'going out' of China into the high-income economies: 'I have you within me but you do not have me within you'

China's stock of outward FDI increased eightfold from $27 billion in 2000 to $230 billion in 2009 (UNCTAD 2010, annex), which has inspired intense media discussion and the widespread perception that China is 'buying the world'. It seems that China's 'going out' policy for its giant state-owned firms has taken off. This perception of China's large firms has strongly influenced the view that firms from developing countries generally are catching up with and overtaking those from the high-income countries on a widespread basis.

China's firms are at the earliest stage of building global production systems. In 2009 China's outward stock of FDI was 27 per cent of that of the Netherlands, 17 per cent of that of Germany, 13 per cent of that of France, 14 per cent of that of the UK and 5 per cent of that of the USA (Table 3.8). It amounted to less than one-fiftieth of that of the high-income countries as a whole. China's total stock of outward FDI (excluding Hong Kong) is just one-fifth of the value of GE's foreign assets ($401 billion) or one-half of ExxonMobil's ($161 billion). China's total global stock of FDI in the manufacturing sector is just $14 billion (SSB 2010), on a par with the international assets of a single medium-sized global company, or the equivalent of a single acquisition by a leading US multinational, such as Kraft's recent $19 billion acquisition of Cadbury, the iconic British confectionary company.

China's outward FDI in the high-income countries is negligible. Sixty-eight per cent of China's outward stock of FDI is in Hong Kong/Macao

Table 3.8. Globalization and FDI: Outward stock of FDI, 1990 and 2009 ($ billion)

	1990	2009
Developed economies	*1,942*	*16,010*
of which:		
USA	732	4,303
UK	229	1,652
Germany	152	1,378
France	112	1,720
Netherlands	107	851
Australia	31	344
Denmark	7	216
Developing and transition economies	*145*	*2,691*
of which:		
Singapore (a)	8	213
Russia	negl.	249
Taiwan (a)	30	181
Brazil	41	158
China	4	230 (76)(b)
India	negl.	77

Source: UNCTAD (2010, annex).
Notes: (a) the World Bank categorizes both Singapore and Taiwan as high-income economies
        (b) excluding Hong Kong and Macao; 67 per cent of China's outward stock of FDI is in
             Hong Kong and Macao (SSB 2009, tables 17–20)

(Table 3.9). Only 11 per cent of China's total outward stock of FDI is in the high-income countries. China's stock of outward FDI in the high-income countries is just $27 billion, compared with an inward stock of FDI of nearly $500 billion, most of which is from the high-income countries. In other words, the high-income countries' stock of FDI in China is almost twenty times as large as China's FDI stock in the high-income countries.

In 2009 China's stock of outward FDI in the USA was $3.3 billion. In Germany it was $1.2 billion and in Japan it was $0.7 billion. The USA's stock of FDI in China was around $100 billion, which is 30 times as large as China's stock of FDI in the USA. Japan's stock of FDI in China was around $85 billion, which is around one hundred times greater than China's stock of FDI in Japan. Germany's stock of FDI in China was around $33 billion, which is 22 times as large as China's stock of FDI in Germany (Table 3.10).

Table 3.9. Distribution of China's outward stock of FDI, 2009 ($ billion)

Region/country	$ billion	%
Total	*245.8*	*100*
of which:		
Hong Kong/Macao	166.3	67.7
Africa	9.3	3.8
Latin America	30.6	12.4
of which:		
Cayman Islands	13.6	5.5
Virgin Islands	15.1	6.1
High-income countries (a)	*27.1*	*11.0*
of which:		
Europe	8.7	3.5
France	0.2	negl.
Germany	1.1	0.4
UK	1.0	0.4
North America	5.2	2.1
USA	3.3	1.3
Japan	0.7	0.3
Singapore	4.9	2.0
Korea	1.2	0.5
Oceania	6.4	2.6

Source: SSB (2010, 257).
Note: (a) excluding Hong Kong

Table 3.10. FDI stock of American, Japanese and German firms in China, compared with the FDI stock of Chinese firms in the US, Japan and Germany ($ billion)

	Stock of FDI in China (a)	China's stock of FDI in the respective high-income country (b)	Ratio of (b) to (a)
USA (2009)	100	3.3	1:30
Japan (2011)	85	0.9	1:94
Germany (2009)	33	1.2	1:28

Chinese firms have been conspicuously absent from major international mergers and acquisitions, which is centrally important for building a global business system. China's giant banks played no role whatsoever in the massive round of mergers and acquisitions during the global financial crisis.

There have been only a tiny number of significant international acquisitions by Chinese companies. None of these has been large by the standards of the world's largest mergers and acquisitions. Moreover, each of these has faced more or less severe difficulties.

In 2005 Lenovo acquired IBM's PC division for $1.75 billion. This was highly significant and has helped make Lenovo a global force in the PC market. However, the reason that IBM was willing to sell the division is the low profitability of this division and the intense competition in the sector. In September 2011 HP, the world's largest producer of PCs, announced that it was planning to spin off its PC division due to its slow profitability. The future of the PC industry as a whole was in serious doubt due to the explosive rise of a new genre of IT communications devices, including 'tablets' and 'iPhones'. Nokia, which was the world's super-giant of the mobile phone industry, has been eclipsed by the new generation of communication devices, led by Apple and Google's 'Android' system. It remains to be seen whether traditional PC companies, such as Lenovo, will be commercially successful in the face of this dramatic technological challenge.

It was not until 2010 that a Chinese company made another significant international acquisition, when the Chinese auto manufacturer Geely acquired Volvo Cars for $1.8 billion. Volvo Cars was a loss-making division within Ford and by late 2012 Volvo Cars was making large losses and faced a bleak future. Its European managers acknowledged that it was too small to compete with the global giants of luxury cars, Mercedes and BMW.

The efforts of China's large firms to acquire businesses in the high-income countries have mostly ended in failure. In June 2005 the third largest Chinese oil company, CNOOC, launched a bid of $18.5 billion to acquire the mid-sized US oil company Unocal. Zhou Shouwei, the president of CNOOC said: 'If the bid succeeds CNOOC's business will be transformed from a Chinese into a global enterprise.' In fact the bid was greeted with a storm of opposition in the US media. In early July the US House of Representatives voted by 398–15 to call on the US government to review the bid on the grounds that it constituted a 'threat to US national security'. On 3 August 2005 CNOOC withdrew its bid. Subsequently, Unocal was acquired by Chevron.

In July 2012 CNOOC made an offer to acquire the Canadian oil and gas company Nexen for $15.1 billion. In a landmark decision in early December, the Canadian government approved the acquisition, by far the largest made by a Chinese company. At the same time it approved the acquisition of Progress

Energy Resources by Malaysia's Petronas. However, the Canadian government simultaneously announced the introduction of tougher rules for acquisitions of Canadian companies by state-owned enterprises. Canada's prime minister, Stephen Harper said: 'When we say Canada is open for business, we do not mean that Canada is for sale to foreign governments… Canadians generally, investors specifically, should understand that these decisions are not the beginning of a trend, but rather the end of a trend.'

A succession of possible international acquisitions by Huawei were all abandoned. In 2005 it was rumoured that Huawei was in negotiations to acquire Marconi, the venerable but loss-making UK telecoms equipment maker. This prompted intense discussion in the UK mass media and rumours that the deal would be referred to the US government's Committee on Foreign Investment in the United States (CFIUS). Huawei made no formal offer to acquire Marconi and eventually it was sold to Ericsson for $2.1 billion. In 2010 Huawei made a bid to acquire the tiny niche telecoms software company 3Leaf for $2 million, a miniscule transaction in global terms. The deal was blocked by CFIUS on national security grounds.

An alternative to full-scale takeover is the acquisition by Chinese companies of substantial minority shares in leading Western companies. In 2007–2008 it was proposed that Huawei would acquire 3Com, the US telecoms equipment company, jointly with the US private equity firm Bain Capital. Despite the fact that Huawei would own only a small minority share, and despite the fact that 3Com is a relatively small company, the proposal led to an intense US media furore focusing on Huawei's 'threat to US national security' and the case was referred to CFIUS. Before a formal ruling was reached, the acquisition offer was withdrawn by Bain and Huawei. In 2010 HP acquired 3Com for $2.2 billion.

One can always speculate about the future. However, up until this point Chinese firms have been extremely cautious in their international mergers and acquisitions, as well as in their international 'greenfield' investments. China's 'going out' strategy has advanced furthest in the critically important energy sector. However, even here China's leading firms have proceeded cautiously in their international expansion in both developing and high-income countries. They have far to go before they can catch up with the global operations of the oil majors, the leading oil service companies[12] or chemical companies. China's large firms from different industries have failed in several efforts to acquire international companies, mainly on account of political obstacles to 'their' firms acquiring 'our' firms. The acquisitions that they have made are small scale compared with the routine mergers and acquisitions that are made continuously by the world's leading companies. Moreover, China's record with even the small number of acquisitions that have been made is mixed, with few well-chosen or successful acquisitions. China's large firms remain far removed from the global production systems that the world's leading firms, mostly with their headquarters in the high-income countries, have established during the three decades of modern capitalist globalization.

Constraints on China 'buying the world'

Gerard Lyons, chief economist of Standard Chartered Bank, has expressed widely held concerns about China 'buying the world' and acquiring Western technologies. In 2007 he said: 'The big worry is that [sovereign wealth funds] see an opportunity to buy strategic stakes in key industries around the globe... The expertise of emerging economies, such as China, in low cost manufacturing could quickly be added to by the acquisition of high tech firms overseas' (Lyons 2007). In 2012 Lyons said: 'The three most important words in the past decade were not the "war on terror" but "made in China". On present trends, the three most important words of this decade will be "owned by China"' (quoted in the *FT*, 6 September 2011). The reality is very different from the widely held popular perception that China is 'buying the world'.

How large are China's foreign exchange reserves?

The perception of most Western commentators and, indeed, ordinary citizens is that China has 'enormous' foreign exchange reserves that it is using to 'buy the world'. It is true that China has very large foreign exchange reserves, totalling $3,200 billion by June 2011, by far the largest in the world. However, the size of China's foreign exchange reserves can be looked at from a variety of perspectives.

China is still a developing country. The 'umbrella' of its foreign exchange reserves has to 'shelter' 1.3 billion people. In mid-2011 its foreign exchange reserves amounted to $2,459 per person, compared with $6,356 per person for Korea, $8,889 for Japan, $39,601 for Hong Kong and $60,571 for Singapore. The Asian financial crisis deeply scarred East Asian countries. Since then they have mostly built up their foreign exchange reserves as a form of insurance against an international financial crisis rather than as a vehicle for international business expansion. The State Administration of Foreign Exchange (SAFE) has the weighty responsibility of managing China's foreign exchange reserves: 'Since China is a large developing country, maintaining sufficient foreign exchange reserves is of great significance to ensure international liquidity, enhance the capability to respond to risk, and safeguard the economic and financial security of the nation' (www.safe.gov.cn, 2011). China's policymakers were for many years deeply concerned that the deregulation of Western financial systems through 'regulatory capture' by giant global banks would cause a global financial crisis. It pursued an extremely conservative domestic regulatory regime completely at odds with that pursued in the West, and in the face of heavy international criticism of their approach. In fact, their fears proved to be well founded.

The current global financial crisis is far from over. It has already had a profound effect on China, leading it to greatly increase bank lending in order to stimulate the economy in the face of the collapse in external demand in 2008–2009. It remains to be seen what long-term impact this will have on the country's banking system. China's leaders are vigilant, fully aware that the international crisis could deepen, which would have profound implications for China. Under these circumstances China's foreign exchange reserves must be managed prudently, with a large share allocated to secure, liquid assets, even if the return on these is much less than alternative investments. This task has become even more difficult due to the sovereign debt crisis in the West.

China's total foreign exchange reserves are small in comparison with the funds managed by Western asset managers. In 2009 the world's top 500 asset managers had a total of $62 trillion of assets under management (Towers Watson 2010). Within this total, US asset managers had a total of $30.6 trillion under management and European asset managers had $24.1 trillion under management, totalling $54.7 trillion, while asset managers in developing countries had just $2.5 trillion under management. The top firm, Blackstone, had $3.3 trillion under management, exceeding China's total foreign exchange reserves today. Funds come in all shapes and sizes in terms of risk profile. However, there is a sense in which the West's asset managers are literally 'buying the world', since the total value of the funds they manage is roughly equal to total world GDP, which amounted to $58.3 trillion in 2008 (WB 2011). Even more meaningfully, they are easily able to 'buy the developing world'. In 2009 the total GDP for all low- and middle-income countries amounted to $16.7 trillion, and in 2010 the total value of their stock market capitalization was $13.4 trillion, compared with the total of $54.7 trillion managed by the leading US and European asset managers (WB 2011).

A great deal of discussion has taken place in the Western press about China's sovereign wealth funds, namely China Investment Corporation (CIC) and SAFE Investment Company (SIC), which are the principal vehicles for international equity investment by the Chinese government. China's sovereign wealth funds are estimated to have a total of around $700 billion of funds under management,[13] and they have made numerous minority equity investments in global companies.[14] In March 2011 the market capitalization of the two largest US companies, ExxonMobil and Apple, totalled $738 billion, roughly the same as the total estimated funds managed by CIC and SIC. In 2011 the market capitalization of the 160 US companies in the *FT* 500 amounted to $9.6 trillion and that of the top 34 UK companies in the *FT* 500 amounted to $2.1 trillion, totalling $11.7 trillion, which is 17 times greater than the estimated combined funds managed by CIC and SIC. In 2010 the stock market capitalization of the high-income countries as a whole totalled $42.8 trillion (WB 2011), 61 times as large as the total estimated funds managed by CIC and SIC. In other words, China's sovereign wealth funds cannot under any circumstances 'buy the world'.

Can China's national champion companies acquire, merge with and integrate global companies?

The culture of China's national champion firms is changing significantly, with intense efforts to raise not only technical management skills, but also to deepen understanding of global culture. A new generation of business leaders is being trained intensively in the skills needed to compete globally. Foreign-trained Chinese graduates are returning to take up positions in the national champion firms. The flotation of part of their equity has led to greatly increased media scrutiny of the firms both within and outside China. Remuneration practices have altered greatly. The appointment of international non-executive directors has deepened awareness of international business practice. As their international operations gradually increase a new generation of Chinese business leaders is able steadily to deepen their understanding of the global economy through daily business experience.

However, 'going out' for China's large national champion firms is just beginning. They have limited experience of conducting international mergers and acquisition. Although the share of international business is growing, most of the assets, employment, revenue and profits of China's national champion firms are derived from the large and fast-growing domestic Chinese market. Success in international mergers and acquisitions requires long experience and practice. The leading global companies make numerous acquisitions and divestitures annually. Skill in this area is a key aspect of their competitive advantage. Identifying potential targets and making a successful offer is just the beginning of a successful merger or acquisition.

There is still a significant gap between the operational systems of China's large state-owned enterprises and those of the world's leading international companies. The management system is typically hierarchical with innumerable layers between the lower and the higher levels. The methods of remuneration and promotion are still very different from those in global companies. At the higher levels, males are dominant with only a handful of top women managers.

There are few non-Chinese people in senior executive positions. These differences might make it difficult for China's large state-owned firms to integrate an international acquisition or to merge with a Western multinational company. However, up until this point, Chinese firms have had few opportunities to acquire or merge with significant multinational firms. The most significant example of an international acquisition by a Chinese firm is Lenovo's acquisition of IBM's PC division. This appears to have been a successful acquisition in terms of integrating the two entities, despite the wide apparent cultural difference. In 2007 China's ICBC acquired a 20 per cent equity stake in South Africa's Standard Bank for $4.5 billion. Standard Bank is the largest bank in Africa, and there appear to have been substantial mutual benefits from the relationship with no significant operational difficulties. These examples suggest that if the high-income countries allowed them to do so large Chinese firms might quickly learn to make substantial international acquisitions and integrate them successfully. Moreover, there are many examples of Western companies that have substantial state ownership, which have successfully acquired and integrated firms from other high-income countries, including the USA. These include the European Aeronautic Defence and Space Company, or EADS (France/Germany/Spain), Électricité de France, or EDF (France), Renault (France), Safran (France), France Télécom (France), ENI (Italy), Finmeccanica (Italy), VW (Germany), Deutsche Telekom (Germany) and Statoil (Norway).

How open are Western governments to large acquisitions of, and mergers with, China's national champion companies?

The leaders of China's national champion firms are all appointed by the Chinese Communist Party, and the Communist Party still has a deep influence on the way in which the state-owned firms are run. Since the 1970s the Chinese Communist Party has changed greatly. China's leaders have made great efforts to upgrade the educational level and technical skills of party members, and to deepen their understanding of the world economy, international relations and global culture. Despite these profound changes, there is deep political and ideological resistance among Western governments to permitting Chinese state-owned firms to acquire substantial assets through merger and acquisition, even though these firms are partially privatized and quoted on global stock markets. Western governments view China's national champion firms fundamentally differently from the way in which they view companies from other Western countries that have substantial state ownership.

The idea that China can 'catch up' technologically by buying high-technology Western firms has so far proven to be incorrect. The main acquisitions by Chinese firms have been of loss-making companies in non-strategic industries, notably IBM's PC division and Ford's Volvo Cars division. Both were small-scale acquisitions. The attempt at more substantial acquisitions in more sensitive sectors, by both state-owned and private firms, failed, most notably the attempt by CNOOC to acquire Unocal and the various attempts by Huawei to acquire small segments of the telecoms equipment sector. The attempt by Chinalco to acquire a substantial minority stake in Rio Tinto encountered strong political opposition in Australia. In July 2012 CNOOC made an offer to acquire the Canadian oil and gas company Nexen for $15.1 billion. Although the Canadian government approved the acquisition, it made it clear that there would be no further acquisitions of Canadian natural resource companies by foreign state-owned companies.

4. The Case of Huawei

Background

Huawei stands out among Chinese companies for its success in penetrating the world's most competitive high-technology markets in the high-income countries. It provides a useful benchmark against which to compare China's state-owned enterprises.

Huawei is a telecoms equipment, software and services company, based in Shenzhen, in southern China. In the 1990s, when China followed the path of 'reform and opening up', both the Chinese and global telecoms equipment markets were dominated by a handful of giant high-technology companies, including Alcatel, Lucent, Siemens, Ericsson, Nortel and Motorola. There was only a negligible role for indigenous Chinese companies. Since then the global telecoms equipment and service industry has gone through a technological and business revolution and an even smaller number of giant firms now dominates the industry. Ericsson stands at the forefront of the global industry. Other leading global firms in the sector have foundered, including Nortel, Motorola and Alcatel-Lucent. Even Nokia-Siemens faces severe competition from Huawei. Against most predictions Huawei has emerged to become the number two firm in the global telecoms equipment industry, with an approximate global market share of around 16 per cent compared with around 20 per cent for Ericsson. In some areas, such as radio base stations, industry experts estimate that Huawei has established a technological lead over all other companies in the sector.

Huawei was founded in 1988 by Ren Zhengfei, who was then aged 40 and had retired from his position as an officer in the Chinese military in 1984. In China, as in Western countries, people with a military background can sometimes be strong business leaders, with a firm grasp of strategy, discipline and motivation. There is no evidence that sales to the People's Liberation

Army (PLA) at any stage have formed an important part of Huawei's sales.[15] Huawei has advanced from a minnow in the global telecoms industry, with no serious hopes to compete with the global giants, to a giant firm with revenues in 2010 of $27.1 billion and an operating profit of over $4.3 billion.

Huawei is a private company owned entirely by its employees. It is not owned by the Chinese state at either the central or the local level and it is not floated on the stock market. It has been run from its inception by a single CEO, Ren Zhengfei, and since 1999 it has had a single chairwoman, Sun Yafang. This provided Huawei with a remarkable continuity of its top leadership. The fact that it is not a state-owned enterprise has put pressure on the company, but it has also provided it with the possibility of pursuing a different strategy from that of the large SOEs. The fact that it is not quoted on the stock market has provided the opportunity to take a long-term view of strategy.

Initially Huawei was an agent for simple imported PBX (private branch exchange) equipment. It quickly began to manufacture PBX equipment itself. Faced with the near monopoly established by the global giants among large urban customers, Huawei focused on the decentralized rural market, selling mainly to small local SOEs and rural collective enterprises. Its strategy was to 'use the countryside to surround the cities', mimicking the strategy that Chairman Mao had used in the Communist Party's guerrilla war before 1949. In the early years Ren Zhengfei urged Huawei's employees to make use of the 'wolf spirit' to fight for sales in difficult circumstances. Once it had consolidated its position in its rural 'base areas' it began to compete in urban markets for core network and access network equipment. By 1998–99 it had begun to compete in the Chinese backbone market against the global giants.

The central Chinese government only began to provide significant support for Huawei once it had become firmly established. In 2004, China Development Bank (CDB) provided Huawei with a credit facility of $10 billion in order to support its international expansion by providing loans to Huawei's customers to purchase its equipment. In the 1990s, there was almost no diplomatic support from the Chinese government for Huawei's overseas sales. However, as Huawei became an important symbol of China's international business success, the government began to provide significant diplomatic support, with Huawei's top managers frequently participating in the international visits of China's leaders.

The fact that it was not a state-owned national champion had important advantages for Huawei. If Huawei had been a state-owned firm that was closely connected with the Chinese political system, it would have provided Huawei with opportunities to earn money from investing in 'rent-seeking' businesses dependent on political relationships, which could have led it to becoming a 'spoilt child'. Numerous Chinese firms were led into diversification, especially property development, away from investment in their core business and away from face-to-face competition with the global giants. The very fact that Huawei lacked such opportunities forced it to re-invest in the telecoms equipment business and look towards international markets. In Ren Zhengfei's view: 'If the government had given Huawei the right to develop the Beijing–Guangzhou railway, Huawei would have left the telecoms equipment business.' Throughout its existence, Huawei has remained focused on its core business of telecoms equipment and services. It has poured its profits back into expanding its core capabilities. It has consistently spent a high share of its revenue on R&D. In 2010 it spent $2.4 billion on R&D, amounting to around 9 per cent of its revenue. It outsources most of its manufacturing activities. Around 51,000 employees out of a total of 110,000 employees are engaged in R&D. In addition to its core campus in Shenzhen, Huawei has 20 research institutes around the world close to its customers, including the USA, Germany, Sweden, Russia and India.

One reason that the central government allowed Huawei to follow its own development strategy is that it couldn't imagine that any Chinese firm would be able to succeed in such a fiercely competitive, high-technology industry as IT hardware. By leaving Huawei to its own devices, the government allowed it space to grow. In many sectors, the Chinese central government used 'industrial policy' to require foreign investors to establish joint ventures with specified local firms. In numerous cases, the central and local governments pushed firms into unwanted mergers and acquisitions. Huawei had to face the full force of competition with the world's leading firms on its own, initially within China and increasingly in the international market. In Ren Zhengfei's view, faced with the intense heat of competition from the global giants, the Chinese market provided a 'furnace in which to refine Huawei'.

In the domestic market, despite the fact that the leading telecoms operators are all majority state owned, by 2004 Huawei accounted for only around 10 per cent of the fast-growing market for mobile equipment. The Chinese domestic mobile networking equipment market was dominated by the international giant telecoms equipment companies. It was precisely because of its relatively weak position in domestic markets that Huawei was forced to put so much effort into building its position in international markets: 'We were forced to go into the international market for our very survival.'

Re-engineering Huawei

In the late 1990s Huawei reached a watershed in its development. In 1997 Huawei's CEO, Ren Zhengfei, and its chairwoman, Sun Yafang, took the momentous step of comprehensively re-engineering the company, shifting from a technology-based firm to a customer-based approach. This involved a comprehensive transformation of Huawei's culture, which caused intense internal debate. Many engineers left the company because they felt that this approach devalued their contribution to the company compared with the sales force. However, if they wished to return they were welcomed back into the company, and many have returned. The Huawei leadership was convinced that the only way to succeed in international competition was to adopt international best-practice management techniques. The re-engineering process was so painful that Ren Zhengfei likened the process to 'cutting our feet to fit American shoes'. No other large Chinese company has gone through such a radical change in its corporate culture.

At great expense Huawei engaged teams from IBM to lead the transformation of its product development, which was the core of its cultural transformation. Between 1998 and 2005 more than 200 IBM employees spent long periods at Huawei headquarters to institute the process of 'integrated product development' (IPD). In the telecommunications equipment industry each customer requires a different configuration, with 'assembly-to-order' depending on the specific customer's requirements. Each site has different requirements and different installation needs. Each product requires a different combination of a large number of physical components and accompanying software. Because of this industry characteristic, Huawei's systems re-engineering under IBM's guidance was critical to its commercial success. IBM introduced the idea of building cross-functional teams focused on particular customers. The process was now market driven, not driven by R&D. Teams from across functions now worked together on specific projects, coming from all parts of the company, including marketing and sales. Product development now incorporates all aspects of the product from the start, including financial assessments, procurement and the ease with which the product can be manufactured and serviced. The IPD approach introduced by IBM tightly links the process of product development from one end of the supply chain to the other. The transformation to a system in which the whole process of product development was geared to the specific needs of each customer was revolutionary in the Chinese business system.

A second important aspect of the cultural change at Huawei involved the introduction of international standards in financial management. The reforms introduced by KPMG after 1998 were essential to Huawei's successful operation in international markets. KPMG helped Huawei to understand the gap that existed between themselves and global best practice in financial control systems. Under KPMG's guidance, Huawei introduced a new internal financial management structure, including a financial system, financial processes, financial coding and practice, and financial monitoring and supervision. Once KPMG had helped Huawei to put the basic infrastructure into place, Huawei restructured the company's budget, cost and financial control systems. It was then able to use its database to monitor the company's internal performance as well as its financial interactions with other companies. The financial reforms introduced with KPMG's guidance helped Huawei introduce a single centralized system controlling all Huawei's operational departments and units both in China and internationally. Henceforth, all Huawei departments and units were subject to strict central financial control in accordance with common financial practice across the whole company. This was a revolution in the way the company was organized.

The third area of re-engineering after 1999 involved human resources. Hay Group played a central role in this process. Under the reforms, Huawei introduced 'Key Performance Indicators' (KPI) to evaluate and reward performance of individual employees across the whole company. In the second phase of re-engineering, Hay concentrated its efforts on the key people at the top of Huawei. It attempted to ensure that the people occupying these positions developed a high level of cross-functional skills. The top tier of managers should be excellent both at research and development, as well as at marketing. These people should also be leaders with a high level of energy. Huawei also used Mercer Management, which specializes in organization design. In the late 1990s Huawei used to think of its organizational style as similar to that of a 'guerilla force' (youjidui), with a culture that rewarded individual 'heroes'. This changed radically after the late 1990s and there was a fundamental shift of style towards team working within systematic structures and measurable performance criteria.

As Huawei's international business expanded, it paid great attention to internationalizing the culture at Huawei. This started from the design and feel of the Huawei campus in Shenzhen. Huawei's CEO, Ren Zhengfei, is passionately interested in architecture, both for its own intrinsic merits and for the effect that the working environment has on people's creativity. The overall design was undertaken by the British architect, Norman Foster, with individual buildings following the style of leading international architects, such as Frank Lloyd Wright. The total cost of the campus was around $1.5 billion, which was a huge expenditure compared to Huawei's annual revenues in the late 1990s. The campus is designed to feel like a university, reinforcing the fact that Huawei is a science-based high-technology company. It is the beating 'heart' of the whole Huawei system. It provides a strong non-financial attraction for scientists and engineers, both Chinese and foreign, to come to work at Huawei. It is a source of pride for all Huawei employees, both in China and across the world. The campus strongly impresses foreign visitors, including both customers and suppliers. International competitors acknowledge that Huawei has been highly successful at attracting the best Chinese students in the field: 'Huawei is close to HP in its early days. It's a place where the brightest people in China want to work.' The Huawei team feels it 'can do anything', and this communicates itself to its potential employees.

The proportion of foreign employees at Huawei is exceptionally high compared with other Chinese companies. Already in 2004, more than one-fifth of Huawei's 23,000 employees were non-Chinese, and the proportion of foreign employees has remained at around that level. In 2010 Huawei had 21,700 foreign employees out of a total of 110,000. As part of the re-engineering of the company since the late 1990s, Ren Zhengfei required senior managers in each functional department to use English as the standard language of communication.

Huawei's foreign sales have grown in a remarkable fashion, rising from $100 million in 1999 to $1.8 billion in 2004, reaching almost $18 billion in 2010. As early as 2004, 40 per cent of Huawei's sales were outside China. By 2007 more than two-thirds of Huawei's revenue came from international sales.[16] Huawei's initial focus in its international revenue growth was on developing countries. In 2004 94 per cent of Huawei's international sales were to developing and transition economies. Africa was Huawei's biggest international market, accounting for one-third of its international sales. Its sales to Nigeria were three times as large as its total sales to Europe. Its sales to the USA were non-existent. It is still the case that sales to developing and transition economies are far greater than those to high-income countries, but they have risen substantially, and now stand at around one-fifth of its total overseas revenue.

However, Huawei has made significant inroads into markets in the high-income countries, especially in Europe. In 2004 Huawei made a significant breakthrough in Europe by winning a contract with Telfort (now merged with KPN), the Dutch mobile phone company. It displaced Ericsson, which had supplied Telfort for almost ten years, installing most of its 2G network. It supplied Telfort with a total of over $500 million worth of equipment. In 2005 Huawei achieved two landmarks in its international expansion. It was certified as a qualified supplier to both BT and Vodafone. Huawei displaced Marconi as one of the suppliers of BT's massive contract for its twenty-first-century network. However, even more significant is the fact that since 2005 Huawei has established itself as a long-term supplier for Vodafone, the world's biggest mobile phone company. In order to qualify as a supplier to BT and Vodafone, Huawei needed to submit to the deepest scrutiny of its products and processes, and all aspects of its performance, including not just technical issues but also its compliance with internationally accepted practices in terms of corporate social responsibility.

Conclusion

Among large Chinese firms Huawei has been uniquely successful in building a globally competitive business system. It is alone in having penetrated the business system of the high-income countries and met the most severe standards of global competition among customers in high-income countries. It stands alone in being 'inside us'. It is alone among large Chinese firms in terms of the continuity of its top management, its focus on core business, the high share of revenue allocated to R&D, the large share of its employees engaged in R&D, the large share of foreign workers among its employees, the open and transparent system of organization and remuneration of its workforce, the intellectual and physical attractiveness of the work environment, and the internationalization of its culture, including the use of English throughout the upper reaches of the company. Is Huawei the 'exception that proves the rule', or the 'shape of things to come'? Will there be a large cohort of Chinese firms in the years ahead that will reproduce Huawei's competitive success and establish themselves 'inside us'?

5. Institutional Change and Globalization in European State-Owned Enterprises

Many of the world's leading firms, which are today at the forefront of innovation and technical progress in their respective sectors, were state-owned enterprises in the recent past. The largest group of such enterprises are from Western Europe. They span a wide range of industries. A relatively short time ago many of Europe's leading global firms were owned by the state and were focused mainly on the domestic market, where they were protected from international competition. They followed a variety of paths from state-owned enterprises to globally competitive firms at the forefront of customer-focused innovation. What lessons can be learned from these examples about China's own reform of its state-owned enterprises?

Telecommunications: The case of Telefónica (Spain)

In most European countries up until the 1990s, the telecommunications system was state owned, usually as part of the ministry of posts and telecommunications. The national state-owned telecoms systems typically procured their telecoms equipment mainly from domestic companies.[17] In the 1990s the main body of the state-owned European telecoms sector was privatized. In the case of the UK's BT, between 1984 and 1991 the company was wholly privatized. In 1999 BT de-merged its mobile operations, which were re-branded as O2.

In the case of Germany and France the state retains a significant minority share ownership and substantial influence over the 'national champion' telecom companies.[18] The companies remained integrated fixed line, broadband and mobile telecoms companies.

In 1945 the Spanish government established Telefónica (then called CTNE) as a state-owned monopoly. It was partially privatized in 1995 and fully privatized in 1999. Like most European state-owned telecoms companies, the main body of its revenues came from the home market. Prior to privatization, Telefónica had begun to expand in Latin America. In 1989 it acquired a 43.5 per cent stake in CTC, the former Chilean state-owned telecoms company, which had over 90 per cent of the country's telecoms market. In the same year it acquired the southern portion of the former state-owned Argentinean telecoms company. This experience in acquiring two former state-owned telecoms companies in Latin America helped to guide the strategy that Telefónica followed subsequently. Following its own privatization Telefónica launched an ambitious international expansion strategy focused on Latin America, taking advantage of the privatization of telecoms companies in the region and the fast growth opportunities in the region's market, including the rapidly growing market for mobile telephony. In addition to its Chilean and Argentinean business, it acquired Telefónica del Peru, and Brazil's Telesp and Tele Sudeste. Within a few years of its own privatization Telefónica had built a large telecoms business in Latin America, based heavily on the acquisition of privatized telecoms companies in the region.

According to the companies' annual reports, by 2002 Telefónica's international revenues had reached 43 per cent of its total revenues, compared with 13 per cent for Deutsche Telekom and 17 per cent for France Télécom. It was the leading telecoms provider in Latin America, accounting for 26 per cent of the region's fixed line market, compared with 18 per cent for its closest rival. By 2002 the share of its home market in Spain had shrunk to less than 50 per cent in terms of the number of customers and 58 per cent in terms of revenue. Latin America accounted for 49 per cent of its customers and 38 per cent of its revenues.

In the following decade Telefónica accelerated its international expansion. In 2003 it established its Brazilian Vivo mobile joint venture and in 2010 it bought the share of its partner, Portugal Telecom, for 7.5 billion euros. In 2008 it acquired Brazil's Telemig, a regional mobile company. In 2004 it acquired Bell South's Latin American assets, including those in Guatemala, Panama and Venezuela. In 2006 it took a 51 per cent stake in Colombia Telecom. In 2008 it consolidated its position in Chile, increasing its ownership share in Telefónica CTC to 98 per cent. In 2011 it acquired a mobile licence in Costa Rica. By 2012 Telefónica was the market leader in Brazil, Argentina, Chile and Peru and its Latin American operations greatly exceeded its domestic operations.

By 2012 Telefónica had 24 million fixed line and 166 million mobile phone customers in Latin America, compared with 16 million fixed line and 70 million mobile customers in Europe (including Spain). In Brazil alone, Telefónica had 77 million mobile phone customers. Between 1997 and 2012 Telefónica's total revenues expanded from 14.2 billion euros to 46.5 billion euros. The share of its revenues from outside Spain had increased to 75 per cent. Latin America's share of its total revenues had risen to 49 per cent.

In 2006, having established its strong foundations in Latin America, Telefónica took the decisive strategic decision to acquire O2, the UK-based mobile phone company that had been de-merged from the former state-owned BT in 1999. It paid £17.7 billion (around US$29 billion) to acquire O2, in one of the biggest acquisitions in the history of the telecoms industry. Through its acquisition of O2 Telefónica added 22 million mobile subscribers in the UK and 19 million in Germany. Telefónica now has twice as many international mobile customers in Europe as it has in Spain itself.

Automobiles: The case of Volkswagen

Europe has had several large automobile companies that were at one point under state ownership, including Renault (France)[19] and British Leyland (UK).[20] Europe's largest automobile maker today is Volkswagen. It was established in 1937 as a wholly state-owned automobile manufacturer. From 1945 to 1949 it was under the trusteeship of the British military and in 1949 the company was transferred to the joint ownership of the federal government and the local government of the state of Lower Saxony. In 1961 the company was partially privatized, with the sale of 60 per cent of the company as 'people's shares'. The federal government and the state of Lower Saxony still held 20 per cent of the equity each. This was a milestone in the history of privatization in Europe. In 1988 the federal government sold its share. However, the state of Lower Saxony retained its 20 per cent share ownership, which allowed VW to focus on long-term strategy by reducing the possibility of being acquired by a competitor.

Up until the 1970s Volkswagen relied heavily on a single vehicle, the VW Beetle, which had not altered fundamentally since it was launched in 1938. By 1973 Volkswagen had sold over 16 million Beetles.[21] Following the partial privatization in 1961 Volkswagen acquired the German automobile producers Auto Union (in 1964) and NSU (in 1969) and combined them into a new Audi division. In 1982 Volkswagen established its joint venture with SAIC, the platform for its expansion in China. In 1986–90 it acquired SEAT, the privatized Spanish national champion in the auto industry,[22] and in 1991 it acquired Skoda, the privatized Czech national champion car company. In the late 1990s it acquired a group of small luxury auto makers, including Bentley, Bugatti and Lamborghini. In recent years it slowly built up majority control of the global truck makers Scania (Sweden) and MAN (Germany), which now form the foundation of its commercial vehicle division. In 2012, after a prolonged and complex strategic battle, Volkswagen acquired Porsche, which reinforced its luxury car division.

In the late 1980s Volkswagen produced less than 3 million vehicles annually. By 2012 it produced more than 8 million vehicles and vies with Toyota as the world's largest automobile producer. Between 1991 and 2012 its revenues grew from $42 billion to $222 billion, while its R&D spending grew from $1.5 billion to $8.3 billion. Today Volkswagen has 94 production plants globally, of which 25 are in Germany, 24 are elsewhere in Europe and 15 are in Asia, including 11 in China. It has an estimated passenger vehicle market share of 14 per cent in Central and Eastern Europe (including Russia), 18 per cent in China, 19 per cent in South America, and 23 per cent in Western Europe. It has a close relationship with key global suppliers such as Bosch, Continental, Johnson Controls and Michelin to develop new technologies that enhance safety and comfort, increase fuel efficiency and improve vehicle ease of operation. Volkswagen also works closely with its leading suppliers to coordinate the construction of global just-in-time supply chains.

Up until the 1970s Volkswagen relied heavily on a single mass vehicle, mainly assembled in Germany. Today it has a portfolio of global brands that span the whole range of vehicles. In 2012 Volkswagen sold 1.1 million Skoda and SEAT passenger vehicles with revenues of 16 billion euros and profits of 490 euros per vehicle; 4.5 million 'VW' brand vehicles with revenues of 95 billion euros and profits of 850 euros per vehicle; and 1.5 million Audi brand vehicles with revenues of 44 billion euros and profits of 3,500 euros per vehicle. The Audi brand provided 46 per cent of Volkswagen's total profits. Its commercial vehicles division had revenues of 22 billion euros and profits of 2 billion euros. Following the acquisition of MAN and Scania, the commercial vehicle division was in a position to compete fiercely with the leading global commercial vehicle producers, Mercedes, Paccar and Volvo. Large trucks are typically built to order for each customer. The average sales price of Volkswagen's Scania brand trucks is 120,000 euros with profits of 16,000 euros per vehicle.

Electricity and gas: The case of GDF-Suez (France)

Gaz de France (GDF) and its sister company, Électricité de France (EDF), were created as French state-owned monopolies in 1946. GDF was a traditional public utility in the gas industry, supplying mainly domestic French customers, both households and businesses, with gas produced from domestic coal. Increasingly natural gas replaced coal as the main energy source for the gas industry. Imported sources of natural gas included Algeria (1965), the Netherlands (1967), Russia (1975) and Norway (1977), which extended GDF's international operations. However, it remained mainly focused on its monopoly of domestic gas supply in France. In 2005 GDF had total revenues of 22 billion euros, of which 64 per cent came from its domestic sales. In that year the French government sold 20 per cent of the equity to the general public, but retained an 80 per cent ownership share.

Suez is an entirely different type of company. It was the product of a merger between two French non-state enterprises in 1997, namely Lyonnaise des Eaux (established in 1880) and Compagnie de Suez (established in 1858 in order to build the Suez Canal). Lyonnaise des Eaux had grown into a leading international company in waste disposal. Suez had built itself into a leading international company in electricity generation and distribution. It had taken advantage of the international move towards electricity privatization to become the world's largest international independent power producer, operating power stations and selling the electricity to public utilities or high consumption customers. By 2005 Suez had a total electricity generating capacity of 54.6 GW and it operated more than 200 power plants in over thirty countries. Within this total, 58 per cent was in Europe, mostly outside France, 20 per cent was in South America, 10 per cent in North America, and 12 per cent in the rest of the world. Its total revenues were 41.5 billion euros, of which around three-quarters (31.8 billion euros) was from outside France.

In 2006 the French government announced the decision to take the privatization of GDF a step further through an agreed merger with Suez. After intense political debate within France the merger was completed in 2008. It resulted in the conversion of the French government's 80 per cent equity stake in GDF into a 35.7 per cent stake in the new entity, GDF-Suez. The French government had the right to nominate four of the directors in the new entity. The CEO of the new company was Gérard Mestrallet, who had been the CEO of Suez prior to the merger. It was thought that Suez would inject the culture of the private sector into the operational mechanism of the new entity. Through the merger GDF-Suez became a giant integrated multi-utility company embracing both gas transmission and distribution, and electricity generation and distribution. In 2011 GDF-Suez was the world's largest producer of non-nuclear energy, with 118.2 GW of capacity, of which the Americas had 26.0 GW, Europe had 55.3 GW, and Asia, the Middle East and the Pacific had 37.0 GW. Almost 60 per cent of GDF-Suez's energy came from natural gas, mainly to supply combined cycle power stations, in close partnership with leading suppliers such as Siemens. Hydro power and coal each accounted for 14 per cent of energy supply. In sharp contrast to the French giant EDF, just 5 per cent of GDF-Suez's electricity is generated by nuclear power. Within GDF-Suez's total revenues in 2011, only 36 per cent came from France, compared with 25 per cent from the rest of Europe and 39 per cent from outside Europe.

Energy privatization in the UK followed a different path from that in France. In 1990 the UK government split the electricity industry into three privatized generating companies, National Power, Powergen and Nuclear Energy, with the National Grid as a separate transmission company. In 1992 National Power established its International Power division as a separate operational unit, which began to expand rapidly overseas, taking advantage of the international privatization in the industry to build its international capacity. In 2000 National Power was split in two and the domestic UK business was acquired by RWE, the German-based energy utility. By 2010 International Power had 11.9 GW of capacity, including operations in the USA, the Mediterranean, Australia and Asia. In 2011 GDF-Suez acquired 70 per cent of International Power, and in 2012 it completed the acquisition of the remaining 30 per cent of the equity, the total acquisition amounting to $36.1 billion. By 2012 GDF-Suez had become the world's largest and most international non-nuclear electricity generator.[23] The company now contained within its structure the former French state-owned gas utility, GDF, as well as a substantial segment of the former British state-owned electricity generator. The French state still held nearly 36 per cent of the company's equity.

Aerospace: The case of EADS

It is only in relation to Boeing that the emergence of EADS can be fully understood. Boeing's planes (B-17s and B-29s) were central to the Allied victory in World War II. After the war Boeing developed the jet-engine B-47 bomber aircraft, of which more than 2,000 were produced, and the giant, eight-engine B-52 bomber aircraft, of which over 700 were produced. These planes helped to lay the foundation for Boeing's jet-engine commercial aircraft. By the 1970s, Boeing had a suite of commercial aircraft with closely related technologies, the B-707, B-727, B-737 and B-747. It was by far the world's largest commercial aircraft producer, with a global market share of over 70 per cent. By the mid-1990s Boeing had produced over 8,000 large commercial jet-engine aircraft as well as several thousand large jet-engine military aircraft. In 1997 Boeing took the momentous step of merging with McDonnell Douglas. Following the merger, Boeing accounted for over 80 per cent of the total world commercial aircraft fleet. Moreover, through the merger, Boeing also became one of the world's largest military equipment manufacturers, with military revenue accounting for almost one-half of its total revenues.

In the 1960s France, Germany and the UK each had their own national aerospace companies. However, they were each far too small to compete with Boeing. Up until the 1970s none of the European manufacturers produced more than 300 units of any commercial jet aircraft, far behind the number of aircraft that Boeing was producing for each aircraft type.[24] In 1969 the German and French governments agreed to combine their principal commercial aircraft capabilities in a single entity, Airbus. They were later joined by Spain (in 1971) and Britain (in 1979). The first Airbus was delivered in 1974. By 1999 Airbus had produced a total of more than 2,000 aircraft. The large commercial aircraft market had become a fiercely contested duopoly between Boeing and Airbus.

The initial corporate structure adopted by Airbus reflected the desire to combine economies of scale and scope with the maintenance of 'national champions' in the aerospace industry within each of the partner countries. In its initial form Airbus was not a company in the usual sense. Rather, it was an 'association for developing commercial interests', which published no detailed accounts and made no profits and losses in its own right. All the profits went directly to the four partners in proportion to their shareholdings. France's Aérospatiale and Germany's DASA (Deutsche Aerospace AG) each owned 37.9 per cent, Spain's CASA (Constructiones Aeronáutica SA) owned 4.2 per cent and Britain's BAe (British Aerospace, later BAE Systems) owned 20 per cent. In 2000 a unified corporate entity, EADS, was created (but without BAE Systems' participation). By 2012, after a long process of restructuring, EADS was 22.16 per cent owned by Sogeade, through which the French state controls 14.97 per cent, 14.77 per cent by DASA, 5.4 per cent by SEPI and 2.75 per cent by KfW, a German state-owned development bank (80 per cent owned by the Federal Republic of Germany and 20 per cent by the states of Germany). Among the 54.92 per cent of the free float shares, the French state controls 0.06 per cent. The four people on the EADS board who represent the French government, Lagardère (the French media and marketing company) and Daimler (DASA) have wide-ranging powers, including the right to nominate EADS's chairman and CEO, as well as to veto investments of above 500 million euros.

In the 1950s France established two state-owned companies, Sud Aviation and Nord Aviation, which included the main body of the country's aerospace assets. In 1957 the government merged the two companies into a single entity, Aérospatiale. In 1999 Aérospatiale was partially privatized and the French state reduced its ownership share to 44 per cent, selling 33 per cent of the equity to its strategic partner Lagardère, 23 per cent to private shareholders and 3 per cent to employees. When EADS was formed a new corporate entity, Sogeade,[25] was established to manage French national interests in the company. Sogeade is owned 66.67 per cent by the French state and 33.33 per cent by Lagardère.

In 1989 the main body of Germany's aerospace assets were combined
under the ownership of Daimler-Benz to form DASA. They included
Daimler-Benz's own aerospace assets together with MTU Munchen and
Dornier Flugzeugwerke. In addition to DASA's 14.77 per cent ownership of
EADS, German national interests are represented by the 14.9 per cent equity
share held by Dedalus, the German banking consortium. Dedalus includes the
German government's own state-owned development bank, KfW, which has a
2.75 per cent equity share in EADS.

Before 1998 the main body of Spain's aerospace assets were in the state-
owned enterprise, CASA. In 1995 CASA was placed under the control of the
state's holding company, SEPI. In 1998 SEPI sold 30 per cent of the shares
in CASA. After the formation of EADS, SEPI took control of CASA's equity
share in EADS.

By 2011 EADS had revenues of 49.1 billion euros and accounted for
roughly one-half of the global market in large commercial aircraft. However,
sales of Airbus aircraft accounted for over 67 per cent of the total revenues of
EADS, while sales of military equipment accounted for only 24 per cent of
its total revenues, compared with almost one-half at Boeing. In 2011 EADS's
sales of military equipment were $16.3 billion compared with $30.9 billion for
Boeing. Apart from powerful technological synergies between the civilian and
military segments, Boeing benefits from the different cycles of the two parts
of the aerospace business. Moreover, there are strong arguments in terms
of national defence strategy for a combined civilian and military aerospace
capability within a single national champion company, irrespective of whether
it is state owned or privately owned.

In the 1950s Britain had over twenty aerospace companies. In 1960 the UK
government orchestrated their merger into two new corporate entities, BAC
(British Aircraft Corporation) and Hawker-Siddeley. In the 1960s they both
made large commercial aircraft as well as military aircraft.[26] However, their
scale was far too small to compete with Boeing. In 1977 the UK government
nationalized the companies and merged them into a new state-owned entity,
British Aerospace (BAe) and in 1979 it acquired 20 per cent of Airbus. BAe was
privatized fully between 1981 and 1985. Following privatization it diversified
into a wide range of non-aerospace businesses, including property development
and automobiles. By 1991 BAe was near collapse. Under new leadership it
sold its non-aerospace businesses, ceased to produce large commercial aircraft,
and focused on developing its military business. In 1998 BAe, DASA and
Aérospatiale announced their intention to merge into a single company, the
European Aerospace and Defence Company (later EADS). The participation
of BAe would have created a company with an even balance between military
and commercial business. However, the French government refused to reduce

its share in Sogeade. Both BAe and DASA made it clear that they wanted the company with which they merged to have no state holding at all (*FT*, 3 September 1998). In 1999 BAe broke off negotiations and announced instead that it was merging with the UK-based company GEC-Marconi (forming BAE Systems), which greatly strengthened its capabilities in military equipment. In 2006 BAE Systems sold its 20 per cent share in Airbus.

By 2011, following further acquisitions in the sector, BAE Systems was the world's second largest producer of military equipment, with over 40 per cent of its sales to the US government. In 2012 BAE Systems and EADS announced that they intended to merge. The new entity would have revenues of over 70 billion euros compared with Boeing's 50 billion euros in revenues, and a roughly equal balance of military and commercial segments of the company. The combined ownership share controlled by the French and German governments would fall to below 20 per cent of the new EADS and it would have greatly enhanced access to the US military equipment market. In October 2012 the German chancellor, Angela Merkel, announced that her government opposed the merger and the deal collapsed.

Conclusion

Throughout the period of 'transition' from the centrally planned economies, the Washington Consensus institutions have argued unceasingly that state-owned enterprises are inherently inefficient.[27] In fact, the relationship between ownership change and globalization has been much more complex than it is usually portrayed. At the start of the modern era of capitalist globalization large parts of the Western European economy were dominated by state-owned enterprises selling mainly within their domestic market, often to other state-owned enterprises. Over the past three decades a large part of these have been transformed into leading global firms at the forefront of innovation in their respective sector. It is widely thought that the essential precursor of this transformation was comprehensive privatization. In fact the process of ownership change and its relationship to the transformation of Europe's former state-owned enterprises has been much more complex. This paper has examined four examples, which illustrate the wide range of paths that ownership reform has taken in Western Europe, as well as its complex relationship to ownership reform elsewhere in the world and its relationship to the construction of globally competitive firms.

Telefónica: Comprehensive privatization

In common with the practice in other Western European countries, up until the 1990s Spain's telecoms system was controlled by a single firm, Telefónica, the state-owned incumbent. Telefónica was fully privatized in the late 1990s. Prior to this it had already begun to expand internationally, taking advantage of telecoms privatization in Latin America to acquire former state-owned assets. Following privatization, its expansion in the region accelerated, based heavily on the acquisition of privatized telecoms assets. It built itself into the biggest telecoms company in Latin America. In 2006 it acquired the UK-based mobile operator, O2, which had itself been spun off from the privatized UK telecoms company, BT. Today 75 per cent of Telefónica's revenues come from international operations.

Volkswagen: Substantial minority state ownership

Volkswagen is today arguably the world leading automobile producer.[28] It was established in 1937 as a wholly state-owned company. Privatization of VW began in 1961 with the sale of 60 per cent of the company's equity as 'people's shares'. In 1988 the federal government sold its equity share. However, the state of Lower Saxony retained its 20 per cent equity share. This permitted VW to pursue a long-term growth strategy without the possibility of being acquired by another automobile company. VW's mass-market automobile brands both came from the acquisition of privatized state-owned enterprises, SEAT (Spain) and Skoda (Czech Republic) respectively. In addition, the core of its expansion in China was based on joint ventures with China's state-owned enterprises. Up until the 1970s VW relied on a single vehicle, the 'Beetle', which was mainly produced within Germany. Today VW produces a full range of both commercial and passenger vehicles and three-quarters of its assembly plants are outside China.

GDF-Suez: Merger of a national state-owned enterprise with a large national private enterprise

Up until 2005 GDF was wholly state-owned, but it had developed considerable international operations in order to secure access to natural gas supplies for its domestic operations in France. In 2005 the French government sold 20 per cent of its equity share, but retained an 80 per cent share. Suez is a long-established private company. By 2005 it had built itself into the world's largest independent power producer operating more than 200 plants worldwide. Its growth had been based mainly on the acquisition of privatized assets, particularly in developing countries. In 2006 the French government orchestrated the merger of GDF and Suez to form a giant vertically integrated energy company, GDF-Suez. Following the merger the French government retained a 35.7 per cent equity share in the new entity. In 2010–11

GDF-Suez acquired the UK-based company International Power, which had been de-merged from the privatized parent company National Power.

EADS: Cross-boundary government-orchestrated industrial policy

In the 1970s Britain, France, Germany and Spain each had their own 'national champion' aerospace company. In the case of Britain, France and Spain they were state owned, namely BAC (later BAe/BAE Systems), Aérospatiale and CASA respectively. They were of insufficient scale to compete with Boeing. The governments of these countries agreed to merge the main body of their aerospace industries into a single entity, Airbus, which became the core of EADS. Following its privatization BAe withdrew from EADS, and focused on military equipment. By 2012 the French state and its strategic partner, Lagardère, together owned 22.4 per cent of EADS. German national interests also owned 22.4 per cent and the Spanish state owned 5.4 per cent. The free float was 49.9 per cent. In 2012 EADS and BAE Systems agreed to merge. This would have created a giant company that was equally balanced between the commercial and the military divisions, and in which the share of ownership controlled by the French and German governments would have fallen below 20 per cent. However, the German government blocked the merger.

These four examples show that the path of ownership change in Western Europe was far removed from the popular view of the relationship between privatization and globalization. Telefónica is the only one in which there was outright privatization. Moreover, Telefónica benefited greatly from privatization in other countries, not only in Latin America, but also in Europe. In the case of VW the continued substantial government ownership share was important to the company's ability to focus on long-term strategy without being concerned about acquisition by another company. VW also benefited greatly from the privatization of state-owned enterprises in other economies. In the case of GDF, the government retained a substantial ownership share. GDF was transformed by the government-orchestrated merger with Suez, which had benefited greatly from privatization elsewhere, especially in developing countries. GDF-Suez also benefited from the acquisition of a substantial segment of the UK's privatized electricity sector. In the case of EADS the construction of a global competitor to Boeing depended crucially on government action. The French and Spanish governments still hold significant direct ownership shares. Both the French and the German governments also have substantial indirect mechanisms of control over EADS through national strategic partners that are shareholders in EADS, as well as the right to veto major decisions, including merger and acquisition, such as the merger that was proposed with BAE Systems.

Conclusion

After three decades of industrial policy, China's industrial policy of nurturing a group of giant state-owned enterprises has succeeded beyond most expectations. By 2012 China had 70 firms in the *Fortune* 500 and 22 firms in the *FT* 500. China's SOEs have made remarkable progress in upgrading management and introducing new technologies, which has transformed their operational mechanism. They have grown rapidly and have large profits. In 2011 the net income of China's four largest banks (Industrial and Commercial Bank of China, China Construction Bank, Agricultural Bank of China and Bank of China), all of which are state-owned, totalled $99.1 billion, compared with a total of $61.2 billion for the four largest global banks (Wells Fargo, JPMorgan Chase, HSBC and Citigroup). The net income of China Mobile reached $19.6 billion, compared with $12.8 billion for Vodafone and $7.0 billion for Telefónica, the world's largest global telecoms services companies by net revenue. The net income of PetroChina reached $21.1 billion, compared with $29.8 billion for Royal Dutch Shell and $24.8 billion for BP. It seems that China has demonstrated that an industrial policy based on state ownership of key strategic industries can succeed.

However, China's SOEs are far from catching up with the global leaders. Their share of the world's most competitive markets in the high-income countries is negligible. Their business systems in the high-income countries hardly exist. Few people in the high-income countries can name any Chinese companies. The vast majority of the sales revenue of China's SOEs comes from the domestic market where they operate in sectors that are protected from direct competition with the world's leading firms. These include telecommunications services, oil and gas production, power generation and distribution, metals and mining, and construction. The state-owned banks form the core of the state-owned enterprise system. Four giant state-owned banks account for 45 per cent of the total market capitalization of China's *FT* 500 firms and a further five state-owned firms in the telecoms and oil sector account for a further 45 per cent, so that just nine giant, heavily protected state-owned enterprises account for almost all of China's market capitalization in the *FT* 500.

The main success of China's SOEs in export markets is building infrastructure in developing countries. They have played an increasingly important role in building roads, railways, ports, airports and public buildings. These projects are typically financed by loans from Chinese banks, especially the China Development Bank, which are typically tied to contracts with China's SOEs. These have made a major contribution to economic development in low- and middle-income countries. China's SOEs have also successfully exported low-technology machinery and electronic goods to developing countries. However, their share of high-technology and branded-goods markets in developing countries is small. China's exports of manufactured goods to developing countries mainly come from firms in the non-state sector that export low-technology, low-value-added and non-branded goods or cheap counterfeit global brands, including footwear, clothing, household goods and consumer electronics.

China has the world's second largest economy and the largest population. Its policy-driven sustained growth after 2007 played a vital role in containing the global financial crisis. However, China's national income (at PPP prices) is still only 13 per cent of the global total (WB 2012, 20–22). The main body of global demand is in international markets, not in China. Despite their deep political and economic difficulties, high-income economies still account for 55 per cent of global income and upper middle-income countries account for a further 32 per cent (WB 2012, 22). During the era of globalization firms from high-income countries have built global business systems and penetrated deep into the markets of low- and middle-income countries, including that of China.

Chinese firms have a small, and in some cases virtually non-existent, share of international markets in both high and mid-technology products. These include IT hardware and software; commercial aircraft and components; automobiles, trucks and components; pharmaceuticals; chemicals and plastics; medical equipment; photographic equipment; lifts and escalators; heating, ventilation and cooling systems; mining and earth-moving equipment; electronic and electrical equipment; and oil equipment and services. The same is true for international markets for branded consumer goods, including beverages, confectionary, tobacco, household goods, personal care products and luxury consumer goods. It is true also for key service industries, including international commercial banking, investment banking, insurance, retail, healthcare, film and TV, media and marketing, and legal services.

The areas in which indigenous Chinese firms do have significant market share in the high-income countries are few, most notably telecommunications equipment (Huawei) and PCs (Lenovo). After three decades of evolutionary industrial policy based mainly around state-owned enterprises, China still faces an immense challenge if it is to achieve its long-stated goal of nurturing a substantial group of indigenous firms that can compete in international markets.

At the same time that China's SOEs have failed to build globally competitive businesses, global high-technology and branded-goods producers have rapidly expanded their investment and market share within China in the many sectors that are relatively open to international competition. Large swathes of the domestic market are dominated by global oligopolies. This is highly visible in some sectors, such as the massively important automobile assembly industry, commercial aircraft, consumer information technology products, patented pharmaceuticals and branded consumer goods. However, global companies also occupy commanding positions in less visible sectors, such as auto components, IT hardware and software used by businesses, heating, ventilation and cooling systems, as well as lifts and escalators.

The approach of relying on majority-state-ownership firms in the commanding heights of the economy has produced the illusion of industrial policy success, but at the cost of the development of the indigenous non-state sector and without producing globally competitive firms. The fact that China's industrial policy has been unsuccessful after three decades of intense effort demonstrates just how difficult it is to construct an industrial policy in the era of capitalist globalization, which has produced intense global industrial concentration along the entire length of the global value chain. This is the case even for the world's largest developing country, China. Protection through state ownership in a massive, fast-growing economy has permitted China's SOEs to earn large profits and achieve high market capitalizations, but this is not the same thing as building globally competitive firms.

The core of China's industrial policy has been state ownership in strategic industries, with direct control of key personnel appointments through the Central Organization Department of the Chinese Communist Party and direct control of operations through the State-owned Assets Supervision and Administration Commission (SASAC). In his widely read article, Chen Qingtai, former vice president of the State Council's Development Research Centre, argued that an 'ownership chasm' has grown up between the SOEs and the non-state firms (Chen Qingtai 2012). He acknowledged that deep public disquiet has developed about the 'ownership chasm' in which SOEs operate 'inside the system' of political networks and the non-state enterprises operate 'outside the system'. Although China's SOEs have failed to develop into globally competitive firms, they take the lion's share of loans from the state-owned banking system. State-owned enterprises produce around one-third of national output but account for around 70 per cent of bank loans (Chen Qingtai 2012). This deprives the non-state sector of necessary funding in order to grow and compete. They are forced to rely on expensive informal credit markets. The SOEs also benefit from being 'inside the glass door' in obtaining government procurement contracts. They are treated as 'near relatives' of the government at every level, while the non-state firms are treated as 'strangers' in gaining access to public projects. The 'ownership label' has become a critical issue for Chinese firms: 'There is no other country in which the issue of the "ownership system" occupies such a prominent position, with the market economy sliced up into separate components' (Chen Qingtai 2012).

There is wide acceptance among China's policymakers that reform of China's SOEs has reached a crossroads. However, the direction of change is uncertain. The possibilities include the following:

Mass privatization along the lines of Russia and Eastern Europe in the early 1990s

This is most unlikely. The social and economic results of Eastern European mass privatization were deeply problematic. In Russia this process resulted in the capture of a large fraction of the state's assets by a small group of well-connected people (Goldman 2003; Kotz and Weir 2007). In China a process such as this would be likely to lead to an even greater concentration of assets in the hands of a small minority of the Chinese population than is currently the case. Nor would it be likely to lead to the development of an extensive group of globally competitive indigenous Chinese firms. Rather, it would permit global oligopolies to replace China's own domestic state-owned oligopolies across those parts of the Chinese economy in which state-owned enterprises are protected from global competition.

'Close the door' to multinational enterprises

In those sectors in which global companies have relative freedom of operation in China, they have demonstrated that they are able to reproduce the form of oligopolistic competition that they have created across large swathes of the global economy since the 1970s. This is resented by substantial segments of the Chinese political class and, indeed, by a significant segment of the Chinese population, even while they buy goods produced by global firms. There is a strong populist sentiment in favour of 'national enterprises', owned and run by Chinese. However, 'closing the door' is not the most likely scenario. There is wide awareness that this would have a deleterious consequence for business competition, technical progress and product quality in both consumer and capital goods industries as well as in services. There is wide dissatisfaction with the dominant position of SOEs and the privileged position they occupy within China. Few Chinese people would be comfortable with an economy that was controlled even more comprehensively than today by SOEs. Such a policy shift would take China away from the approach of 'reform and opening up' that has characterized China's economic policies since the 1980s. It would mark a decisive break from China's main trend of political economy since the 1970s.

Gradual privatization along the lines of Western Europe's state-owned enterprises

The four examples examined in this paper show that in Western Europe there was no single path of institutional transformation from state-owned national champion to globally competitive firm. Telefónica was comprehensively privatized. However, Volkswagen has retained substantial minority state ownership. GDF-Suez was a merger, which was orchestrated by the French state, of a national state-owned enterprise with a large national private enterprise. EADS involved cross-boundary government-orchestrated industrial policy, with a significant state minority ownership until today. The process of privatization has often been gradual and frequently incomplete. Wholly or partially privatized European firms often have expanded through the extensive acquisition of privatized assets in developing countries. The lessons for industrial policy in developing countries are more complex than they are commonly portrayed.

From reform of state-owned enterprises to reform of state assets

Chen Qingtai has argued that reform of state-owned enterprises should switch towards the reform of state-owned assets (Chen Qingtai 2012). In his view there should be an 'orderly retreat of state-owned capital from ordinary production sectors' and a switch towards publicly owned funds which aim to maximize returns from their investments, thereby putting pressure on SOEs to improve their management and corporate governance. The commanding heights of the SOE system should be transformed into genuine corporate entities with diversified ownership rights. The state should 'consider setting aside 30–50 per cent of the state-owned capital in ordinary productions sectors'. It should 'switch the capital into funds for social livelihood guarantees and public welfare, for medical insurance, housing guarantees, the elimination of poverty, education, scientific and technical innovation, in order to supplement the inadequate investment in these areas'. This would 'allow state-owned assets to return to their basic characteristic of all-people ownership'. This would enable a true separation of ownership rights and management rights. In his report to the 18th Party Congress President Hu Jintao said: 'By 2020 China should generally achieve equal access to basic public services... Social security should cover all the people. Everyone should have access to basic medical and public health services' (Hu Jintao 2012).

In his opening speech at the Party Congress in November 2012, President Hu Jintao said that 'Chinese companies should expand their overseas presence at a faster rate, enhance their cooperation in an international environment, and develop a number of world-class multinational corporations.' He said also that a greater proportion of government investment should be concentrated in a few industries 'that comprise the lifeline of the economy and are vital to national security'. He emphasized that China should 'ensure that economic entities under all forms of ownership have equal access to factors of production in accordance with the law, compete on a level playing field and are protected as equals'. The concrete content of this policy shift remains to be seen.

Notes

1 I use the term 'administratively directed economy' because the so-called 'planned' economies were not planned in the strict sense, because they were unable to reach their stated goals in terms of technical progress and improvement in living standards. Rather, they were anarchic, unable to break out of the path-dependent pattern of development that they were locked into. It was only when they began to allow market forces to have a greater role in the economy that they were able to move away from this pattern of development (Nolan 1995).

2 It was reported that the total order could amount to as much as 22,000 MW in generating capacity and be worth $7 billion, but it remains to be seen if this huge order comes to fruition.

3 Japan's high-speed *shinkansen* train system has been in operation since 1964 without a single fatal accident. However, the worst high-speed rail crash in the world took place in Germany in 1998 at Enscheda, in which 101 people were killed. The accident did little to dent the export of high-speed trains from Germany or to dent the image of Germany as a high-technology powerhouse.

4 COMAC is headquartered in Shanghai. The principal shareholders in COMAC are SASAC, the State-owned Assets Supervision and Administration Commission, with 31.59 per cent, Shanghai Municipal Government's Shanghai Guosheng Company with 26.33 per cent and AVIC with 26.33 per cent. Sinochem, Baosteel and Chinalco each have 5.25 per cent.

5 The consortium included several of the main subsidiaries of AVIC.

6 After 2007 the DTI was successively renamed the Department for Business Enterprise and Regulatory Reform (BERR) and the Department of Business, Innovation and Skills (BIS). In 2008 the number of companies in the survey increased to 1,400, but in 2009 the number was reduced to 1,000, and in 2010 the decision was made for budgetary reasons to cease publication of this invaluable piece of research.

7 The main exception is the luxury vehicle sector. In 2009 the top two luxury vehicle assemblers, Mercedes and BMW, produced only 1.7 million and 1.2 million passenger vehicles respectively. However, within the luxury vehicle sector they have a global market share of around 70 per cent.

8 In 2000 CAT acquired Bucyrus for $7.6 billion, which greatly strengthened its position across the range of mining equipment.

9 These are joint ventures with Shanghai Auto (SAIC) and First Auto Works respectively. However, the management, brands, vehicle development, technology and strategy are firmly in VW's hands. 'SAIC' is technically a *Fortune* 500 company, but its revenues are almost entirely from its two joint ventures, one with VW and the other with GM. It has a limited capacity to compete as an independent auto manufacturer within China, let alone on the international stage.

10 Methylene diphenyl diisocyanate, which is usually abbreviated as MDI.

11 Although several indigenous companies, including Lenovo, ZTE and Huawei, have established significant market shares within the Chinese smartphone market, their core technology is Android (Google).

12 For example, in the oilfield services sector, among the top 20 firms ranked by revenues, 13 are from the United States, and the others are from France, the UK, Italy, Norway and Australia. There is not one firm in the top 20 from a developing country. The top ten firms in the sector all have revenues of over $10 billion, and include the US giants Schlumberger ($27.2 billion), Halliburton ($18.3 billion), National Oilwell ($13.4 billion) and Transocean ($12.7 billion), and the Italian giant Saipem ($14.8 billion).

13 There are numerous estimates, mostly of around the same level.

14 The rationale for these investments and their performance is intensely debated in the Chinese press, with heavy public criticism when the fund managers have made losses on their investments.

15 Despite intense efforts by Western investigators, none has found any evidence Huawei has enjoyed preferential access to military contracts.

16 The share reached 70 per cent in 2007 and in 2010 it was 65 per cent.

17 For example, Siemens was the main supplier to Deutsche Telekom, Alcatel was the main supplier to France Télécom, and GEC was the main supplier to British Telecom.

18 The German government retains a 32 per cent ownership share in Deutsche Telekom through its own direct shareholding and that of the government-controlled bank KfW. The French government retains a 27 per cent ownership share in France Télécom through its own direct share ownership and that of its holding company ERAP. The French government retains the right to appoint the CEO of France Télécom.

19 Renault was nationalized in 1945. Although it was privatized in 1996, the French government retains a 15 per cent equity stake in the company and appoints two of the company's directors. Following privatization Renault launched an ambitious international expansion plan, including its alliance with Nissan, under which Renault owns 44.4 per cent of Nissan and Nissan owns 15 per cent of Renault. However, Renault faces severe challenges. It produces over 3 million vehicles per year but this means that it lacks the scale of the largest global auto companies, Toyota, GM, Ford and Volkswagen. Moreover, it sold its truck division to Volvo (in 2001) and does not have a globally competitive luxury vehicle brand.

20 When it was nationalized in 1975, British Leyland combined most of the British automobile industry within a single state-owned firm, including many brands with international reputations. Despite the wealth of experience and technical capabilities of its constituent companies, British Leyland failed to make the transition to a globally competitive company. Its different brands either ceased production, or were sold off to international automobile companies. Passenger vehicle production in the UK today consists almost entirely of global firms, with Japanese companies at the forefront. In 1998 Leyland's truck division was sold to Paccar (US), which now produces almost all the trucks manufactured in the UK.

21 Volkswagen eventually produced over 21 million Beetles, of which 15 million were made in Germany.

22 SEAT was established in 1950 with 51 per cent state ownership and 42 per cent ownership by a group of large Spanish banks.

23 EDF is the world's largest electricity generator with a total capacity of 120 GW in 2011, of which around 75 per cent is from nuclear energy. In 2005 the French state sold 15 per cent of the equity to the public but retained an 85 per cent state

ownership share. Despite the fact that until 2005 EDF was 100 per cent state owned and 85 per cent state owned thereafter, and that even after 1999 only 20 per cent of the domestic market was open to competition, EDF was extremely active in international expansion as energy privatization and market liberalization advanced across the world. Among its most significant acquisition was the purchase of the privatized UK generator, British Energy Group (formerly Nuclear Electric), which generates around one-fifth of British electricity. By 2011 even though it was 85 per cent owned by the French state, over three-quarters of its revenues came from outside France, with its operations distributed widely across the world.

24 Sud Aviation produced 282 Caravelle aircraft, Germany's Dasa Aerospace produced less than twenty VFW 614s, Britain's De Havilland produced 114 Comets, BAC produced 244 BAC111s, Hawker-Siddeley produced 117 Tridents and Vickers produced 54 VC10s.

25 Societé de Gestion de l'Aeronautique, et de la Défense et de l'Espace.

26 Each of them produced two large jet-engine commercial aircraft. BAC produced the VC10 and the BAC111, while Hawker-Siddeley produced the Comet and the Trident.

27 The classic text was the World Bank's publication *Bureaucrats in Business* (1995).

28 Its closest rival, Toyota, does not produce commercial vehicles.

Chapter 4

GLOBALIZATION AND COMPETITION IN FINANCIAL SERVICES

In a single generation, our financial system has been transformed…into a highly concentrated oligopoly of enormous, diversified, integrated firms. This revolution has gone largely unnoticed.
—Henry Kaufman, *The Road to Financial Reformation* (2009)

The development of capitalism has arrived at a stage when, although commodity production still 'reigns' and continues to be regarded as the basis of economic life, it has in reality been undermined and the bulk of the profits go to the 'geniuses' of financial manipulation. At the basis of these manipulations and swindles lies socialised production; but the immense progress of mankind, which achieved socialisation goes to the benefit of…the speculators.
—V. I. Lenin, *Imperialism, the Highest Stage of Capitalism*
(1968 [1917], 24)

Introduction

Of all sectors, banking is the most strategic. This sector is at the centre of the supply and use of money. During the era of modern globalization, the strategic importance of the banking sector increased relentlessly as the global economy became ever more 'financialized'. In the USA household debt rose from 60 per cent of household income in the 1980s to 120 per cent in 2004. The ratio of global financial assets to global GDP rose from 109 per cent in 1980 to 316 per cent in 2005. By the year 2000, the global stock of household wealth had risen to $125 trillion, around three times global GDP. By early 2007, the volume of outstanding derivatives ($516 trillion) stood at ten times global GDP. The global financial crisis was intimately linked to the behaviour of financial firms and their central position in the process of credit creation. The process of endogenous money creation by financial firms sat at the centre of the asset bubble and the 'great unwinding' that began in mid-2007, which still profoundly affects the global political economy.

This chapter examines the evolution of the industrial structure of global financial firms during the period of globalization after the 1970s, during which free market policies dominated theoretical and practical policy discussion. It contrasts this with the evolution of the Chinese banking system, which has taken a very different direction. The contrast between the two systems is of central importance for the way in which global competition and regulation develops in the financial sector.

1. Contrasting Views on Globalization and Industrial Structure

The nature and determinants of industrial structure is one of the most important issues in economics. In the history of economics, there have been radically contrasting views on the basic determinants of industrial structure. There is a substantial empirical literature analysing the nature and determinants of industrial structure prior to the era of modern 'globalization'. However, there is still a dearth of empirical analysis of the nature and causes of the trends in industrial structure in the era of globalization, and of the implications of these trends for both theory and policy. The assembly and interpretation of evidence on this issue is critical for understanding the current era.

Mainstream view

The 'mainstream', 'neo-classical' view of the competitive process believes that the perfectly competitive model best describes the essence of capitalist competition. Departures from it are viewed as exceptional and typically arising from government intervention, including protection and nationalization. At the heart of the mainstream view is the self-equilibrating mechanism of market competition. It is believed that the basic driver of the capitalist process, competition, ensures that if any firm enjoys super-normal profits rivals will soon enter to bid away those profits and undermine any temporary market dominance that the incumbent enjoys. The neo-classical approach emphasizes the importance of competition among small firms as the explanation for the prosperity of the advanced economies. It considers that there is a general bias and tendency to overemphasize the importance of the big versus the small.

Mainstream economists generally believe that managerial diseconomies of scale set in after firms reach a certain size. The classic expression of this view was contained in Alfred Marshall's *Principles of Economics* (1890) in which industrial structure was likened to the 'trees in the forest', in a perpetual state of flux, with a powerful tendency towards decline of trees as they became old and lacking in vitality:

> One tree will last longer in full vigour and attain a greater size than another; but sooner or later age tells on them all. Though the taller ones have a better access to light and air than their rivals, they gradually lose vitality; and one after another they give place to others, which though of less material strength, have on their side the vigour of youth... In almost every trade there is a constant rise and fall of large businesses, at any one moment some firm being in the ascending phase and others in the descending.

During the era of globalization, mergers and acquisitions reached new heights. Global mergers and acquisitions increased from around $700 billion in 1995 to $3,300 billion in 2000. After 2000 the level slumped, before rising to a new peak in 2007, when they reached $4,300 billion. Despite the explosive advance of mergers and acquisitions, it is widely argued that global concentration levels have not increased. It is observed that there is a high rate of disappearance of companies from the *Fortune* 500. Based mainly on the analysis of shareholder returns, mainstream economists believe that mergers and acquisitions mostly fail. One of the most influential studies of mergers and acquisitions is evocatively entitled *Disappointing Marriage* (Meeks 1977). It is argued also that in the era of globalization markets have become so large that it is hard for any firm or small group of firms to dominate a given sector.

Insofar as there is evidence of increased industrial concentration over the course of the twentieth century, the argument was made by mainstream economists that this was due to government policies rather than to the advantages of large-scale production. In recent years, the argument has gained ground that advances in information technology have created the possibility of a radical change in the nature of the firm. Activities that it was formerly rational to carry out within the firm can now be performed by networks of small firms connected by the internet. Mainstream economists believe that technological changes in the last 25 years have transformed the business to the disadvantage of large firms, and that more and more large firms, particularly in the traditional production industries, have found themselves outperformed by smaller, nimbler competitors. This is widely thought to herald the rise of a new form of 'Post-Fordist' economic system based around 'clusters' of small businesses that can both compete and cooperate at different times. This view appears to be strongly reinforced by the rapid rise in the extent of outsourcing activities that were formerly carried on within the firm. It is a common proposition in business schools that the large corporation is being 'hollowed out', and rapidly becoming an 'endangered species'.

The spread of global markets has led to the widely held view that there are limitless opportunities for firms from developing countries to 'catch up' if they compete on the free market of the 'global level playing field'. This view is expressed powerfully in Thomas Friedman's book *The World is Flat* (2005): 'The explosion of advanced technologies now means that suddenly, knowledge pools and resources have connected all over the planet, levelling the playing field as never before, so that each of us is potentially an equal – and competitor – of each other.' The view that the 'World is Flat' is strongly reinforced by the explosive growth of China during the era of globalization. The world is widely thought to have become 'flat' for individuals, countries and firms from developing countries, due to liberalization, privatization and the IT revolution.

Non-mainstream view

From the earliest stages in the development of modern capitalism, there were economists who believed that capitalism contained an inherent tendency towards industrial concentration. Karl Marx, in *Capital* Vol. 1 argued that there was a 'law of centralization of capital' or the 'attraction of capital by capital'. The driving force of concentration was competition itself, which pressured firms to cheapen the cost of production by investing ever larger amounts of capital in new means of production and in 'the technological application of science', which in turn creates barriers to entry. In the early 1970s, on the eve of the modern era of globalization, Stephen Hymer visualized the possible outcome of the capitalist process if the restrictions on merger and acquisition were lifted (Hymer 1975 [1972]). He imagined a situation at some point in the near future in which giant multinational corporations (say 300 from the US and 200 from Europe and Japan) had established themselves as the dominant form of international enterprise and controlled a significant share of modern industry in each country. The world economy would then resemble more and more the US economy, where large corporations spread over the entire continent and penetrate almost every nook and cranny.

Despite his view that competition is analogous to the trees in the forest, Marshall's *Principles of Economics* provides numerous reasons to explain the advantages that a large business of almost any kind nearly always has over a small one. These include economies in procurement, transport costs, marketing, branding, distribution, knowledge, human resources and management. By contrast, his explanation of 'managerial diseconomies of scale' resorts to an analogy ('the trees in the forest') without logic or evidence.

Edith Penrose's path-breaking book *The Theory of the Growth of the Firm* (1995) examines the limits to the growth of the firm. Like Marshall, she identifies a number of potential advantages that can be enjoyed by the large firm. She considers that the most significant advantages for the large firm are those that she terms 'managerial economies'. Penrose concludes that there are no theoretical limits to the size of the firm. She finds nothing to prevent the indefinite expansion of firms as time passes, and clearly if some of the economies of size are economies of expansion, there is no reason to assume that a firm would ever reach a size in which it has taken full advantage of all these economies.

Conclusion

As has been seen in Chapter 3, the era of capitalist globalization has been accompanied by intense industrial consolidation in the non-financial sector. In almost every sector global oligopolies have been established among 'systems integrator firms' and they are deep in their global value chain. The transformation of global non-financial firms corresponds closely to the predictions of the non-mainstream view of industrial structure. To what extent have the same processes been at work in the financial sector? It is widely considered that mergers and acquisitions in the banking industry are stimulated mainly by the greed of the senior officers rather than by industrial logic. This view is strongly reinforced by the enormous incomes earned by the senior managers of the world's largest financial firms. Given the critically important role of the banking industry in the global business system, it is especially important to investigate the nature and determinants of industrial structure in this sector, and examine the extent to which this process is different from that in other sectors.

2. Deregulation and Liberalization in the OECD Countries

From the early 1980s onwards, financial markets were liberalized step-by-step across the advanced economies in the belief that this would bring the benefits of competition in the banking sector as much as in other economic sectors. Those parts of the financial sector that were state-owned were gradually privatized. By the late 1990s, in both Europe and the USA, most of the legislative restrictions on national cross-regional mergers and acquisitions and many of the restrictions on international mergers and acquisitions had been removed. The barriers that separated different segments of the financial services industry were widely broken down.

Anglo-Saxon approach

UK. In the UK the 'Big Bang' of financial market liberalization took place in 1986. The Big Bang consisted of a set of measures that were intended to open up the City of London's hitherto highly protected investment banking and stock-broking sector to international competition: 'The core belief was that industries would benefit from being exposed to competition and that Government interference should be minimal' (Augur 2000, 46–47). When plans for the Big Bang were announced in 1983, the Department of Trade and Industry (DTI) said: 'The [UK] Authorities are anxious to see the emergence of strong British securities firms, capable of competing with the big Wall Street and Japanese houses' (Augur 2000, 5). The head of Goldman Sachs International 'stressed that fears that Americans will subsume British securities firms after the City's Big Bang are exaggerated' (Augur 2000, 6).

However, within a few years, almost all of the City's investment banks and stockbrokers had been acquired by global giant financial firms. Morgan Grenfell was sold to Deutsche Bank; Warburgs was sold to UBS; Kleinwort was sold to Dresdner; Smith New Court was sold to Merrill Lynch; Barings was sold to ING; Schroders was sold to Citigroup; Flemings was sold to Chase Manhattan; and Cazenove was sold to JPMorgan. Since the Big Bang London has enhanced its position as the world's leading financial centre, with a central role for global banks. The UK accounts for almost half of the global total of interest rate derivatives, around two-fifths of the total of foreign exchange trading, and around one-fifth of the global total of cross-border bank lending and hedge fund assets (*FT*, 2 April 2013).

USA. In the USA in the 1930s, in the wake of the Great Depression and massive failures of financial institutions, new legislation established strict barriers between the different parts of the financial services industry, notably in the form of the Glass–Steagall Act, which separated investment banking from deposit-taking commercial banking. The US also placed tight restrictions on inter-regional bank mergers.

From the early 1980s onwards these regulatory restrictions were removed piece by piece. The barriers to cross-regional mergers and acquisitions in this sector were broken down, especially through the passage of the Riegle–Neal Act in 1994. In 1982, the Garn–St Germain Act allowed the first tentative moves to permit financial institutions to move across the borders of the main fields of financial sectors. The conclusion of this process was the passage of the Gramm–Leach–Bliley Act in 1999. Commercial banking, mortgage provision, investment banking, insurance and asset management could all now be carried on within a single corporate entity.

Continental Europe

Across Continental Europe, the 1990s saw a widespread dismantling of the barriers that separated the different branches of financial business, notably insurance, commercial banking and investment banking. There also took place widespread privatization of those banks that had been in state ownership. In terms of cross-border relationships, the integration of the internal market in financial services is a central plank of EU policy.

However, despite formal commitment to open markets in financial services within the EU, liberalization of cross-border mergers and acquisitions has been a long, slow process and is still far from complete. The main Continental European countries have only slowly removed the barriers to cross-border mergers and acquisitions. The banking regulators in each country reserve the right to reject takeovers of domestic banks if they believe it will undermine the national banking system. They each have signalled that it would not be in the national interest to allow the national champion banks to be acquired by foreign banks. They have made clear that they would not fully liberalize the ownership rules in their respective financial sectors until they had each overseen the emergence of a powerful group of 'national champion' banks. Each large Continental European country has nurtured a group of powerful 'national champion' financial institutions that are far stronger than those from developing countries. Merger and acquisition has played a central role in this process.

Germany. In 2003 several international financial institutions asked the German government whether it would oppose an acquisition of a domestic bank. Germany's deputy finance minister, Mr Koch-Weiser, cautioned that the failure of Germany's banks and insurance groups to restructure sufficiently meant that they were easy targets for foreign rivals intent on acquiring a presence in the German market:

> When one looks at the banking and financial markets in other countries to gauge the international position of Germany, one must admit that there is only one German grouping in both the banking and primary insurance industries that has a significant position in the 'champions league'… Even large German banks could fast become takeover candidates. (Quoted in the *FT*, 5 December 2003)

Not only the German government, but also Germany's leading industrial corporations expressed alarm that other countries' financial firms might acquire the country's main banks. Following the rumour that Citigroup or HSBC might acquire Deutsche Bank, the Bundesbank announced its opposition to a foreign takeover of a major German bank: 'For an important national economy such as Germany, it is an asset to have at least one big German bank' (Bundesbank official, quoted in the *FT*, 24 March 2004). The publicly expressed concerns of the German government caused international banks to shelve their plans to attempt to acquire major German banks. Germany subsequently supported a process of domestic merger and acquisition in order to produce a group of banks that could compete on the global stage.

France. The French government has long been concerned to develop 'national champions' in 'strategic sectors', including banking. In 1982 it nationalized the commanding heights of the banking industry. It has made it clear that its major banks cannot be acquired by other countries' banks, and has used industrial policy to nurture giant domestic banks through merger and acquisition. It has made use of the privatization process to support this goal. Despite the great difficulties experienced by Société Générale in 2007–2008 it was made clear by the French government that no foreign bank would be permitted to acquire it.

Italy. During the twelve years in which Antonio Fazio was governor of the Italian central bank (1993–2005) no foreign bank was allowed to take over an Italian bank. In 2005, in the teeth of intense opposition from the European Commission, the attempts by two foreign banks (BBVA (Spain) and ABN Amro) to acquire two leading Italian banks (Banca Nazionale del Lavoro and Banca Antonveneta) were blocked by the Italian banking regulator. Since then the Italian government has supported a process of intense mergers and acquisitions of domestic banks in order that they could achieve global scale.

Belgium, the Netherlands, Switzerland and Spain. All were highly sensitive to the possible acquisition of domestic banks by international competitors. Each of them encouraged the emergence of 'national champion' banks through merger and acquisition.

Within the Washington Consensus the Continental European countries were forceful advocates of liberalization of financial markets in developing countries. This is ironical in view of their own efforts to nurture 'national champion' banks, even in small European countries. It is as if they advocated the approach: 'Do as I say, not do as I do.'

3. The Process of Consolidation

The logic of industrial consolidation in financial services

The pursuit of power and income is a significant motive for mergers and acquisitions in the financial services industry. However, there also is a powerful industrial logic behind the pursuit of increased scale in this sector, including both economies of scope and economies of scale.

Economies of scope

There have been two principal aspects to economies of scope in modern banking: sharing knowledge and providing a globally integrated service for global customers.

Sharing knowledge. It has increasingly been realized that there are large economies of scope (i.e., common processes contributing to improved performance across different segments of the firm) in financial firms in the epoch of deregulation. A central weapon in building competitive advantage in the financial services industry is the ability to share knowledge across different segments of business activity. This process has been greatly facilitated by the application of information technology, which has undergone a revolution in the past 20–30 years, and has been at the heart of a comprehensive transformation of the nature of banking, greatly to the advantage of giant financial firms.

Giant financial firms benefited from economies of scope by creating a new type of firm that spans the main categories of financial services, especially the reintegration of investment and commercial banking. These produced powerful economies of scope achieved through a deep intertwining of different aspects of banking business, including trading (including both trading for customers and proprietary trading of currencies, commodities and equities), corporate advice (mergers and acquisitions, IPOs) and wealth management: 'Sales, research, trading, underwriting, advisory, asset management and brokerage are under one roof and work together easily' (Augur 2005, 108).

As banks have grown in size in recent years, they obtain an increasing body of knowledge about different financial activities that can be shared across the company. Sheer size and market share become competitive advantages through the accumulation of greater quantities of knowledge that can be shared across the company. A leading global bank can have over 300 million global customers. It can build up a detailed knowledge of their financial behaviour and use it to the advantage of all operations within the bank: 'The higher the market share, the more information flows in... Their big market share is a virtuous circle for the largest firms' (Augur 2005, 110). The dramatic increase in the application of information technology allows an explosive increase in the potential to share knowledge across the modern giant financial firm:

When a firm like Morgan Stanley writes in its form 10-K of managing the business 'on a Company-wide basis, on a worldwide trading division basis, and on an individual product basis', it is referring to [the] constant sharing of information upwards, downwards, sideways and crossways. (Augur 2005, 113)

Globally integrated services for global customers. It is widely said that in banking today, the top 10 per cent of customers account for around 80 per cent of bank revenue. Giant financial firms are able to offer global 'one-stop shop' services both to giant, non-financial sector firms and to wealthy individuals. Rapidly growing industrial concentration and vast differences in wealth distribution mean that a relatively small number of customers can generate a large share of the income and profits for giant global banks.

We saw in Chapter 3 that the era of capitalist globalization has seen a process of explosive merger and acquisition among non-financial firms. Giant systems integrator firms have widely dispersed production systems, with plants across the globe. However, we have also seen that in order to meet the needs of the systems integrator firms, the upper reaches of global value chains have also experienced high-speed consolidation. Leading sub-systems integrators and specialized global components suppliers also established global production systems in order to meet the needs of global systems integrators by supplying inputs from close at hand in order to achieve 'just-in-time' supply.

As the era of capitalist globalization progressed, global banks increasingly provided global financial services for systems integrators, sub-systems integrators and global components suppliers. Global supply chains are increasingly linked by electronic transactions through global banks. They provide a wide range of services for global companies in other sectors, including syndicated loans, trade finance, payables and receivables, hedging foreign exchange and commodity prices, payrolls and taxes. It is estimated that around 95 per cent of all money movements undertaken by global corporations are undertaken by global banks. A wide range of global companies' financial needs are 'outsourced' to global banks. It is more efficient for global non-financial companies to subcontract many of these services to global banks than it is to undertake them in-house.

In the era of the global business revolution global shipping companies such as Maersk and Evergreen have emerged as the physical representation of the interconnected global economy. In a similar fashion, global banks emerged as the 'glue' that bound together the global corporation and global supply chains in the era of capitalist globalization. Only a handful of giant global banks had the capability of providing such a service. Their ability to do so is critically dependent on their purchase and use of massive investments in IT hardware, software and human resources.

It is estimated that in the year 2000 total global household wealth amounted to $125 trillion, around three times as large as global GDP. The top 10 per cent of the world's households were estimated to account for 85 per cent of the total wealth. Leading international banks derive around 80 per cent of their income from the top 20 per cent of customers. Giant global banks are able to 'get close' to a relatively small number of global businesses and individual household customers and service their global needs.

Economies of scale

There are powerful economies of scale in many aspects of financial services in the modern era; procurement and operation of IT hardware and software, mergers and acquisitions, human resources, marketing, spreading risk and best practice.

Procurement and operation of IT hardware and software. IT systems have substantially replaced the intimacy of face-to-face contact with customers. These have increasingly become a key instrument of competitive advantage in this industry. Leading financial firms each spend many billions of dollars annually on IT systems. In 2006 the world's financial services firms altogether spent around $380 billion on IT hardware and software. The largest global banks also employ a large number of IT engineers. One of the top 20 global banks is likely to employ 20,000–30,000 IT engineers. For global banks 'technology is our number one competitive advantage'.

Modern IT systems allow giant banks to have 24-hour-a-day linkage on a worldwide basis both within the bank and with their customers. A giant global bank can have as many as 300 million customers around the world and undertakes many millions of transactions each day. Only the largest banks have the resources to invest in IT systems that enable them to provide such a service. It is vital that giant banks have the most reliable and most rapid IT systems. If the IT system of a global bank is out of operation for just five minutes, 'a quarter of a million customers will be angry'. The entry costs into global banking are extremely high. Banks that lack sufficient scale to invest in such IT systems are unable to compete for the business of global customers. In the view of the head of technology at one of the world's largest banks, the minimum scale of IT systems required to compete for global customers is so great that only 20 banks in the world have the necessary scale. This makes it hard to compete internationally as a medium-sized bank, let alone a small bank, which must rely on some form of niche position in the banking market, either geographical or sectoral.

Intense pressure from the huge procurement spending of the world's leading banks has helped to produce dramatic institutional change in the sectors that supply IT products to the financial services industry. The commanding heights of the IT hardware industry have become an oligopoly of giant global firms. Giant banks, which purchase an enormous value of IT hardware and software, are in a better position to secure lower prices and superior service terms from these giant suppliers than smaller banks are able to obtain. A key aspect of mergers and acquisitions in the banking industry has been the ability of giant banks to acquire or merge with other banks and reduce unit costs by merging the IT systems.

The IT hardware and software sector has the largest R&D spending of any sector in the G1400 (BIS 2009). There is a total of 228 firms from this sector in the G1400, of which three-fifths (134) are American. The R&D spending of the firms in this sector amounts to $139 billion, which is one-quarter of the total R&D spending of the G1400. The IT software and computer services subsector in the G1400 has a total of 69 firms, of which the top ten account for 74 per cent of the subsector's R&D spending. Eight of the top ten firms are American, including the industry's super-giants Microsoft, IBM, Google and Oracle. The IT hardware subsector has a total of 159 firms, of which the top ten firms account for 46 per cent of the total spending in the subsector. Five of the top ten firms are American (Intel, Cisco, Motorola, Hewlett-Packard and Qualcomm).

In the 1970s apart from IBM there were more than a dozen global mainframe manufacturers, including Burroughs, UNIVAC, NCR, Control Data, Honeywell, GE and RCA. Outside the USA, competitors included Siemens, Telefunken, ICL, Olivetti, Fujitsu, Oki and NEC. Since then the number has steadily shrunk. The mainframe market became increasingly specialized, focused on tasks requiring the high-speed processing of vast amounts of data. The market within global banks is especially important. Today, IBM has reached a position of complete dominance in the global mainframe market, accounting for over nine-tenths of the total world market.

Servers have taken over many of the functions that were formerly performed by mainframes. The server market for global banks is dominated by IBM and HP, which between them have around three-fifths of the global market. IBM and HP are giants of the world's IT industry. In 2008–2009 their respective revenues were $95 billion and $114 billion, and their respective R&D spending was $6.0 billion and $3.5 billion (BIS 2009).

Desktop software for global banks is a virtual monopoly for Microsoft, which has a revenue of over $58 billion and spends over $9 billion annually on R&D (BIS 2009). Business software for global banks is close to a duopoly, with Oracle and SAP accounting for around three-quarters of the global market. The huge cost of investment in R&D that is needed to remain competitive in this sector has driven most competitors out of the industry. Oracle has revenues of $24 billion and spends $2.8 billion on R&D (BIS 2009). In recent years Oracle strengthened its already powerful position in business software through the acquisition of PeopleSoft (for $10.3 billion), BEA (for $8.5 billion), Sun (for $7.4 billion), Hyperion (for $3.3 billion) and I-flex (for $0.9 billion). I-flex is one of the biggest Indian software companies, with around 10,000 employees, and a focus on business software for global banks. In 2007 SAP greatly strengthened its position in business software with its acquisition of Business Objects for $6.7 billion. The main threat to Oracle and SAP arises from IBM's rapid advance in software and computer services through a series of acquisitions. The most important of these was IBM's acquisition of the leading business software company Cognos for $5 billion in 2007.

The ATM has revolutionized the most basic and ubiquitous of banking operations. Three firms, NCR, Diebold and Wincor-Nixdorf, account for over 80 per cent of the market in automated telling machines (ATMs) for global banks. The ATM manufacturers have invested heavily in technical progress, including increased speed, modularized servicing, and greater ease of use. Most ATM machines across the world use Intel processors and a high proportion use Microsoft software. Intel has revenues of over $38 billion and spends $5.7 billion on R&D (BIS 2009).

The fastest-moving part of the IT industry is the tablet and smart phone, essential accoutrements of the international banker. This, the newest of all IT industries, has rapidly assumed a duopolistic shape. Over 70 per cent of the world's 'tablet' devices are produced by Apple and over nine-tenths of the operating systems for smart phones are supplied by Google-Android and Apple. The key innovator, Apple, has a 70 per cent global market share. Apple's main rival in the 'tablet' market, Samsung, trails far behind. Other powerful rivals, including Sharp, HP and Dell have all left the business.

Human resources. Global giants are able to offer more attractive terms of service to employees than smaller financial firms, and consequently they can attract the best human resources in the industry, bidding them away from smaller firms. Giant global banks offer superior terms in order to attract the scarce supply of brilliant mathematicians and physicists (the 'Sorcerer's Apprentices') who are critical to the development of new products. Instead of living the lives of impoverished scholars, leading young mathematicians today can earn enormous incomes as the creators of new financial products, which are of such a high degree of complexity that they are often barely understood by those who run global banks.

Marketing. Marketing, including branding, has become an increasingly important aspect of competition in financial services. Global financial firms spend large amounts on brand and trust-building campaigns to attract customers and expand revenue. The media and marketing industry has itself become highly concentrated, with a handful of global firms (WPP, Omnicom, Publicis and Interpublic) constituting an intensely competitive global oligopoly.

Spreading risk and best practice. Large banks can spread risk across business sectors and countries. If one sector or region is performing badly another sector or region may be performing well. Most of the global banks have encountered severe problems in one part or other of their global business, including money laundering in Mexico (HSBC), breaking US government regulations on dealing with Iran (Standard Chartered), or losses on credit derivatives (JPMorgan). However, a giant global bank is able to withstand even substantial damage to one part of their business. Moreover, a global bank, with a wider diversity of cultures and markets is able to benefit from sharing best practice across the global organization.

Oligopolistic competition. There have been examples of collusion between the major banks. The most notable has been the allegation of long-standing collusion among major banks in setting the London Interbank Offered Rate (LIBOR). However, in most areas, there is intense competition among global banks for both corporate and retail customers' business.

Industrial concentration in the high-income countries' financial services sector: The evidence

Merger and acquisition. In the era of globalization after the 1980s a handful of giant financial firms emerged, in each of which merger and acquisition played an important role. Although some of these were unsuccessful, the majority of them made a positive contribution to the construction of globally competitive banks. *Citigroup* was formed from the combination of Travellers Group, Salomon, Smith Barney, Citicorp, Schroders, Banamex and Bank Handlowy. *JPMorgan Chase* was formed from the combination of Chase Manhattan, JP Morgan and Robert Fleming. *HSBC* was formed from the combination of HSBC Holdings, Midland Bank, Republic New York, CCF (Crédit Commercial de France), Banque Hervet and Bital. *Deutsche Bank* was formed from the combination of Deutsche Bank, Morgan Grenfell and Bankers Trust. *Bank of America* was formed from the combination of BankAmerica, Bank Boston, Fleet Boston, MBNA and Nations Bank. *UBS* was formed from the combination of United Bank of Switzerland (UBS), Swiss Bank Corporation, Phillips and Drew, Dillon Read, S. G. Warburg, O'Connor Associates and Paine Webber. *Crédit Agricole* was formed from the combination of Crédit Agricole, Banque Indosuez and Crédit Lyonnais. *BNP Paribas* was formed from the combination of BNP, Paribas and Compagnie Bancaire.

Within a few weeks of the explosion of the crisis in 2008, a further round of super-large mergers and acquisitions took place. These included JPMorgan's acquisition of both Bear Stearns and Washington Mutual; Wells Fargo's acquisition of Wachovia; Bank of America's acquisition of Merrill Lynch; BNP Paribas' acquisition of Fortis (Belgium); Santander's acquisition of ABN Amro (Latin America) and Abbey National; Nomura's acquisition of Lehman Brothers (Asia and Europe); Barclays' acquisition of Lehman Brothers (USA); and Commerzbank's acquisition of Dresdner Bank. The total price of these acquisitions was less than $100 billion, while the combined market capitalization of the acquired banks in 2007 before the crisis had been over $500 billion.

Share of total assets. During the era of globalization the super-large banks greatly increased their relative importance within the global financial system. In less than a decade between 1997 and 2006, the top 25 banks increased their share of the total assets of the world's top 1,000 banks from 28 per cent to 41 per cent (*The Banker*, July 2006). However, due to the round of mergers and acquisitions during the financial crisis, the top 25 banks further increased their share, which reached 45 per cent in 2009 (*The Banker*, July 2010). Indeed, in different subsectors of the global financial services industry, the degree of industrial consolidation was even higher.

Asset management. In 2010 the world's 500 largest asset managers had $64,000 billion (i.e., $64 trillion) in funds under management (Towers Watson 2010). The top 50 firms accounted for 61 per cent of the total funds under management and among the top 100 firms none was from a developing country. The top firm, Blackrock, had $3.3 trillion in funds under management. In other words, the assets under management by a single global financial firm are roughly the same amount as China's total foreign exchange reserves.

Foreign exchange trading. In 2010 a total of $4 trillion was traded each day on the world's foreign exchange markets. The top five banks (Deutsche Bank, Barclays, UBS, Citibank and JPMorgan) accounted for 52 per cent of the total amount traded and the top ten accounted for 77.3 per cent (Euromoney 2011). All of the top ten banks were from the high-income countries. In Asian foreign exchange trading, the top five banks (Deutsche Bank, Barclays, Citibank, HSBC and UBS) accounted for 58 per cent of total foreign exchange traded and all of the top ten banks were from high-income countries.

Investment banking. In 2012–13 global investment banking revenues totalled $69 billion, including bonds (34 per cent), mergers and acquisitions (24 per cent), equity (21 per cent) and syndicated loans (21 per cent) (*FT*.com). The top ten banks accounted for 53 per cent of total revenue from investment banking and the top 20 banks accounted for 66 per cent of the total. All of the top five banks were from the US (JPMorgan, Bank of America, Goldman Sachs, Morgan Stanley and Citibank) and all of the top 20 investment banks were from high-income countries (Dealogic.com).

It is abundantly clear that the 'law of industrial concentration', outlined by Karl Marx in *Capital* around 150 years ago, applies at least as strongly to the financial services industry as it does to the non-financial sectors of the global economy. Indeed, the two processes of industrial concentration are deeply intertwined and mutually supportive. Marx's comments on financial concentration seem wholly applicable to the current era:

> Talk about centralization! The credit system, which has its focus on the so-called national banks and the big money-lenders and usurers surrounding them, constitutes enormous centralization, and gives to this class of parasites the fabulous power, not only to periodically despoil industrial capitalists, but also to interfere in actual production in a most dangerous manner – and this gang knows nothing about production and has nothing to do with it. (Marx 1967b [1886], 544–45)

4. The Drive into Developing Countries

Washington Consensus and financial institutions in developing countries

The Washington Consensus institutions have played a critical role in shaping thinking about financial institutions. Since their inception in the 1940s, they have been firmly controlled by the high-income countries. On the eve of the global financial crisis the OECD countries, which account for only 16 per cent of the global population, had 61 per cent of the votes in the IMF. The head of the IMF is always a European and the head of the World Bank is always an American. This remains so even after the global financial crisis. Throughout the era of capitalist globalization the Washington Consensus institutions worked tirelessly to promote the global free market in finance, in order to serve the interests of giant American and European banks.

The IMF and the World Bank argued strongly for the benefits to be derived from allowing global banks to grow freely in developing countries. The following is a representative selection of World Bank observations on financial market liberalization: (i) 'the arrival of reputable foreign banks is generally associated with an improvement in prudential regulations' (WB 2002, 90); (ii) 'foreign banks bring better accounting and information disclosure standards, since they adhere to their home country regulations' (WB 2002, 90); (iii) 'financial globalization stimulates economic growth by increasing the global supply of capital and promoting domestic financial development that improves allocative efficiency, creates new financial instruments and raises the quality of banking services' (WB 2000, 36); (iv) 'In terms of foreign entry, existing evidence does not indicate that such entry, either *de novo* or through the purchase of an existing domestic bank, had adverse consequences. In fact, such entrants bring competition, which improves efficiency and can also strengthen the demand for better institutions to support banking' (WB 2002, 96); (v) those transition economies that have been 'more willing to cede majority control of their banks to foreign interests' have enjoyed higher growth rates (WB 2002, 86); (vi) 'the benefits associated with the entry [of foreign banks into developing and transition economies] appear to outweigh the risks associated with concentration of foreign ownership' (WB 2002, 90); and (vii) 'experience suggests that foreign institutions do not undermine domestic banking systems: they are rarely dominant and tend to exhibit long-term commitment' (WB 2000, 36).

In his widely read and influential book, *Why Globalization Works*, Martin Wolf, a former World Bank economist, argued: 'Countries with a higher proportion of foreign-owned banks and a smaller proportion of state-owned banks are less prone to financial crises, perhaps because the foreign-owned banks are better regulated, better managed or merely more immune to pressures for imprudent lending' (Wolf 2004, 285).

In the 1990s Washington Consensus policies to dismantle restrictions on cross-border mergers and acquisitions to establish a 'level playing field' between local and global banks were implemented across a wide swathe of transition and developing economies, including much of Latin America and Eastern Europe.

Central and Latin America

Across most of Latin America the liberalization of banking resulted in a rapid growth of market share held by the global giants. By the year 2001, the share of foreign banks in total bank assets stood at 49 per cent in Brazil, 59 per cent in Venezuela, 61 per cent in Argentina and Peru, and 62 per cent in Chile (Chang Song 2005).

Mexico. The Mexican case is highly instructive, since Mexico is an upper middle-income country, with a relatively sophisticated banking system and a large population (almost 100 million).

In the late 1990s Mexico had a group of relatively powerful indigenous banks, including Bancomer, Banamex, Serfin, Bital and Banorte, themselves the product of large-scale merger and acquisition. They accounted for more than three-quarters of total assets and capital in the Mexican banking sector. At the time that Mexico was negotiating with the US about the establishment of the North American Free Trade Agreement (NAFTA), the Mexican government said: 'The one thing we want to preserve is Mexican ownership of Mexican banks. That is the essential element of our sovereignty, we must not give it up.' However, to a considerable degree due to the fragile state of Mexico's banks after the financial crisis of 1994–95, the Mexican government permitted comprehensive liberalization of ownership in the financial sector. The Mexican government was said to have spent $60–70 billion in public funds to bail out the bankrupt banks.

In 2000 Santander won the bid to acquire Serfin, Mexico's third largest bank. In the same year, Banamex attempted to take over Bancomer, in order to create a Mexican-owned 'national champion' in the banking sector. However, in the newly liberalized environment of Mexico's financial services sector, Banamex was defeated by Spain's BBVA, which acquired Bancomer. In May 2001 it was announced that Citigroup (US) was taking over Banamex, for $12.5 billion, in 'the largest financial services transaction of any emerging market' and the 'biggest corporate deal in Mexico's history' (*FT*, 18 May 2001). Citigroup offered a premium of more than 40 per cent on Banamex's share price the day before the deal was announced and Banamex's share price rose more than 30 per cent on news of the deal. Banamex's chairman Roberto Hernandez was offered a seat on Citigroup's board. Banamex was to become part of what he termed a 'global champion'. Citigroup retained the Banamex brand. The *Financial Times* commented: 'The acquisition [of Banamex] underscored the rapacious appetite of Citigroup, owner of Citibank, for assets in the developing world, and executives made it clear that they will pursue similar banking deals in other emerging markets' (*FT*, 18 May 2001). Sandy Weill, Citigroup's chairman and CEO, portrayed the take-over as 'part of a thrust to strengthen US–Mexican ties that have been championed by the new leaders of both countries, George W. Bush and Vicente Fox' (*FT*, 18 May 2001). In September 2002 it was announced that HSBC had taken over Bital for $1.4 billion (*FT*, 18 September 2002). The only substantial indigenous bank left in local hands was Banorte, and this 'was widely expected to sell itself within the next few years for about \$1.8–2.5 billion' (*FT*, 18 September 2002). Following HSBC's acquisition of Bital, foreign banks controlled over 80 per cent of Mexico's banking assets (*FT*, 10 September 2004).

Eastern Europe

In the 1990s, the global giants began to engage in 'a bruising battle' for the Eastern European banking market, with consolidation already 'sweeping across the region' (*FT*, 20 October 2000). Across the whole region banking sector liberalization resulted in a surge in take-overs by global giants of the financial services industry.

The market share of the international banks in the region reached 20 per cent by 1997, but leaped to 41 per cent by 1999. Already in 2001, foreign banks accounted for 99 per cent of bank assets in Estonia, 90 per cent in the Czech Republic, 89 per cent in Croatia and Hungary, 86 per cent in Slovakia, 78 per cent in Lithuania, 75 per cent in Bulgaria and 73 per cent in Bosnia-Herzegovina (Chang Song 2005). By 2004 the share of foreign banks in Eastern European bank assets had reached 75 per cent, as further important acquisitions took place by the international giants (*FT*, 8 August 2004). After the latest round of privatizations, by 2006 90 per cent of Romania's bank assets were controlled by foreign banks (*FT*, 17 October 2006).

Poland. Within the 'transition' economies the example of Poland is especially instructive as it is a large, upper middle-income transitional economy, with a relatively sophisticated banking sector compared with its poorer neighbours. After the mid-1990s global banks advanced rapidly in the liberalized environment of Polish banking. By 2000 the global giants already accounted for over one-half of the total Polish banking market (*FT*, 20 October 2000).

In 2000 Bank Pekao, the second largest Polish bank, was bought by UniCredito, and soon afterwards UniCredito also bought Poland's third largest bank, BPH (*FT*, 27 March 2006). In 2001 Citigroup purchased the fourth largest Polish bank, Handlowy. Following the take-over of Bank Handlowy, Citigroup announced that increasing its operations in China was 'top of our radar screen' (reported in the *FT*, 18 January 2002).

Following this take-over, global banks accounted for over three-quarters of the total Polish banking assets (*FT*, 17 April 2001). In 2006 a Polish government investigative commission concluded: 'It would have been better if Poles had gritted their teeth and not privatized for fifteen years. Then we would have a banking sector in Polish hands like Germans have German banks and Italians have Italian banks' (*FT*, 7 September 2006).

5. China

Groping for a reform path

During the years in which the global banking revolution was taking place in the outside world, China's banking system was struggling to find its reform path. In the years either side of 2001, in which China joined the WTO, the prospects for successful reform of China's large state-owned banks appeared bleak. The Asian financial crisis, particularly through the medium of Hong Kong, exposed deep shortcomings in China's non-bank financial institutions. There was extensive concern that in-depth investigation of the formal banking sector might reveal that it contained equally serious problems as those that had been exposed in the non-bank financial sector.

In the wake of the Asian financial crisis, and as China's entry to the WTO came closer, it became increasingly clear that there were profound shortcomings in China's commercial banks which meant that they would find it extremely difficult to compete with the giant global banks on the 'global level playing field' of the WTO. China's commercial banks had a high level of non-performing loans (NPLs), weak human resources, a simple operating mechanism far removed from the sophisticated operations of leading global banks, backward technologies, and deep problems of corporate governance, including weak risk management, serious corruption and persistent interference from politicians in bank lending decisions. Many experts considered that China's main state-owned banks were 'too big to fail' and that they suffered from serious moral hazard as a consequence of the fact that the state would bail them out no matter how poor their performance might be.

As we have seen, during the period of capitalist globalization the leading banks from the high-income countries participated in an explosive process of merger and acquisition, and industrial concentration in the sector increased relentlessly. By the early 2000s, the leading banks had established dominant positions in the banking industry throughout most of Latin America and Eastern Europe. They hoped that after China joined the WTO the banking sector would be opened up in the same way as in Latin America and Eastern Europe. This would provide them with extensive opportunities for them to build their business in China, not only through organic growth, but also through mergers and acquisitions. In the midst of their explosive international expansion and high-speed growth of profits and market capitalization, the leaders of giant global banks were profoundly optimistic about their growth prospects in China. They were confident that within a few years they would take the lion's share of the profitable 'cream' in the Chinese banking industry, leaving the indigenous banks to serve the financial needs of small- and medium-sized enterprises, rural areas and poor people. Many Chinese policymakers were apprehensive that this might indeed happen. Global banks exerted great efforts to win over China's policymakers to support their proposals for bank liberalization in China.

In the early years of this century there was deep scepticism among international commentators that China could successfully reform the five main state-owned banks, which dominated the financial system. It was widely argued that the only way to reform such poorly functioning institutions was through privatization, splitting up the banks into many smaller units, and opening the sector to foreign ownership.

In a widely distributed analysis published in 2003, Citigroup argued that China should 'tear apart (*chaifen*) the big four banks into relatively small units in order to switch on the process of bank reform': 'If the big four are not broken up soon they will face bankruptcy.' It considered that the new, smaller units should have either a regional or a sectoral basis. It suggested that the break-up of the big four banks is the 'only way out' (*biyou zhi lu*), and that this would 'encourage competition' and 'promote reform'. Citigroup argued that to have a small number of super-large banks poses a serious threat of moral hazard, because the state will go to any lengths to avoid bankruptcy of one of the big four banks.

Citigroup argued that tearing apart the big four banks would promote the reform process, and would be 'useful in making effective the plan produced at the State Council Financial Work Meeting in February 2002'. The plan passed by the meeting included the decision to accept both domestic and foreign strategic investors, 'so that within five years the banks could have made good preparations for listing'. Citigroup concluded:

> The hope that the big four commercial banks can be transformed into entities possessing competitive strength is manifestly unrealistic, but once the state-owned big banks were split up into several relatively small banks, then the whole picture would be transformed. Moreover, if in the future some newly-established small banks are bankrupt, then it will not be serious for the whole macro-economic situation.

Apart from this, such a break-up would also be helpful for absorbing foreign strategic investors and carrying through the banks' future public flotation.

The solution proposed by Citigroup would have left the door wide open for the global giants (such as Citigroup), making it far easier for these firms to grow within the Chinese market in 'partnership' with newly established small banks, or even to perform an outright take-over. In Chinese military philosophy, this strategy is called '*gege jipo*', or 'routing the enemy one by one'.

Finding the reform path

Following intense policy debate in 2002–2003, China's leaders resolved to continue to greatly restrict the role of foreign banks in China, principally by limiting severely their permitted share of ownership in China's indigenous banks. A new regulatory body, the China Banking Regulatory Commission (CBRC) was established. China's policymakers resolved not to split up the main banks, but rather to reform them as 'complete entities' (*zhengti gaige*). The reforms included removal of NPLs from the balance sheet, bringing in strategic partners from among the world's leading banks, investing large sums in state-of-the-art information technology, centralizing risk management, and upgrading human resources. The final step in the reform process was flotation of minority shares of the main banks on international and domestic stock markets, which subjected the banks' management to intense media scrutiny.

CBRC. A critically important part of the Chinese bank reform was the establishment in 2003 of a powerful bank regulatory authority, CBRC, under the chairmanship of Liu Mingkang, who had previously been chairman and president of the Bank of China and deputy governor of the People's Bank of China. CBRC exercised firm control over China's banking system. It was criticized strongly by many experts, especially those in international banks, for its conservative approach to regulation, tightly limiting the areas of business that China's banks were allowed to operate in. CBRC's chairman was famously extremely tough in limiting the banks from entering the derivatives business. CBRC likens itself to the 'parent' and even the largest Chinese banks are the 'children': 'the parent teaches the child, the child does not teach the parent'. The Chinese government was able to exert tight control over the country's banks through the mechanism of selection of the banks' leading personnel, as well as being able to strongly influence bank behaviour through the Chinese Communist Party. The party secretary remained a key figure even in banks that were floated on international stock markets. In the sharpest contrast to the developments in the financial system of the high-income countries, there was no possibility of 'regulatory capture' in the Chinese banking system.

Restrictions on foreign banks. China has maintained a cap of 20 per cent on any individual investment and a 25 per cent cap on overall foreign investment in domestic banks. The US was infuriated by the refusal of the Chinese government to allow a 'level playing field' for American banks. When he was US treasury secretary, Hank Paulson argued relentlessly for China to liberalize ownership rules in commercial and investment banking.

He repeatedly said that his argument for liberalizing the ownership rules in China's banking sector was in the interests of Chinese people and the Chinese economy: 'So many of the things they need to do for their own well-being are also the things that benefit the rest of the world... We have pressed hard on capital markets. I do not understand why there are ownership caps' (Paulson, quoted in the *FT*, 25 May 2007). Confronted by tight restrictions on foreign ownership and tight regulatory requirements enforced by CBRC, international banks still play a small role in the Chinese economy. Their share of China's total banking assets stands at less than 2 per cent (CBRC 2012, 33).

The US Chamber of Commerce pressed China to roll back foreign ownership restrictions on international banks and securities firms so that they would be allowed to own 100 per cent of the operations in which they invest. They argued that expanding market access for international banks and securities companies would 'allow China to realize important benefits from having greater access to world-class financial services' and that it would benefit the Chinese economy and Chinese consumers through the transfer of technology, through 'technical assistance to reform and modernize its financial system' (US Chamber of Commerce 2006). At high level international meetings such as the annual China Development Forum the heads of global banks argued ceaselessly for China to liberalize the constraints on foreign banks' investments in China.

Strategic investors. Although there were strict limits on foreign share ownership, the Chinese government welcomed selected minority equity share ownership by global banks. The introduction of overseas strategic investors was an important, bold and controversial measure to support the restructuring and reform of the state-owned commercial banks into joint shareholding banks. CBRC established a strict criterion for selecting international strategic investors, with five specific requirements. The proportion of shares held should not be less than 5 per cent. Based on the spirit of long-term cooperation and mutual benefit, strategic investors were required to hold the equity shares they acquired for at least three years. They were requested to send directors to participate in the management and decision-making process of the board of directors, and were encouraged to send experienced senior managers to participate in the daily business operation and management. The strategic investors were chosen for their rich experience in banking, hands-on experience, technical skills and willingness to cooperate with the Chinese partner.

HSBC was the pioneer of this form of international cooperation with China's leading banks. In 2004 it purchased 19.9 per cent of the equity of Bank of Communications. In the following two years, several leading international financial firms each became a strategic investor in China's largest commercial banks. In the following two years Goldman Sachs acquired 6.1 per cent of the equity of Industrial and Commercial Bank of China (ICBC), RBS acquired 10 per cent of the equity of Bank of China (BOC) and Bank of America acquired 8.5 per cent of the equity of China Construction Bank (CCB).

The main purpose of introducing strategic investors was not to attract funds but to support a fundamental change in the wholly state-owned ownership structure and thus strengthen the core competitiveness of the Chinese banks. It was hoped that the strategic investors would help to introduce the best business and management practices, introduce the most advanced information systems, improve corporate governance, risk management and internal control mechanisms, and enhance the banks' capabilities in product innovation and value creation. In other words, the objective of having overseas strategic investors was to introduce 'system, experience and technology' into the banks. The most important was introducing 'system', which placed the banks under the supervision of strategic investors, thus advancing changes in the banks' operational mechanisms.

Since the global financial crisis, Bank of America, Goldman Sachs and RBS, sold the main part of their equity investments in Chinese banks. RBS sold its shares entirely, while Goldman Sachs and Bank of America's shares in the respective Chinese banks have fallen to less than 1 per cent. However, HSBC maintained its large minority ownership share of Bank of Communications. The bank is unique in the depth of interaction between a global bank and large Chinese state-owned bank, including the presence of two HSBC directors on the board of Bank of Communications.

IT systems. Almost unnoticed, China's largest banks quietly implemented a comprehensive and high-speed transformation of their IT systems. This involved enormous investment, but it contributed greatly to modernizing the banks' operational mechanism and helped to centralize risk control. Instead of the 30–40 different hardware systems that they used to have, the main banks each unified their hardware into a single centralized system. From a negligible proportion ten years ago, over 60 per cent of the business of China's main banks is now conducted online. China's top banks now compare favourably with their global peers in terms of the sophistication of their IT systems.

IBM's mainframe computers are the first choice for China's 'Tier 1' state-owned banks, with a 100 per cent market share. The implementation of a huge programme of mainframe acquisition in China coincided with a step change in the capabilities of IBM's mainframe computers. IBM's mainframe computers are steadily advancing in terms of the number and speed of transactions they can undertake. The immense processing capacity of IBM's mainframes has enabled the consolidation of data processing in China's large banks into a single central data centre. Once giant customers have bought IBM's mainframes as the foundation of their data system, it is difficult to move to another system.

The market for servers in China's large banks is essentially a duopoly, shared between IBM and HP. Between them they have over nine-tenths of the market for servers in China's large banks.[1] The market for storage hardware in China's large banks is a duopoly between IBM and HDS (Hitachi Data Storage).[2] The core business software platforms for China's large 'Tier 1' as well as its 'Tier 2' banks are provided principally by Oracle, with SAP its closest competitor. China's main banks have invested heavily in the installation of a countrywide network of ATMs. These have greatly improved the ease and convenience for money withdrawals across China. Most ATMs in China are from one of the world's top three ATM manufacturers, NCR and Diebold and Wincor-Nixdorf.

Competition. The Chinese government has made it clear that a slow but relentless process of interest rate liberalization will take place. This places pressure on China's banks to seek out non-interest forms of income. Moreover, the big five banks face intensified competition from other segments of the Chinese banking industry. Their share of total banking assets has shrunk from 58 per cent in 2003 to 47 per cent today while the combined share of the joint stock commercial banks and city commercial banks has grown rapidly, from 16 per cent of total assets in 2003 to 25 per cent in 2011 (CBRC 2012, 119).

Human resources. China's state-owned banks have undertaken a comprehensive programme of skills upgrading for top level management. Regular training programmes are held in leading international universities. The banks have recruited a large body of highly qualified young graduates from China's leading universities and attracted many young Chinese who have graduated from leading international universities. Competition for entry to the leading banks is intense. China's leading banks have appointed senior international experts as independent non-executive directors to assist the banks to upgrade their competitiveness, improve their corporate governance and control risk more effectively. These include Sir Callum McCarthy, former chairman of the UK's Financial Services Authority (at ICBC), Joseph Yam, former chief executive of the Hong Kong Monetary Authority (at CCB), and Nout Wellink, former chairman of the Basel Committee on Banking Supervision (at BOC).

Flotation. After 2004 each of the main state-owned banks undertook huge international IPOs of minority stakes, including the $19 billion flotation of ICBC, which was the largest IPO in history. A succession of smaller mainland banks also undertook IPOs of minority shares. As late as 2006 there was just one Chinese bank in the *FT* 500 list of the world's largest companies by market capitalization. This was BOC (Hong Kong), ranked 59th among the banks in the *FT* 500. By 2012 the remarkable position had been reached that China had 12 banks in the *FT* 500, more than any other country, including the US. Moreover, there were four Chinese banks in the top ten, including first and second place (ICBC and CCB, respectively). In 2011–12 the net income of the four largest Chinese banks totalled $99.1 billion compared with $61.2 billion for the top four US banks in the *FT* 500.

The rise of China's banks astounded and confused both the global banks themselves and Western governments. In its July 2010 issue, the *Banker* magazine issued a stark warning:

> Western banks as we know them are in serious decline and this century looks like the turn of Asia, and of China in particular... A new world order in banking is emerging, with the traditional dominant players in the post–Second World War period, the Western banks, no longer playing the role they once did.

Given the centrality of banks to a country's economic and political system, the fact that China's banks had apparently overtaken the leading global banks was a fact of great historic significance.

Contrast with global banks

China's financial sector reforms have been remarkably successful, far exceeding the expectations of most international observers. However, there remain fundamental differences between Chinese and global banks. The areas in which they directly compete with each other are still small. The fact that China has so many banks in the *FT* 500 list of the world's largest companies ranked by market capitalization does not mean that they are globally competitive. China's top policymakers face complex and difficult decisions about the direction of reform in both the country's state-owned banks and the closely related industrial system.

Corporate governance. Superficially, Chinese and global banks are little different. Indeed, in key aspects of corporate governance, China's banks have explicitly adopted best practice at leading global banks, including extensive involvement of officials from global banks inside the Chinese banks themselves in order to improve their operational mechanism. However, there are some fundamental differences in terms of corporate governance. In the first place, a majority of the shares in China's main commercial banks are owned by the government. Although minority shareholders can express their views freely, and the mass media can exert great pressure on the bank management, ultimately, the most important strategic decisions are taken by the Chinese government. The most important of these is the appointment of the top managers at the banks, including the president and chairman. The top level appointments at the main banks are all decided by the Central Organization Department of the Chinese Communist Party. Moreover, every bank has a party secretary, who has enormous influence within the bank, especially in relation to human resource issues.

The deep penetration of the Communist Party into the commercial banks and the fact that the main banks are state owned has mixed implications in terms of competition with the global banks.

On the one hand it has the competitive advantage that the party and the government can think in terms of the long-term interests of the banking sector, and indeed of the whole Chinese system of political economy, and not merely the short-term pursuit of profit. This means that the government and party can take personnel decisions which would be difficult to take in global banks. For example, talented personnel can be moved from one state-owned bank to another to the overall benefit of the whole banking system. It means that the government can avoid the regulatory capture that has so deeply damaged the Western banking system and, in turn, the whole system of political economy in the high-income countries. It means that the state-owned banks and the state-owned large industrial enterprises can work closely together in order to build a team of globally competitive national firms. It is difficult for multinational banks to break into this network of relationships. It means that bank officials can receive extensive education from the party in terms of the wider social and national interest, so that bank officials at all levels can better understand the duty of the bank to maintain social stability and serve the wider social interest.

On the other hand, the deep-rooted presence of the Communist Party in the banks creates difficulties for corporate governance. This is a problem at all levels, from top to bottom, due to the close relationship between party members inside the banks and party members in entities outside the banks. It creates an environment in which it is difficult for bank officials to make lending decisions entirely on commercial grounds. It makes it more difficult to make decisions on appointments and promotions on the basis of ability rather than wider political criteria, which may tend to discourage talented people from entering or staying in the bank.

Human resources. China's banks remain strikingly parochial in their employment policies. In this sense they are strongly reminiscent of Japanese banks in the 1980s. There are only a tiny number of non-Chinese people working for China's commercial banks. The foreigners who have worked at a high level within China's commercial banks have sometimes found the experience difficult and left. Cultural homogeneity may provide some advantages. It may make it easier for the employees to communicate with each other and work together to a common purpose. It may be a competitive advantage in dealing with foreign competition within the domestic market and in working with Chinese firms in international markets.

However, cultural homogeneity may also constitute a potential weakness. Global customers form the core part of the business of global banks. The vast bulk of these are themselves multinational in their employee composition, including using English as the common language across the company. The cultural narrowness of the employees in Chinese banks may hinder them in competition outside China and in dealing with international customers. Also, Chinese banks sometimes have encountered difficulties in their overseas operations due to relationships with criminal enterprises run by overseas Chinese people. The possibility of such links is increased if the bank's employees are mostly Chinese.

Revenue structure. The revenue structure of China's commercial banks is strikingly different from that of global banks. China's commercial banks have increased the proportion of their income derived from non-traditional sources, including wealth management products, credit cards, auto loans and mortgages. However, the vast majority of bank revenue and profits is derived from the margin between deposit and loan interest, which is tightly controlled by government policy (CBRC 2012, 27). In 2011 over three-fifths of the revenue of China's domestic banks came from net interest income. The world's leading banks have a wide portfolio of business, within which they are continually seeking to enhance revenue from high-margin activities. They have, for example, all greatly increased their investment banking business, a process that accelerated during the global financial crisis, as leading stand-alone investment banks, such as Merrill Lynch, Lehman Brothers and Bear Stearns, were acquired by commercial banks. Revenues from trading in currencies, commodities and fixed income products, as well as fees from IPOs, corporate advice, and mergers and acquisitions, now form core high-margin business for the world's leading commercial banks. By 2012 only two of the world's top ten 'investment banks', ranked by investment bank fees, were stand-alone investment banks. The world's largest 'investment banks' in terms of investment banking fees were JPMorgan and Bank of America, ahead even of Goldman Sachs and Morgan Stanley. Moreover, investment banking business now provides a large fraction, in some cases more than one-half, of the profits at the world's biggest banks. China's largest banks have a very small role within the most profitable and intensely competitive segments of global banking.

International presence. The factors analysed above help to explain why and also reflect the fact that the international presence of China's commercial banks is still extremely limited. China's commercial banks are able to earn enormous profits mainly due to the fact that they operate in a highly protected domestic market, which is growing at high speed. If, for example, we compare two banks of similar size, Bank of Communications and Standard Chartered Bank, they superficially look similar (Table 4.1).

However, there is a wide difference in the nature of their respective operations. In June 2010 Bank of Communications employed 80,137 people within China, and only 1,611 people outside the mainland, of whom 1,407 were in Hong Kong. Out of the total outstanding loans of RMB 2,071 billion on 30 June 2010, RMB 1,860 billion were domestic (BoCom 2010, interim report, 82). Standard Chartered Bank has its headquarters in London. However, out of a total of 75,000 employees, just 2,000 are employed in the UK. Out of its total operating income of $15.2 billion in 2009, just $1.8 billion came from the Americas, the UK and Europe combined. The rest of its income was generated from a broad spectrum of countries and regions across the world. Standard Chartered and Bank of Communication present mirror images of each other, which in turn reflect and help to sustain a comprehensively different banking culture. For Bank of Communication, markets outside China employ only a tiny fraction of their employees and generate only a tiny fraction of their revenue. For Standard Chartered, their markets are almost everywhere. Only a tiny fraction of their employees work in the UK and only a tiny fraction of their revenues is generated in the UK. Their mindset must be comprehensively global in order to survive and prosper. The place in which the two entities come into sharpest direct and open competition is in Hong Kong, where both of them have relatively large operations (Table 4.2).

Banks' role in industrial policy. The corporate structure of the high-income countries has changed dramatically. The global business revolution has produced an extraordinarily high degree of industrial concentration across almost every industrial sector, including the 'commanding heights' of

Table 4.1. Bank of Communications and Standard Chartered compared, 2011

	Tier 1 capital ($ b.)	Assets ($ b.)	Capital assets ratio (%)	Pre-tax profits ($ b.)	Profits on av. capital (%)	Return on assets (%)	Market capitalization ($ b.)	Rank in FT 500 (2012)	Rank in Global 1000 (2012)
Standard Chartered	37.0	599	6.18	6.7	18.1	1.12	59.4	22	34
Bank of Communications	41.8	732	5.71	10.4	24.8	1.42	46.5	27	30

Source: *The Banker*, July 2012.

Table 4.2. Operating income of Standard Chartered Bank, 2009

	$ million
Hong Kong	2,370
Singapore	1,592
Other Asia-Pacific	2,888
India	1,813
Middle East/Other South Asia	2,078
Africa	1,089
Americas, UK, Europe	1,800
Total	*15,184*

Source: Standard Chartered, 2009 annual report.

the systems integrator firms, down through large swathes of the supply chain, due to the operation of the 'cascade effect'. In order for its large firms and their Chinese suppliers to survive and compete on the global stage, China has had no choice other than to implement a powerful state-led industrial policy. The core elements of this include maintaining state ownership over a wide array of 'strategic industries', using government procurement policy to favour indigenous firms, requiring multinational firms to establish joint ventures with domestic partners, and requiring localization of production and transfer of technology as a condition of gaining market access ('exchanging markets for technology').

However, a further important element in the expansion of the 'national champions' has been the provision of credit from the state-owned commercial banks. In the late 1990s much of this was used to facilitate industrial restructuring, including enormous lay-offs of workers. However, increasingly bank loans were used to support new capital investment, which embodied upgraded technologies, as well as supporting investment in research and product development. In addition, bank loans became increasingly important as an instrument to facilitate sales through credit to customers. As China's national champion firms have begun the process of 'going out', the state-owned commercial banks have been increasingly important in financing the international expansion of indigenous firms, through both capital investment and natural resource acquisition as well as through credit for customers.

In other words, bank credit has been centrally important in sustaining the overall growth rate through its role in financing China's high rate of investment, channelling the country's huge savings from bank deposits into productive investment. It has been crucially important also in enabling China's fledgling global firms to gain a foothold in the brutally competitive global level playing field.

Banks' role in maintaining socio-economic stability. In the high-income countries only a small share of the banking industry, such as the '*Landesbanks*' in Germany, is state owned. In China the Communist Party sits at the core of the country's state-owned banking system. The country's leading government officials, its leading regulators and the leaders of the country's banks are all Communist Party members. Every bank has a party secretary, who wields great authority within the respective bank. The central objective of the Communist Party in relation to the banking system is to ensure that all parts of the banking system work towards a common goal of the national interest. This means, above all, maintaining socio-economic stability in the wider common interest of the mass of the country's citizens. Western banks increasingly pay attention to 'corporate social responsibility', which they fulfil through charitable, educational and 'green' activities. However, the degree to which the bank's behaviour is connected with the achievement of a common social purpose is far weaker than is the case for China's banks, where the connection with that wider purpose is ensured through the in-depth penetration of the Communist Party into the very fabric of the banks, from top to bottom, including the government regulators.

Conclusion

The era of capitalist globalization has been characterized by an explosive increase in industrial concentration in the financial sector. Merger and acquisition has been a central driving force in this process, including the years since the onset of the global financial crisis. Marx's 'law of industrial concentration' provides a penetrating insight into the determinants of industrial structure in both the financial and the non-financial sector. This has resulted in a massive disparity in competitive capabilities between large financial firms from the high-income countries and those in developing countries. This difference is especially marked in the most profitable segments of the global banking business. Giant global banks are critically important to the globalization of non-financial business. They are the glue that binds the system together. However, the consequent high degree of industrial concentration in the hands of a relatively small number of giant financial firms is a two-edged sword. It was this very concentration of power that permitted the regulatory capture that was the underlying cause of the global financial crisis. It permitted the weakly regulated financial system to generate a vicious circle of endogenous money creation and asset price increase, with wide support from the mass of the population who welcomed the illusory increase in paper wealth and corresponding debt that was permitted by the increase in wealth. The fact that the system was poorly regulated and high-level employees in the sector were fabulously remunerated should not blind us to the underlying capabilities of global banks.

In Central and Latin America, as well as in Eastern Europe, liberalization of financial services provided a vivid demonstration of the fact that the 'global level playing field' in financial services is hugely skewed to the advantage of the incumbent giants based in the high-income countries. The evidence refutes the Washington Consensus view that liberalization of financial markets tends to strengthen local banks through the force of competitive pressure. On the contrary, where financial markets have been liberalized and a 'global level playing field' in financial services has been established, large local banks typically have been acquired by the global giants rather than being 'stimulated' by them. Numerous small local banks tend to survive only as niche players, serving poor people and local, internationally uncompetitive small- and medium-sized enterprises. The experience of developing countries contradicts the optimistic view expressed by the Washington Consensus institutions and European and American policymakers, of the impact of liberalization upon local financial institutions. Such views are either ill-informed or wilfully misleading.

Among developing countries China has by far the biggest potential financial market for global financial firms. They viewed China's entry to the WTO as an unprecedented business opportunity. To their intense disappointment, China chose not to implement the policies of the Washington Consensus, despite intense lobbying from the US government and the US banking industry, as well as from the EU and from European giant financial firms. If China had followed the advice of the Washington Consensus and the incessant urgings of policymakers from high-income countries, China's leading banks would have been broken into pieces and the most profitable segments acquired by the global giants.

Instead, China followed its own path, quite different from that advocated by the Washington Consensus institutions. The share of foreign ownership has been strictly controlled and the state remains the majority shareholder of the main banks. Moreover, China's banks are under tight regulation by the country's banking regulatory authority, with strict limits on the range of products they are permitted to provide. Tight regulation of its banks was critically important in permitting China to surmount the huge policy challenge presented by the global financial crisis. China has achieved enormous progress in the process, constructing profitable, well-regulated banks, which provide an improving quality of service to both corporate and retail customers. Only a few years ago the international media had concluded that China's banking system was terminally ill, that only comprehensive privatization and large-scale entry of the global giant banks could save China's financial system. Against most international expectations China now has the world's most profitable banks with the highest market capitalization.

However, the fact that China's large banks are highly profitable and have high market capitalization does not mean they are globally competitive. The structure and operational practice of China's banks remains radically different from that of the leading global banks. China's banks are tightly controlled by CBRC, with control mechanisms reinforced through the Communist Party, which deeply penetrates the banking sector at all levels. China's banks have strict controls on the range of products they are permitted to offer to their customers. Consequently, the main basis of their revenue remains the interest rate margin between deposits and loans. Deposits constitute the main source of their funding, with tight control exercised over the ratio of deposits to loans. Only a small fraction of the revenue of Chinese banks comes from outside the country. A large majority of loans are provided to state-owned enterprises within China. Only a small fraction of their revenues comes from global corporate and retail customers. The vast majority of employees are Chinese people, with Chinese as the main language of communication within the banks. China's banks face great difficulties in their international expansion due to the high degree of political sensitivity about the possibility of China's state-owned banks acquiring banks in the high-income countries. Even during the height of the global financial crisis, when the share price of Western banks collapsed, no Chinese bank has attempted a significant acquisition in the banking sector in the high-income countries.

After three decades of capitalist globalization, the areas of direct competition between Chinese and global banks are minimal. Global banks have a small penetration of the Chinese banking market and Chinese banks have only a small penetration of the banking markets of the high-income countries. The respective banking systems are at the heart of the entire fabric of political economy in the West and in China. The way in which they engage in the years ahead will be fundamentally important in terms of both competition in the global financial industry and for the way in which the global financial system is regulated.

Notes

1　Dell is also a powerful force in the overall Chinese server market. Dell estimates that due to its deals with Chinese internet companies such as Tencent, 60 per cent of the Chinese internet runs on Dell servers (*FT*, 19 September 2011).

2　In 2009 Hitachi had annual revenues of $124 billion and invested $4.7 billion in R&D.

Part III

INTERNATIONAL RELATIONS

Chapter 5

CHINA, WESTERN COLONIALISM AND THE UN CONVENTION ON THE LAW OF THE SEA (UNCLOS)

Introduction

In the Western media China is widely perceived to be engaged in a state-sponsored 'resource grab' in developing countries. It is also involved in a high-profile dispute with Japan over a group of tiny uninhabited islands, the Diaoyu (in Chinese) or Senkaku (in Japanese) Islands, which are on the edge of the South China Sea. The Western media are full of reports about China's claims to territory in the South China Sea and the fact that if the claims were successful this might bring China access to the natural resources that might be in or under the sea. The Western media routinely refer to China's alleged 'bullying behaviour' in the South China Sea. Some commentators have suggested that a new 'Peloponnesian War' might begin with the disputes in this sea. The territory in dispute is of great historical and strategic significance, and it may well possess substantial natural resources. However, the resources of the South China Sea are dwarfed in every sense by those involved in the United Nations' 'revolutionary' decision of 1982.

In 1982 the United Nations enacted a 'revolutionary' piece of legislation, the United Nations Convention on the Law of the Sea (UNCLOS) which allows countries to establish an 'exclusive economic zone' (EEZ) of 200 nautical miles from their coastline.[1] China is a signatory to UNCLOS and the dispute over the South China Sea revolves primarily around the extent of the EEZ that is claimed by China compared with that of the countries with which it is in dispute. However, the area and the potential resources involved are dwarfed by the vast maritime territories that the former colonial powers have amassed as a consequence of UNCLOS. A large part of these territories is in and around the Pacific Ocean. Up until the late eighteenth century this was China's own 'backyard' with negligible Western presence. The colossal resource grab by the former colonial powers arises from the 'scattered remnants' of tiny territories that they still retain from their former empires. This process has almost entirely escaped international attention, while China's complex dispute with its neighbours over a vastly smaller EEZ, in an area with which it had a close relationship over a long span of history,[2] has dominated international media discussion of the control over maritime resources in the Asia-Pacific region.

1. Decolonization

In the late 1940s the West began decolonization in earnest and the process was basically completed by the early 1980s. Only a few widely scattered remnants remain of the West's former gigantic colonial empire that had once spanned the entire globe. At this point the West, led by the United States and its European allies, began the process of economic liberalization that was to become known as the Washington Consensus, which it urged upon the rest of the world. Throughout the era of modern globalization, which began in the 1970s, the West has dominated the key international institutions. Right through to the present day the head of the IMF has always been a European and the head of the World Bank has always been an American. Even though the developing countries have somewhat increased their share of IMF votes since the global financial crisis, their share is far below their share of world population and the USA has a veto on key decisions due to the size of its shareholding. Within a few years, large parts of the world went through a process of privatization of state-owned enterprises, trade liberalization and liberalization of flows of foreign direct investment (FDI). There is a superabundance of literature in international political economy devoted to the analysis of almost every conceivable aspect of globalization, not least the rise of China.

The 'few remaining scattered remnants of the old colonial structure' turned out to be far more significant than most people realize. Indeed, they formed the basis for a veritable re-establishment of the colonial empires of the high-income countries. The remaining colonial territories each has a small land area, sometimes just a few square kilometres, often with a small or non-existent human habitation. Those people in the high-income countries who know anything about them typically regard them as eccentric anachronisms.[3] Some of them are exotic tourist destinations. Many of them constitute wildlife reserves to protect endangered species. They often support eco-tourism, such as bird watching or whale watching. They frequently have scientific research stations. Few people can name many of these far-flung territories or, if they can name them, have little idea of where and what they are. How many British people know what or where the British Indian Ocean Territory is? How many French people know what or where the Kerguelen Islands are? How many Americans know what or where the North Mariana Islands are?

However, these far-distant territories are often of immense strategic significance, with many of them containing American naval and air force bases, as well as reconnaissance facilities. They have also become extremely important in relation to the distribution of legally enforceable property rights over the world's natural resources.

UNCLOS

From the 1970s onwards there was increasing global concern at the perceived decline in stocks of exhaustible resources. The most obvious area of concern was the rapidly falling global fish stocks (Roberts 2007). Technical progress also opened up the possibility for greatly increased extraction of fossil fuels and other resources from deep-water and climatically challenging areas. Consequently, international interest in property rights in the world's oceans intensified. In 1982, after nine years of negotiations, the United Nations adopted the Convention on the Law of the Sea (UNCLOS). The convention established a legal framework to govern all uses of the world's oceans. By 2011, 161 individual states and the European Union were parties to UNCLOS. Once a state becomes a party to UNCLOS, it is under obligation to bring its maritime claims and national laws into conformity with UNCLOS. Five of the parties involved in the dispute over the South China Sea (China, Malaysia, Indonesia, the Philippines and Vietnam) had all ratified UNCLOS by 1996. The other disputant, Taiwan, could not ratify UNCLOS as it is not a member of the United Nations, but it brought its own internal legislation into line with UNCLOS.

Prior to UNCLOS maritime states had sovereign authority over their territorial waters, which extended to a distance of 22 km (12 nautical miles) from the shore. Many disputes developed about the extent and nature of rights beyond the 12-mile limit. UNCLOS made a 'revolutionary' change in the law of the sea by establishing a new resource zone called the 'exclusive economic zone' (EEZ), which is adjacent to the territorial sea and which extends 200 nautical miles from the baselines from which the territorial sea is measured. UNCLOS permitted a massive extension of the legally controlled territory of the former colonial powers, based on the 'scattered remnants' of their former empires. Within the EEZ coastal states have sovereign rights for the purpose of exploring and exploiting the living and non-living natural resources of the waters lying immediately above the seabed as well as those of the seabed itself and its subsoil, as well as the rights to other activities for the exploitation and exploration of the zone, such as the production of energy from the water, currents and winds. As the depletion of natural resources increases and global population expands to reach a peak of as much as 10 billion, the significance of the EEZ has greatly increased.

A critically important part of UNCLOS is the provision that islands are entitled to the same maritime zones as land territory, including an EEZ of 200 nautical miles (370 kilometres). Although the colonial empires were largely dismantled between the late 1940s and the early 1980s, there were numerous small islands that remained either as formal colonies or in other ways under the administration and control of the high-income countries. The overseas EEZs of the United States (including Alaska), France and the UK, vastly exceed those of their home territories. Many of these consist of groups of small islands stretching across large expanses of ocean, which allows these countries to claim sole authority over access to the resources within their vast EEZs. This authority is frequently enforced by their respective armed forces, including the USA's huge coastguard and naval fleets.

The USA, France, the UK, Australia, New Zealand and Russia, are the six countries with the largest EEZs (Table 5.1). Each of them is a developed, former colonial country, with a mainly white population. Their total population is 604 million compared with 1,338 million for China. Each of them established the territorial basis of their vast overseas EEZs during the colonial era, from the fifteenth century to the mid-twentieth century. Their total EEZs amount to 54 million sq. km, of which almost three-quarters (39 million sq. km) is separate from their home territory. Moreover, the very existence of the 'home territory' of the United States, Australia and New Zealand, is

Table 5.1. EEZs, selected countries ('000 sq. km)

	Mainland	Overseas territories (% total EEZ)	Total
USA	2,450 (a)	9,786 (80)	12,236
France	335	10,700 (97)	11,035
Australia	6,633	2,611 (29)	8,974
Russia	1,400 (b)	6,696 (83) (c)	8,096
UK	774	6,031 (89)	6,805
New Zealand	3,423	3,273 (49)	6,696
China (d)	c.900 (e)	< 2,000	<3,000

Source: Pew Trust (2012).
Notes: (a) the 48 continental states, excluding Alaska, as well as Hawaii and other offshore islands
    (b) European Russia
    (c) Pacific and Siberia
    (d) these are rough, maximum figures – the precise calculation of China's EEZ is extraordinarily complicated; a large proportion of China's claims in the South China Sea are disputed by the countries that also border the sea.
    (e) undisputed EEZ

attributable to their settlement by white European colonists, who forcibly and often violently deprived the indigenous people of their property rights over their own resources. China's undisputed EEZ is only around 900,000 sq. km, the size of one of the smaller overseas EEZ areas of the United States, France or the UK. If it is successful in all its disputed claims, it is unlikely that its total EEZ would be more than 3 million sq. km.

China has only around 900,000 sq. km of undisputed EEZ adjacent to the mainland. There is a further area of probably less than 2 million sq. km of EEZ that China claims in the South China Sea.[4] Apart from its claims in the South China Sea, which are vigorously disputed by countries in the region, and the adjacent island of Taiwan, which has long been a Chinese province, China has no overseas island territories to which it lays claim. In the sharpest contrast to the European powers and their colonial settler descendants, China did not seek to construct an overseas empire. This difference has had profound consequences for the global distribution of national property rights over the oceans' resources, especially under UNCLOS.

Britain

In the case of Britain, the EEZ attached to its overseas territories amounts to over 6 million sq. km, which is eight times the total EEZ around the UK itself (Table 5.2). These territories were all acquired during Britain's colonial past. They typically have small populations and a small land mass. However, in most cases the land mass consists of islands spread over a wide area. Few people in the home country know where these are and even fewer are aware that attached to these territories is a vast EEZ within which the UK lays sole claim to the resources.

The largest concentration of Britain's overseas EEZ is in the South Atlantic, with a total area of over 3.6 million sq. km. Britain first claimed sovereignty over the Falkland Islands in 1765, and Captain Cook claimed British sovereignty over South Georgia and the Sandwich Islands in 1775. When Britain went to war with Argentina in 1982 far more was at stake than Argentina's claim to the 16,000 sq. km of windswept territories on the Falkland Islands and the neighbouring South Georgia and the Sandwich Islands. The EEZ of the Falklands, South Georgia and the Sandwich Islands amounts to 2 million sq. km, nearly three times that of the UK itself. The Falklands War aroused a near-universal nationalist hysteria in the UK. Those who opposed the war, such as the former Labour Party minister, Tony Benn, were vilified in the popular media.[5] Around 1,500 Argentinean troops and 1,000 British troops were killed or wounded in the brief war. Britain's continued occupation of these 'far distant islands' is based mainly on the

Table 5.2. The UK's overseas EEZs

Territory	Land area (sq. km)	EEZ ('000s sq. km)	Population	Date first occupied by Britain
UK	–	*774*	–	–
Anguilla	91	92	13,500	1650
Ascension Island	88	442	880	1815
Bermuda	53	450	64,268	1609
British Indian Ocean Territory (a)	60	639	4,000	1810
British Virgin Islands	153	80	27,800	1666
Cayman Islands	264	119	54,878	1670
Falkland Islands (b)	12,173	551	3,140	1765
Montserrat	102	8	5,164	1632
Pitcairn Islands	47	836	67	1838
St Helena	122	445	4,255	1651
South Georgia and South Sandwich Islands (b)	3,903	1,450	30	1775
Tristan da Cunha	207	755	275	1815
Turks and Caicos Islands	430	154	44,819	1678
South Atlantic	*16,493*	*3,643*	*8,580*	–
Caribbean/North Atlantic	*1,093*	*903*	*210,429*	–
Indian Ocean	*60*	*639*	*4,000*	–
Pacific Ocean	*47*	*836*	*67*	–

Source: Pew Trust (2012).
Notes: (a) disputed with Mauritius
        (b) disputed with Argentina

argument that the handful of British colonists in this 'far-off land' have a 'right to self-determination'.

In 1657 Oliver Cromwell granted the East India Company a 'charter to govern St Helena'. It came under the company's control in 1659 and later became a British colony. Ascension Island and Tristan da Cunha were colonized by Britain at the end of the Napoleonic Wars. The three British-ruled South Atlantic territories have a total land area of just 417 sq. km and a population of 5,400, the equivalent of a medium-sized English village. However, due to the fact that each of them consists of numerous widely distributed islands, their total EEZ amounts to 1.64 million sq. km.

Britain retains several exotic 'scattered remnants' of its eighteenth-century slave empire in the Caribbean and North Atlantic, including Anguilla, Bermuda, the British Virgin Islands, the Cayman Islands, Montserrat and the Turks and Caicos Islands. Their total land area is only 1,093 sq. km, and their population is only around 201,000 people. However, their EEZ is 903,000 sq. km, around the same as China's undisputed EEZ.

The British Indian Ocean Territory consists of a group of widely dispersed islands, which have a total land area of just 60 sq. km, but an EEZ of 639,000 sq. km. The Chagos people originally inhabited the main body of islands, principally Diego Garcia. By the mid-twentieth century they numbered around 2,000. The islands were charted by Vasco da Gama in the sixteenth century and claimed by France in the eighteenth century as part of their Mauritius Territory. French interests established coconut plantations using African slaves and Indian labourers. In 1810 Mauritius, including the Chagos islands, was ceded by France to Britain. In 1965 Britain split the Chagos archipelago from Mauritius to form the British Indian Ocean Territory. The main purpose was to allow the UK to lease Diego Garcia to the United States in order that it could construct an air base on the island. The 2,000 or so indigenous inhabitants were forcibly relocated to Mauritius and to the Seychelles to allow US military occupation of the island. Construction began in 1971, and included a 3,000-metre-long runway able to accommodate heavy bombers such as B52s. The base was used for US Air Force operations during the 1991 Gulf War, the 2003 Iraq War and the 2011 war in Afghanistan. The population consists of around 4,000 people of whom around 2,000 are American military personnel, and around 2,000 people, mainly from the Philippines, who work for contractors.

The main British overseas territory in the Pacific Ocean is the Pitcairn group of islands. In 1790 Pitcairn Island was the refuge for the mutineers from the *Bounty*. The group of islands became a British colony in 1838, and were joined in 1902 by three island groups: the Henderson, Oeno and Ducie Islands. The total land area of the whole group of Pitcairn islands is 47 sq. km, with a population of less than 70 people, the size of a small English village street. However, due to the wide distribution of the islands, the EEZ is 836,000 sq. km, around the same size as China's undisputed EEZ.

France

Even though the UK's EEZ is extremely large, it pales by comparison with that of France. Its overseas EEZ, the legacy from its colonial empire, is more than thirty times the size of that of metropolitan France (Table 5.3). Its former slave-based sugar colonies in the Caribbean and North Atlantic have a total EEZ of 903,000 sq. km. Those in the Indian Ocean total 2.58 million sq. km, but its EEZ in the Pacific Ocean is no less than 6.9 million sq. km. French Polynesia contains several groups of islands. It has a total land area of 4,167 sq. km, and a population of 260,000, the equivalent of a medium-sized French city. However, its 130 islands spread across an area of 2.5 million sq. km of ocean. Its EEZ is a total of 4.8 million sq. km. Until 2007 Clipperton Island was administered together with French Polynesia. It consists of a single uninhabited coral atoll in the eastern Pacific Ocean. Its total land area is just 6 sq. km, but France's EEZ on account of this territory is 431,000 sq. km. New Caledonia is located in the southwest Pacific. It became a French colony in 1853. The archipelago is spread widely across the ocean and has a total land area of 18,500 sq. km. Its population is 252,000, equivalent to that of a medium-sized city. It has an EEZ of 1.4 million sq. km.

Table 5.3. France's overseas EEZs

Territory	Land area (sq. km)	EEZ ('000 sq km)	Population	Date acquired
France	–	*335*	–	–
French Guiana	83,534	134	236,250	1814
Guadeloupe	1,628	96	405,500	1674
Martinique	1,128	48	403,795	1638
French Polynesia	4,167	4,767	260,000	1842
Wallis and Futuna	264	258	15,000	1837
New Caledonia	18,500	1,423	252,000	1853
Clipperton Island	6	431	0	1711
Crozet Islands	352	574	0	1772
Kerguelen Islands	7,215	568	0	1772
St Paul and Amsterdam Islands	61	509	0	1843
Scattered Islands in the Indian Ocean	–	352	–	various
Reunion	2,512	315	800,000	1638
Tromelin Island	negl.	270	0	1810
Caribbean	*86,290*	*278*	*1,045,545*	
Pacific Ocean	*22,937*	*6,879*	*527,000*	
Indian Ocean	*10.140*	*2,588*	*800,000*	

Source: Pew Trust (2012).

One segment of the French territories in the Indian Ocean consists of the uninhabited Subantarctic archipelago of Crozet Island and Kerguelen, which together have a land area of 7,500 sq. km but command an EEZ of 1.1 million sq. km. Another segment consists of the tiny uninhabited islands of Amsterdam and St Paul, which have a total land area of only 61 sq. km. However, their EEZ is 509,000 sq. km. France's subtropical territory of Réunion has a land area of 2,512 sq. km and a population of 800,000. Its EEZ is 315,000 sq. km. France's other subtropical territory in the southern Indian Ocean is Tromelin Island, which consists entirely of 'one large sandbank', 1.7 km in length and less than a kilometre wide. However, it has an EEZ of 270,000 sq. km.

USA

In 2011 in his speech to the Australian parliament President Obama proclaimed: 'The United States has been, and always will be, a Pacific nation' (Obama 2011). US secretary of state Hillary Clinton declared that this century would be 'America's Pacific century' (Clinton 2011). In the second half of the nineteenth century the United States acquired a string of overseas territories that formed the foundation for an enormous EEZ, based mainly on its Pacific 'empire'.

The United States chose not to sign the UN Convention on the Law of the Sea, but formally recognized the legality of the EEZ (Woodworth 1994). A year after UNCLOS was enacted by the United Nations, President Reagan proclaimed the EEZ of the United States. It is the largest of any nation by a wide margin, encompassing more than 12 million sq. km (Table 5.4). The area is one-fifth larger than the land area of the United States: 'President Reagan's proclamation can be characterized as the largest territorial acquisition in the history of the United States' (Woodworth 1994, 366).

The 48 states of the USA have an EEZ of 2.45 million sq. km in total. The 48 states were united into the USA as a result of the long westward extension of the frontier, primarily through both regular and irregular military action. America's original 13 states at Independence came into existence through the violent expropriation by white colonial settlers of the lands occupied by Native American Indians. The Louisiana Purchase of 1803 transferred to the USA the ownership of France's enormous colonies stretching across the centre of North America, from Louisiana in the south to Montana and North Dakota in the north. The Mexican War (1846–48) concluded with the absorption of the vast territories of New Mexico, Utah, Arizona, Nevada, and parts of Colorado, California and Texas. The Native American population formed

Table 5.4. The USA's EEZs

Territory	Land area (sq. km)	EEZ ('000 sq km)	Population	Date acquired
East Coast	–	*916*	–	–
Gulf of Mexico	–	*708*	–	–
West Coast	–	*826*	–	–
Subtotal: 48 states	–	*2,450*		
Alaska	1,518,000	3,770	723,000	1867
Subtotal: Pacific islands	*29,602*	*5,804*	*5,521,000*	
of which				
Pacific Guano Islands (a)	*87*	*1,547*	*0*	
Islands without permanent inhabitants	*90*	*1,954*		
American Samoa	197	404	60,000	1904
Guam	541	222	159,000	1898
Hawaii	28,311	2,475	1,375,000	1898
Howland and Baker Islands	3	435	0	1856
Jarvis Island	5	317	0	1856
Johnston Atoll	3	443	0	1858
Northern Marianas	463	749	77,000	1944
Palmyra Atoll and Kingman Reef	76	352	0	1856
Puerto Rico	9,104	178	3,700,000	1898
Wake Island (b)	3	407	0	1899

Source: Pew Trust (2012).
Notes: (a) islands claimed under the 1856 Guano Islands Act, i.e., Howland and Baker Islands, Jarvis Island, Johnston Atoll, Palmyra Atoll and Kingman Reef
(b) Wake Island has no permanent civilian inhabitants, but there are estimated to be around 150 US military personnel on the island

a constant roadblock to the white settlers' expansion into the interior of the continent:

> If they could eliminate the Indians, the settlers could make North America their own... Americans chose the most effective means of subjugating the Indians they faced. They sent groups of men, sometimes a dozen, sometimes hundreds, to attack Indian villages and homes, kill Indian women and children, and raze Indian fields. (Grenier 2005, 12)

The massacre of Native American Indians at Wounded Knee in 1890 brought the creation of the continental state of America to a conclusion, with a long east and west coast, as well as the Gulf of Mexico. In that year the US Bureau of the Census officially declared the frontier complete.

In addition to the EEZ of the 48 states, the US has a further 9.6 million sq. km of EEZ in the Pacific Ocean. This reflects several different sources of territorial acquisition. The largest component consists of the state of Alaska and the Aleutian island chain, which Imperial Russia colonized in the eighteenth century. In 1867 the United States government purchased this vast colonial territory from Russia for $7.2 million. The total EEZ of Alaska is 3.8 million sq. km, which is more than 50 per cent greater than that of the entire 48 states of mainland America. Alaska's Aleutian island chain is 1,900 km long. It stretches out from mainland Alaska across the Pacific Ocean towards Russia's Kamchatka Peninsula. The island chain runs from 163 degrees west to 172 degrees east, the latter being roughly the same longitude as the main body of New Zealand. It has a population of just over 4,000 people, and its EEZ accounts for around one-third of the whole EEZ of Alaska.

The second group of US territories in the Pacific are those acquired in 1856 under the Guano Islands Act, which expropriated for the United States a number of uninhabited island groups scattered widely across the Pacific Ocean. In the late nineteenth and early twentieth century guano was a valuable source of agricultural fertilizer, and could be used also for saltpetre for gunpowder. The USA still possesses most of these islands groups. They include the Howland and Baker Islands, Jarvis Island, Johnston Atoll, Palmyra Atoll and Kingman Reef. They are little more than rocks and have no permanent human inhabitants. Their combined land area is just 87 sq. km. However, due to the fact that each of them consists of tiny islands that are widely scattered across the ocean, they have a total EEZ of 1.55 million sq. km, almost as much as the EEZ of the entire east and west coasts of the United States combined, and considerably larger than China's undisputed EEZ.

By the 1890s the United States had completed its westward expansion on the North American continent. The military and administrative challenges of the ever-expanding frontier had dominated America's foreign policy since Independence. Now the USA turned towards expansion outside the mainland. An editorial in the *Washington Post* on the eve of the Spanish–American War said:

A new consciousness seems to have come upon us – the consciousness of strength – and with it a new appetite, the yearning to show our strength… Ambition, interest, land hunger, pride, the mere joy of fighting, whatever it may be, are animated by a new sensation. The taste of Empire is in the mouth of the people even as the taste of blood in the jungle. (Quoted in Zinn 1999, 299)

As a result of its defeat of Spain in 1898 the US not only controlled Cuba[6] and Puerto Rico, but also acquired a string of territories across the Pacific, including the Philippines, Guam and Wake Island. Although the Philippines became fully independent of the USA in 1946, Guam and Wake Island remain US territories today. From 1801 until 1893 Hawaii was an independent kingdom. In 1893 a group consisting mainly of American businessmen overthrew the monarchy. After a brief period as a republic, the United States annexed Hawaii in 1898. Hawaii was fully incorporated into the United States. Guam and Hawaii are key parts of the USA's military command in the Pacific Ocean, which is by far the largest part of the USA's global military structure.

The island of Okinawa occupies a particularly complicated position in the United States' relationship with the Pacific Ocean. It has huge and highly controversial military facilities on the island, which is part of the Liuqiu/Ryukyu island chain (McCormack 2010). The Liuqiu/Ryukyu Islands are the most strategically important of all the world's small island groups. The Liuqiu/Ryukyu island chain stretches out over 700 miles to the southwest of mainland Japan into the East China Sea. It culminates in the group of tiny uninhabited islands, called the Diaoyu in Chinese and the Senkaku in Japanese.[7] The largest of the Liuqiu/Ryukyu islands is Okinawa, which is 70 miles long. It is around 400 miles from Okinawa to China's Fujian province and around 800 miles to Tokyo. For centuries Liuqiu/Ryukyu was a tiny independent kingdom inhabited by seafaring traders, similar to those in Japan's southern islands (Kerr 2000 [1958]). However, the culture of the Liuqiu/Ryukyu was arguably more strongly influenced by Chinese than by Japanese tradition. Prior to Japan's Meiji dynasty (1868–1912) the Liuqiu/Ryukyu kingdom was 'a toy state, with its dignified kings, its sententious and learned prime ministers, its councils and its numerous bureaus, its organization of temples and shrines, and its classical school, its grades in court rank and its codes of law, all developed in an effort to emulate great China' (Kerr 2000 [1958], 15–16). Five years after the Meiji Restoration in 1868 Japan asserted its authority over Ryukyu and in 1879 it forcefully incorporated the Liuqiu/Ryukyu kingdom into Japan as 'Okinawa prefecture', ruled by Japanese officials.

After the Japanese defeat US troops occupied Okinawa. In 1951 the San Francisco 'Treaty of Peace' gave the United States 'all powers of administration, legislation and jurisdiction' over the territory, 'including the inhabitants and their territorial waters'. The US constructed massive military facilities on Okinawa, using it as a key base in both the Korean and the

Vietnam Wars. In 1972 the Liuqiu/Ryukyu Islands, including Okinawa, as well as the Diaoyu/Senkaku Islands, were 'returned' by the US to Japan. The US military presence on Okinawa continued to grow. Today there are around 25,000 military personnel on the island, around one-half of the total number of US troops in Japan.

The US occupation of Okinawa as a 'virtual US colony' is hugely controversial in Okinawa itself as well as in mainland Japan (McCormack 2010). In 1995 when Joseph Nye was defense secretary, the US government produced a strategy document (US Department of Defense 1995) for the Asia-Pacific region. Nye enunciated a policy of 'deep engagement' (1995), which he argued was necessary on the grounds that 'rising powers create instability in the international state system': a 'forward-based troop presence ensures the US a seat at the table on Asian issues' and 'enables us to respond quickly to protect our interests, not only in Asia but as far away as the Persian Gulf'. For the foreseeable future, Japan and the Okinawa base would serve as the 'cornerstones of our security strategy for the entire region'. The governor of Okinawa remarked that Nye spoke of Okinawa as if it were 'American territory'.

The acquisitions of the Mariana Islands and American Samoa each occurred in a different fashion. Guam is part of the Mariana Islands, which run north to south in the same latitude as the Philippines. They constitute the eastern edge of the Philippine Sea and are in roughly the same longitude as Port Moresby in Papua New Guinea. Prior to the arrival of Spanish forces in 1521, the Mariana Islands were inhabited by the Chamorro and Refaluwasch people. The whole of the Marianas were annexed by Spain in 1565. In 1899 Spain sold the Northern Mariana Islands to Germany. At the end of World War I the League of Nations 'awarded' them to Japan, which developed sugar plantations on the islands. After Japan's defeat the islands were placed under US trusteeship by the United Nations, and in 1976 the Commonwealth of the North Mariana Islands (CNMI) was formally integrated in political union with the United States. The whole of the Mariana island chain, including both north and south (Guam) are American territories. American Samoa is in the South Pacific, to the northeast of New Zealand. By the late nineteenth century the harbour at Pago Pago had become a regular re-fuelling station for coal-fired ships. The 1899 Tripartite Convention between Britain, Germany and the United States divided Samoa in two, with Germany taking control of the western islands and the United States the eastern islands, including the harbour at Pago Pago. It remains an American territory.

The total US EEZ around its Pacific Ocean island territories, excluding the Aleutian island, amount to 5.8 million sq. km. Within this total, just

90 sq. km of land area of uninhabited islands, widely scattered across the ocean, accounts for an EEZ of 1.95 million sq. km.

When the US president or secretary of state speaks of the United States as a Pacific nation, the minds of Americans inevitably recall the battles in the Pacific during World War II. At the forefront of American consciousness is Japan's attack on Pearl Harbor in Hawaii, and Pearl Harbor remains the headquarters of the US Pacific Fleet. Many of the territories that the USA still possesses in the Pacific Ocean were the scene of terrible battles conducted between American and Japanese forces, including Midway Island, Wake Island and the Aleutian Islands. A series of major battles were fought in and around the Mariana Islands, including the Battles of Saipan, the Philippine Sea, Guam, Tinian, Peleliu and Angaur. A total of 108,504 US troops died and more than 248,000 were wounded or missing in the War in the Pacific.[8]

'String of pearls'

It is commonly alleged in the Western media that China has a long-run 'string of pearls' strategy to build a succession of overseas bases in Southeast Asia and the Indian Ocean. Three great powers on the US Security Council, namely the USA, France and the UK, have between them a total of around 23 million sq. km of EEZ that they hold as a consequence of their colonial past. If the acquisition of Alaska is included, the total rises to over 26 million sq. km. Their respective EEZs dominate vast areas of the Pacific Ocean, the Indian Ocean and the south Atlantic Ocean. They are of enormous strategic benefit, providing a 'string of pearls' necklace around the entire globe, forming the platform for a web of overseas military bases. At the same time they are of massive potential importance in terms of the world's scarce natural resources. Their possession has been secured by a revolutionary decision by the United Nations. The dimensions of the combined territorial acquisition under UNCLOS dwarfs by an enormous margin the territories that are in dispute between China and its immediate neighbours in the South China Sea. It is as though the global media has succeeded in focusing the minds of their population on a mouse when a mighty elephant stands behind them unnoticed.

Australia and New Zealand

Australia and New Zealand both benefit greatly from UNCLOS as their main territory contains a long coastline. They each have exceptionally large EEZs on account of this fact alone. Moreover, their existence as countries, occupied principally by white people of European origin, is due entirely to the British colonial conquest. However, the 'colonial bequest' is especially large also in relation to their large body of overseas islands, far removed from their respective main territories. Eastern Australia was claimed by Britain in 1770. On Wednesday 22 August James Cook landed on an island off eastern Australia that he named Possession Island. He said:

> The Eastern Coast from the Latitude of 38 degrees South down to this place I am confident was never seen nor visited by any European before us, and Notwithstand I had in the name of His Majesty taken possession of several places upon this coast, I now once more hoisted English Coulers and in the Name of His Majesty King George the Third took possession of the whole Eastern Coast from the above Latitude down to this place by the name of New South Wales, together with all the Bays, Harbours Rivers and Islands situate upon the said coast, after which we fired three Volleys of small arms which were Answered by the like number from the Ship. (Cook 1999, 170–71)

The whole of Australia was claimed by Britain in 1829. New Zealand was claimed by James Cook in 1769 and annexed by Britain in 1840. In both cases there was a relatively large indigenous population whose rights were ignored and towards whom the British colonial occupiers behaved brutally. In the colonial era Britain acquired several groups of island territories in the southern Indian and Pacific Oceans. In the case of inhabited islands the pattern of treatment of the indigenous people was repeated. Each of these had a small land area, but they were each spread over a wide area of the ocean.

Australia has two groups of offshore island territories, one in the Pacific and one in the Indian Ocean, both of which were annexed by Britain and afterwards transferred to the Commonwealth of Australia (Table 5.5). The Indian Ocean territories include Christmas Island, the Cocos Islands, and the Heard and McDonald Islands in the Arctic. Their combined land area is 517 sq. km with a total population of only 2,003 people. The combined EEZ is 1.1 million sq. km. Australia's Pacific Ocean territories include Lord Howe Island, Macquarie Island and Norfolk Island. They have a combined land area of 178 sq. km and a population of 2,649 people, with an EEZ of 1.5 million sq. km. Australia's overseas island territories have a total area of 695 sq. km and a population of 4,652, equivalent to a small town in the Australian outback. However, the combined EEZ is 2.6 million sq. km.

New Zealand's largest area of EEZ is the Cook Islands in the South Pacific (Table 5.6). They were part of the British Empire before being transferred to New Zealand. They contain 15 major islands with a total land area of just 240 sq. km and a population of 20,000, the size of a small town. However,

Table 5.5. Australia's EEZs

Territory	Land area (sq. km)	EEZ ('000 sq km)	Population	Date acquired (a)
Mainland	–	*6,363*	–	*1770–1829*
Christmas Island	135	277	1,403	1788
Cocos Islands	14	467	600	1888
Heard and McDonald Islands	368	417	0	1910
Lord Howe Island	15	543	347	1788
Macquarie Island	128	478	0	1810
Norfolk Island	35	431	2,302	1788
Indian Ocean	*517*	*1,161*	*2,003*	–
South Pacific	*178*	*1,452*	*2,649*	–
Subtotal	*695*	*2,613*	*4,652*	

Source: Pew Trust (2012).
Note: (a) date of acquisition by Britain, later transferred to Australia

the islands are spread over 2.2 million sq. miles of ocean and their total EEZ amounts to 2 million sq. km, equal to twice the size of China's undisputed EEZ (see Table 5.1). New Zealand's three South Pacific island groups, the Kermadec, Tokelau and Niue islands have a total land area of just 303 sq. km and a total population of only 2,800, the size of a small English or French village. However, due to the fact that they are spread over such a wide area, their combined EEZ amounts to 1.3 million sq. km.

Table 5.6. New Zealand's EEZs

Territory	Land area (sq. km)	EEZ ('000 sq km)	Population	Date acquired (a)
Main Islands	–	*3,243*	–	*1769*
Cook Island	240	1,960	20,000	1888
Kermadec Islands	33	678	0	1788
Niue	260	316	1,400	1900
Tokelau	10	319	1,400	1877
Subtotal: South Pacific	*543*	*3,273*	*22,800*	–
Total		6,516		–

Source: Pew Trust (2012).
Note: (a) date of acquisition by Britain, later transferred to New Zealand

Russia

The vast size of the modern state of Russia is mainly due to its colonial expansion into Siberia. In the mid-fifteenth century Moscow Principality was a landlocked territory to the south of the Baltic and far to the north of the Black Sea. By 1600 the main body of European Russia had been unified under the rule of Moscow. At the end of the sixteenth and in the seventeenth centuries Moscow expanded into the vast Siberian territories. The Russian Empire reached the Pacific Ocean in 1639, and between 1742 and 1867 included even Alaska. After the collapse of the USSR, Russia lost many of its territorial acquisitions in Central Asia. However, it firmly maintained its grip on the vast territories it had acquired in Siberia. Russia's coastline stretches from Murmansk in the west to the Chukchi Sea in the east, and down the Pacific coast to Vladivostok in the Sea of Japan. Russia's EEZ in Europe is less than one-fifth of the country's total EEZ, the main body of its EEZ having been acquired in the conquest of Siberia (Table 5.7).

Table 5.7. Russia's EEZs

Territory	EEZ ('000 sq. km)	Date acquired
European Russia	1,400	–
Pacific	3,419	Sixteenth–seventeeth centuries
Siberia	3,277	Sixteenth–seventeeth centuries
Total	8,096	–

Source: Pew Trust (2012).

2. Impact of Western Colonialism on the Pacific Ocean

An important justification for the UN's establishment of the concept of the 'exclusive economic zone' was the desire to reduce damage to exhaustible natural resources within the zone. It was hoped that establishing clear national property rights over those resources would transform these vast areas from open-access 'global commons' into areas of resource conservation. The West's own experience in managing the resources within these areas, especially in the early phase of Western colonialism, was gravely deficient.

Taking possession. In 1497 Vasco da Gama set out from Europe with his tiny fleet. It sailed around the southern tip of Africa, reached Calicut on the Indian coast and returned to Europe two years later. Thereafter, European merchants steadily deepened their trading activities in Southeast Asia. In 1519 Ferdinand Magellan set out on his voyage to find a westward route to the

Spice Islands of Southeast Asia. He rounded the tip of South America and reached the Philippines, where he was killed in 1521. In 1565 Spain claimed the Philippines as its colony. Manila became the base for Spain's trans-Pacific trade to Central America. Spain's associated island colony of Guam was an important resting place for Spanish galleons on their journeys between Manila and Mexico. However, apart from the Philippines, up until the late eighteenth century the West's impact on the main body of the Pacific Ocean territories was negligible.

Thereafter, the West's impact increased radically. The expeditions of Captain James Cook were the critically important stimulus to the West's impact on the region between the late eighteenth and mid-nineteenth centuries. Cook was an archetypal figure of the British Enlightenment. He was a naval captain, a navigator, a cartographer and a fellow of the Royal Society. His three expeditions to the Pacific Ocean were conducted under the orders of the British Admiralty and were supported by the Royal Society. One of their goals was to identify and map new territories, including a possible southern continent, Terra Australis, and to try to find a passage through the Antarctic. However, a major purpose of Cook's voyages was to 'take possession of Convenient Situations in the name of the King of Britain' (Cook 1999, 11). His three voyages between 1768 and 1779 resulted in detailed maps of large parts of the Pacific Ocean, from inside the Antarctic Circle in the extreme south to the Bering Straits in the north. Among his extraordinary achievements was the circumnavigation of the entire Antarctic. Cook's voyages also resulted in a large extension of the territories claimed by Britain, including New Zealand and the entire east coast of Australia, as well as South Georgia and the South Sandwich Islands. Cook's travel journals were widely read and immensely influential in shaping the West's view of the Pacific Ocean, including that of the fledgling American republic.

Animals. A key issue for UNCLOS is the preservation of the ocean's natural resources. The era of early colonialism had a profoundly negative impact on the Pacific Ocean's animal population.

Each of James Cook's voyages included scientists who provided a detailed record of the wildlife they encountered. One of the most surprising and striking results of the expeditions was the superabundance of wildlife they discovered in the Great Southern Ocean. These included vast numbers of birds, seals and whales. Cook 'stumbled on what was probably the largest congregation of wildlife that existed in the world, and he was the first man to let the world know of its existence' (Morehead 1968, 236). The detailed account of the location and maps to accompany the accounts in Cook's journal stimulated a wave of commercial exploitation of the southern seas by European and

American ships. Seals were killed mainly for their valuable skin and whales mainly for their oil. By the 1830s fur seals in the southern ocean were virtually extinct (Morehead 1968, 242). The main attack was then directed at the whale population, which came south in the summer breeding season. The United States was the leader in this industry. By 1846 New England alone had 735 whalers. Each of them averaged 100 whales on every voyage: 'They came south round the Horn and out into the Pacific where their bases in the tropics were Hawaii and Tahiti, and in the south, the Bay of Islands in New Zealand, Sydney and Hobart Town in Tasmania. It was a tremendous killing' (Morehead 1968, 245). The killing went on and on until there was virtually nothing left to kill: 'In a period of little more than 50 years – roughly from the 1780s to the 1840s – these little ships with their polyglot crews...combed these vast icy oceans so thoroughly that no large marine animal was to be easily found any more' (Morehead 1968, 251–52).[9] By the 1880s commercial whaling had been abandoned over vast areas of the Pacific Ocean (Roberts 2007).

People. Prior to Western colonialism the combined indigenous population of Australia, New Zealand and the Pacific islands was relatively small. Establishing colonial rule did not present a challenge comparable to those presented by India, China or the countries of the South China Sea. Nevertheless, numerous small-scale conflicts occurred between the Western colonists and the indigenous people, particularly over land claims. The most severe conflict was in New Zealand between 1843 and 1872. As many as 20,000 Maoris may have been killed in a series of brutal confrontations with British troops. The war frequently involved 'scorched earth' tactics by the colonial forces, laying waste to Maori villages and destroying crops. Although much smaller in scale the war in New Caledonia between French colonists and indigenous forces was equally bloody. France annexed the territory in 1853. Violent conflicts developed from the 1850s onwards as French settlers attempted to expropriate land from the native Kanaka inhabitants. The full-scale 'Kanaka uprising' erupted in 1878. Rebels attacked French civilian settlers, including their families. The French authorities responded with attacks on Kanaka villages and crops in the traditional 'first way of war' against a guerrilla force. In almost every case of white colonial settlement in the Pacific small-scale violent confrontations took place between the Western colonial forces and the indigenous population. Indigenous people in the Pacific were typically treated as subhuman and often killed without compunction. In the case of Tasmania the settler population, mainly convicts, cleared the indigenous people off their land through a ferocious manhunt. In 1830 Tasmania was put under martial law. Aborigines were 'continually hunted and tracked down like fallow deer, and, once captured, are deported, singly or in parties, to the islands of the Bass Strait' (quoted in Morehead 1968, 213). Within just five years just a couple of hundred of the aboriginal population survived out of an estimated original population of 5,000 (Morehead 1968, 213).

However, an even more serious impact on the Pacific territories' demography took place through the spread of disease. Sexually transmitted diseases played an important role in the widespread demographic decline. From the late nineteenth to the late twentieth century, the great increase in the number of sealers and whalers, as well as ordinary commercial shipping, brought with it a widespread sex industry along with violent sex attacks on indigenous women. A combination of venereal disease, tuberculosis, smallpox and dysentery were mainly responsible for the large declines in population in many Pacific islands, including Hawaii, Tahiti, the Marquesas and Easter Island. Prior to Cook's arrival in Hawaii its population was at least 200,000–300,000, and it may have been as high 800,000 or even one million. The impact of infectious diseases produced a 'genocide' in which the population fell to as low as 30,000 indigenous Hawaiian people by 1900 (Bushnell 1993). In the case of Tahiti, which was annexed by France in 1843, it is estimated that the population fell from 40,000 in the 1770s to just 9,000 in the 1830s, before falling to 6,000 in the late nineteenth century (Morehead 1968, 117). It is estimated that in the Marquesas, which were annexed by France in 1842, the population fell from around 70,000–80,000 in the late eighteenth century to around 4,000 in 1900.[10] The Easter Island population is estimated to have fallen from 4,200 in 1860 to just 500 in 1871 (Thomas 2010, ch. 7).[11]

The number of Australia's indigenous people is estimated to have fallen from around 200,000 in 1800 to just 20,000 in 1900 (Broome 2010, 172). In Australia, the white settlers also brought new diseases, including venereal disease, to which aborigines had low immunity. To a considerable degree the catastrophic decline was caused by deterioration in the health of the indigenous population resulting from the forcible alienation of their lands by white settlers. The effect of this was especially serious in the case of hunters and gatherers such as Australia's aboriginal people. When Charles Darwin visited Australia in 1836 he wrote: 'Wherever the European has trod, death seems to pursue the Aboriginal. We may look to the wide extent of the Americas, Polynesia, the Cape of Good Hope and Australia, and we find the same result' (quoted in Morehead 1968, 212).

Conclusion

In recent years the international media have devoted great attention to the analysis of the dispute over the South China Sea. Most of the analysis has focused on the possibility that China might gain control over the natural resources that might be in or under this Sea. The 'revolutionary' and legally endorsed acquisition by the world's former colonial powers of control over the natural resources in a vast marine territory through the mechanism of UNCLOS has received negligible attention other than in specialist legal journals. This vast resource grab by the former colonial countries, which took place through the legal mechanism of the UN's legislation, eclipses the maritime area and resources that might be in or under the South China Sea.

China is located at the edge of the vast Pacific Ocean. It has existed as a unified state occupying roughly its current territory for most of the past 2,000 years, with the Pacific Ocean forming its 'backyard'. From early in its history China possessed the technological and administrative capability to invade Southeast Asia, as well as the sparsely populated territories of the Pacific Ocean, including today's Australia, New Zealand, the Pacific islands, Siberia, Alaska and the west coast of North America. However, it chose not to do so. Instead China's rulers concentrated on governing the mainland effectively. Nor did China seek to colonize the territories around the South China Sea, despite the fact that it was comprehensively dominant in East Asia for at least two millennia, and had military superiority over the rest of the region and deep trade links with these territories.[12] China did not seek to colonize Southeast Asia because it was a 'land-bound society', and had a 'continental mind-set' with a continual pull from its 'powerful political and cultural centre' (Wang Gungwu 2000, 23, 37). Over the long sweep of its history China has emphasized the importance of regulating the market in a non-ideological fashion to serve the interests of the mass of the population within its own territory. This philosophy has the potential to make an invaluable contribution to the survival of the human species in the face of the surging contradictions of capitalist globalization (Nolan 2009).

Up until the late eighteenth century the West had minimal presence in the Pacific Ocean. Captain Cook's three epic voyages between 1768 and 1780 constituted the great turning point of world history. Beginning in the late eighteenth century, the Western colonial powers invaded the Pacific territories, which had profoundly destructive consequences for both the animal and human populations. By the end of the nineteenth century, the Western colonial powers had turned the Pacific Ocean from China's 'backyard' into their own 'backyard' and had colonized most of the territories around the South China Sea. China had been reduced to the position of a beggar. Its drastically altered position was symbolized by the flood of millions of impoverished Chinese migrants who came to work in the mainly Western-owned mines and plantations in the areas around the South China Sea and on the widely scattered Pacific islands.

In the Pacific Ocean the EEZ derived from the West's colonial expansion between the late eighteenth and late nineteenth centuries includes Alaska, the Pacific Island territories still held by the USA, France, Britain, Australia and New Zealand, and Russia's Pacific Ocean territories, as well as the mainland of New Zealand and Australia. The total EEZ in and around the Pacific Ocean that exists as a direct consequence of Western colonial expansion amounts to 30.9 million sq. km (Table 5.8).

Table 5.8. Pacific Ocean EEZs of the former colonial powers

Country	EEZ ('000 sq. km)
USA (a)	9,574
France	6,879
Britain	836
Australia	3,500 (b)
New Zealand	6,696
Russia	3,419
Total	*30,904*

Source: Pew Trust (2012).
Notes: (a) excluding the USA's west coast
(b) a rough estimate of the EEZ on Australia's Pacific Ocean coastline

The West's preoccupation with China's involvement in the South China Sea is in the sharpest contrast to the complete absence of analysis of the West's vast EEZ that it derived from its colonial past, and which includes areas in China's 'backyard' of the Pacific Ocean. This raises deep questions about the nature of the international media and the way in which perceptions among the general public in the West are shaped. The contrast in treatment of the two issues is especially disturbing in view of the possibility that there might be a new 'Peloponnesian War' that begins with disputes over the South China Sea. We in the West have a painfully blinkered view of who we are and how we are perceived by the rest of the world at this fragile point in the evolution of the human species.

Notes

1 Under certain circumstances a country's EEZ may extend beyond this limit.
2 This complex topic will be the subject of a subsequent study by this author.
3 See, for example, Winchester (1985).
4 China's claim to an EEZ in the South China Sea relates to the areas around the 'islands' in the sea rather than to the whole of the sea. The number of them that are simply

'rocks' rather than 'islands' is hotly disputed. Only 'islands' are entitled to an EEZ. The total area of the South China Sea is roughly 3.5 million sq. km. If the areas of undisputed coastal waters and undisputed high seas are excluded, then the area that China eventually claims as its EEZ in the South China Sea is likely to be substantially less than the total area of the whole sea.

5 A cartoon in the *Sun* newspaper depicted Tony Benn as 'Chicken Benn' flying over a convoy of British troops, dropping eggs on them, on their way to fight in the Falklands. Long after the war ended, Tony Benn was interviewed on a late-night, little-watched programme about World War II. In it he recalled calmly how he and his brother had volunteered for the army and air force respectively. As he recalled his brother's death on his first flying mission he collapsed in tears and the interview was terminated. A similar issue arose in relation to George McGovern. In the 1972 US election he was crushed by Richard Nixon, with only 37 per cent of the popular vote compared with 61 per cent for Nixon. McGovern ran on a platform of opposition to the Vietnam War. In 1941, after the bombing of Pearl Harbor, McGovern volunteered for the US Air Force. He flew 35 missions over Europe in World War II and was awarded the Distinguished Flying Cross for his bravery and skill in achieving an improbable safe landing of his damaged B-24 Liberator on a tiny airstrip in Yugoslavia. Asked why he had not made more of his own war record in the presidential campaign against Nixon he replied simply that he did not know how to speak of it (quoted in Martin 2012).

6 Cuba was not made a formal American colony, but the new Cuban constitution gave the United States the 'right to intervene for the preservation of Cuban independence, the maintenance of a government adequate for the protection of life, property and individual liberty' (quoted in Zinn 1999, 311).

7 The Diaoyu/Senkaku are geologically separate from the main body of the Liu Qiu/ Ryuku island chain. They are located 120 nautical miles northeast of Taiwan, 200 nautical miles east of the Chinese mainland and 200 nautical miles southwest of the island of Okinawa, from which the prefecture takes its name in Japanese.

8 In World War II overall, there were 417,000 American military deaths, including the merchant marine and the coast guard, but less than 2,000 civilian deaths. Japan suffered over two million military deaths and between 0.5 million and 1.0 million civilian deaths due to military action and 'crimes against humanity'. The USSR suffered between 9 million and 11 million military deaths and 13 million and 15 million civilian deaths due to military action and 'crimes against humanity'. Germany suffered 5.5 million military deaths and around one million civilian deaths due to military action and 'crimes against humanity'.

9 For a comprehensive account of the destruction of the whale and sea population by the West's commercial whaling and sealing fleets in this period, see Roberts (2007, chs 7 ['Whaling: The First Global Industry'] and 8 ['To the Ends of the Earth for Seals']).

10 Thomas (2010, ch. 2), gives a detailed account of the ravages that sexual disease wrought upon the Marquesas in the nineteenth century.

11 Forcible recruitment of Easter Islanders to work in Peru also played a role in the catastrophic decline in the Easter Island population (Thomas 2010, ch. 7).

12 The only significant exception to this is the fact that for around 1,000 years China ruled over North Vietnam, which is contiguous to the southwest Chinese border province of Guangxi. North Vietnam broke away from Chinese rule at the end of the Tang dynasty in 907 AD.

Chapter 6

A NEW PELOPONNESIAN WAR? CHINA, THE WEST AND THE SOUTH CHINA SEA

Introduction

The era of wild capitalist globalization has produced profound contradictions. Many of these involve potential conflict between the USA and China, including climate change, human rights, the struggle for access to natural resources and regulation of the global financial system. There has been increasing discussion in the West about the possibility of a new 'Peloponnesian War' between the United States and China. For example, Graham Allison of the Kennedy School of Government at Harvard University warned:

> If leaders in China and the US perform no better than their predecessors in classical Greece, or Europe at the beginning of the twentieth century, historians of the twenty-first century will cite Thucydides in explaining the catastrophe that follows. The fact that war would be devastating for both nations is relevant but not decisive. Recall the first world war, in which all the combatants lost what they treasured most. (Allison 2012)

Much international attention has focused on the possibility that the South China Sea might be a key channel through which a US–China conflict develops. From the point of view of the USA, and indeed the West as a whole, this would be a 'quarrel in a far-country between people about whom we know nothing' (Neville Chamberlain, cited in Kagan 2003, 2). However, the region is one about which a great deal is known in China. There are deep connections between the people of mainland China and the 30 million or so descendants of Chinese migrants who settled in Southeast Asia over the centuries. The United States is closely involved in the region. US secretary of state Hillary Clinton recently has warned China against the use of 'coercion, intimidation and threats' to resolve disputes over the South China Sea. In fact, in both the distant and the more recent past today's high-income countries have made extensive use not only of 'coercion, intimidation and threats' in the region around the South China Sea, but also extreme military violence, often directed against civilians. In 2011–12 the United States announced a comprehensive 're-balancing' of its military strategy towards the Western Pacific, with the self-evident goal of 'containing China'. This dangerously escalates the possibility of a new Peloponnesian War erupting.

The Peloponnesian War

The Peloponnesian War took place between Sparta and Athens around 431–404 BC. It was immortalized through Thucydides' study *The History of the Peloponnesian War*, written during the war itself. Western scholars have long been drawn to the Peloponnesian War in analysing international relations. Interest in the war surged during the Cold War: 'Generals, diplomats, statesmen and scholars alike have compared the conditions that led to the Greek war with the rivalry between NATO and the Warsaw Pact' (Kagan 2003, xxiii). Robert Kagan is arguably the best-known American scholar of the Peloponnesian War. His best-selling study, which is a synthesis of his other works, presents a glowing picture of Athens. The 'astonishing victory' of the Spartan alliance, which included Athens, over the Persians in the early fifth century BC 'opened a proud era of growth, prosperity, and confidence in Greece':

> The Athenians, especially, flourished, increasing population and establishing an empire that brought them wealth and glory. Their young democracy came to maturity, bringing political participation, opportunity, and political power even to the lowest class of citizens, and their novel constitution went on to take root in other Greek cities… [It was] the first democracy in the history of the world… It was a time of extraordinary cultural achievement as well, probably unmatched in originality and richness in all human history. (Kagan 2003, xxi)

Sparta is portrayed as an oppressive regime, based on exploitation of helots, 'who stood somewhere between serfdom and slavery, farmed the land and provided Spartans with food, while the *perioiki*, personally free but subject to Spartan control, manufactured and traded for what the Spartans needed' (Kagan 2003, 3). In Kagan's view, the Spartan social structure was 'potentially dangerous', since the helots outnumbered the Spartans by seven to one and 'would have gladly eaten the Spartans raw'. To meet the challenge of their occasional rebellions, the Spartans 'created a constitution and a way of life like no other, subordinating individual and family to the needs of the state'. Sparta was the organizing force behind the Peloponnesian League, which had its core in the city states in the Peloponnesus, bound to Sparta through a 'loose network of alliances' (Kagan 2003, 4).

In Kagan's view, Sparta and Athens were 'probably as different as any two [states] in the Greek world' (Kagan 2003, 3). Cold War American scholars such as Kagan viewed the United States as the 'Athens' of the modern world and the USSR as a latter-day 'Sparta'. American politicians across the political spectrum continue to share an astounding certainty about their country's unique role as the global guardian of the values of enlightenment and democracy that were first displayed in Athens. During the 2012 presidential election campaign President Obama declared 'Providence is with us, and we are surely blessed to be citizens of the greatest nation on earth' (speech at the Democratic Convention, September 2012). Secretary of State Hillary Clinton said: 'The United States consistently over history seeks to advance not just our own good, but the greater good. And this is part of what makes America's leadership exceptional. There is no real precedent in history for the role we play or the responsibility we have shouldered' (Clinton 2012). Obama's opponent, presidential candidate Mitt Romney declared: 'The US is the greatest nation in the history of the world… Americans have that unique blend of optimism, humility and the utter confidence that when the world needs someone to do the really big stuff you need an American' (speech at the Republican Convention, September 2012). Condoleezza Rice, former secretary of state, said: 'The US is not just any country; we are exceptional in the clarity of our conviction that free markets and free peoples hold the key to the future and in our willingness to act on those beliefs… Mobilizing human potential is something the US has done better than any country in history' (Rice 2012).

This is not the way in which the United States is regarded by much of the rest of the world. Many people would agree with de Tocqueville's judgement:

> I know of no country in which there is so little independence of mind and real freedom of discussion as in America… The majority raises formidable barriers around liberty of opinion; …if [an author] goes beyond them he is exposed to continued obloquy and persecution. His political career is closed forever… The majority lives in the perpetual utterance of self-applause… (Tocqueville 1994 [1863], I: 263–64)

The near-universal American view of Athens as the model of enlightenment and democracy does not bear close scrutiny. In fact, there are some significant parallels of a different nature with America's own history. Kagan's study fails even to mention the word 'slavery' in relation to Athens. At its peak, Athens had a total population of around 220,000, of whom only 30,000 were full citizens. In addition there were around 40,000 resident aliens, of whom only a few would become citizens in due course. There were around 150,000 slaves (Dunn 2005, 35). In other words, democracy among one social group was compatible with tyranny over another group, who were regarded as not fully human. Moreover, by 450 BC Athens had constructed an empire that embraced most of the lands around the Aegean Sea (Finley 1978). Athens quickly asserted its control over the Delian League, which was formed in order to resist the Persian invasion: 'Athens not only acquired the decision-making power for the league but also was prepared, in manpower, ships and psychology, to exert force in the strictest sense, to impose her decisions and to punish recalcitrants' (Finley 1978, 107). Its conquests frequently were harsh, the populations of the conquered territories enslaved and Athenians settled as colonists. Cities that attempted to leave the Delian League were brutally crushed. The empire brought large material benefit to most citizens of Athens including the poorest strata. There is 'no evidence that a single Athenian opposed the empire' (Finley 1978, 106). The fact that a group of people who are democratic in their internal relations can decide democratically to conquer and oppress other peoples is a cause for deep reflection among Chinese scholars and policymakers.

After the collapse of the USSR Western interest in the Peloponnesian War waned: 'enlightened Athens' had defeated 'despotic Sparta'. Interest was revived by China's remarkable rise. However, the interpretation altered sharply to suit the times. The principal message from Western scholars of the Peloponnesian War today is the dangers posed to the West by a 'rising power'.[1] Susan Shirk's influential study *China Fragile Superpower* (2007) summarizes the reinterpretation of the Peloponnesian Wars to suit the new needs in international relations: 'History teaches us that rising powers are likely to provoke wars… In the twentieth century, rising powers Germany and Japan were the cause of two devastating world wars' (Shirk 2007, 4). However, the message is muddied by the fact that China is also seen to be 'Sparta' in terms of political and social structure:

> China's leaders face a troubling paradox. The more developed and prosperous the country becomes, the more insecure and threatened they feel. The PRC today is a brittle, authoritarian regime that fears its own citizens and can only bend so far to accommodate the demands of foreign governments. (Shirk 2007, 5)

The relevance of the Peloponnesian War to international relations has increased since 2008. The relative decline of the West has been accelerated by the impact of the global financial crisis. The OECD countries, with the USA at their core, are mired in economic stagnation and social disruption, while China continues to grow rapidly. Fears of China's rise have intensified, gripping the popular imagination in all branches of the Western media. A careful reading of the significance of the Peloponnesian War for today's international relations is more necessary than ever. Thucydides' provides a meticulous account of the debate in Sparta at which the decision was taken to declare war on Athens. It contains a chilling message for the United States today, and indeed for the West as a whole. In that debate the Spartan king Archidamus said:

> Spartans, in the course of my life I have taken part in many wars and, I see among you people of the same age as I am. They and I have had experience, and so are not likely to share in what may be a general enthusiasm for war, nor to think that war is a good thing or a safe thing. And you will find, if you look carefully into this matter, that this present war which you are now discussing is not likely to be anything on a small scale... [W]e must not bolster ourselves up with the false hope that if we devastate their land, the war will soon be over. I fear that it is more likely that we shall be leaving it to our children after us. (Thucydides 1972, 82–83)

However, in the final speech before the assembly, Sthenelaidas urged the Spartans to declare war on Athens: 'Do not allow the Athenians to grow still stronger' (Thucydides 1972, 86). Thucydides' study of the Peloponnesian War traces the way in which the war emerged from a complex set of mutual complaints and clashes of interests between Sparta and Athens. However, in his opinion 'the real reason for the war is most likely to be disguised by such an argument': 'What made war inevitable was the growth of Athenian power and the fear which this caused in Sparta' (Thucydides 1972, 49). The impact of the war was devastating: 'The [war] not only lasted a long time, but throughout its course brought with it unprecedented suffering for Hellas. Never before had so many cities been captured and then devastated; ...never had there been so many exiles; never such loss of life' (Thucydides 1972, 48).

The South China Sea

The international relations issues involved in connection with the South China Sea are complex. China's territorial and jurisdictional claims in the South China Sea stem largely from the pre-1949 maps compiled by the Kuomintang government (KMT). As early as 1936 the official Chinese government map showed most of the South China Sea, including both the Paracels and the Spratly Islands, as Chinese territory. The KMT's official map of 1947 shows 'nine dotted lines' around a large part of the South China Sea. Chinese maps published since 1953 have all shown the nine-dotted line for the boundary of China's territory in the South China Sea. Within China itself there is considerable difference of opinion about the significance of this line. For example, writing in 1994 Professor Gao Zhiguo, director of the National Institute for Marine Development Strategy, was of the opinion that the nine-dotted line delineated 'ownership of islands rather than being a maritime boundary'. He concluded that 'China never has claimed the entire water column of the South China Sea, but only the islands and their surrounding waters within the lines' (quoted in Li Jinming and Li Dexia 2003, 291). While there are some Chinese experts, who consider that 'the dotted line relates only to the enclosed islands', others believe that 'it asserts Chinese sovereignty over the waters', and still others believe that it indicates a 'claim of historic title over the waters' (Li Jinming and Li Dexia 2003, 291). In fact, on those occasions that China has exercised exclusive rights over the area within the line, it has mainly done so in relation to the islands rather than the waters.

Up until the 1970s there was limited international interest in the issue of sovereignty over the South China Sea. Non-Chinese vessels sail freely across the waters within the 'nine-dotted line'. One-half of the world's super-tanker traffic passes peacefully through the region's waters. The issue came alive with the discovery of oil in the region and was further stimulated by the development of deep-sea oil exploration technologies. However, China's investment in oil exploration and production in the South China Sea is still very limited, confined mainly to areas close to Hong Kong (USCESRC 2010, 129). The most complicated disputes relate to the Spratly Islands, in the central and southern part of the sea. There are 96 'islands' in the Spratly archipelago, but most of them are tiny and many of them are submerged at high tide. They are of negligible intrinsic value. The People's Republic of China, Taiwan, Vietnam, Malaysia and the Philippines each have constructed military installations on some of the islands over which they claim sovereignty. However, these are small-scale installations, far removed from the size of the US military bases in East Asia. Resolving the disputes over sovereignty in the South China Sea region is likely to be prolonged and complicated.

China's relationship with the Association of Southeast Asian Nations (ASEAN) countries has deepened in recent years. Although China is not a member of ASEAN it has participated in numerous summit meetings with the grouping itself, as well as meeting regularly with ASEAN countries in other regional groupings. China's share of ASEAN's trade has risen to roughly equal that of the EU (USCESRC 2010, 125). However, China's share of

ASEAN's trade is still only about one-third that of the OECD countries as a whole. Moreover, China's foreign direct investment (FDI) in Southeast Asia is far below that of the OECD countries. In 2007–2008 China's cumulative FDI was less than one-quarter of that of either Japan or the USA, and less than one-sixth of that of the EU (USCESRC 2010, 127). In 2002 the foreign ministers of the ASEAN countries and China signed a declaration pledging the signatories to resolve disputes peacefully and through direct negotiations among the countries concerned. Although there have been clashes both before and since then, these have almost all been small-scale skirmishes, not warfare and most of them relate to disputes over fishing rights.[2]

There are similar territorial disputes in other parts of the world. For example, Greece and Turkey both border the Aegean Sea and have a roughly similar length of its total coastline. However, there is a chain of Greek islands (Lesbos, Samos, Chios and the Dodecanese Islands) lined up only a short distance from the Turkish coast, far across the Aegean Sea from the Greek mainland, and numerous complex issues, including intense arguments about aviation and navigation rights, have resulted from this. As will be seen later in this chapter, even today there are a large number of similar island territories that are far from the home territory of the respective high-income countries, including the overseas possessions of the USA, the UK and France. In 1982 Britain fought a large-scale war in order to defend its right to occupy the Falkland Islands, a territory that is several thousands of miles from the UK and is claimed by Argentina, which is only a few hundred miles from the Falklands. The war commanded wide support in the British media and among the British public. Britain's continued occupation of these 'far distant islands' is based on the argument that the handful of British colonists in this 'far-off land' have a 'right to self-determination'.

There are several 'enclave' territories far away from their respective home country that are inside the land mass of other countries. For example, Gibraltar, in the extreme south of Spain, is occupied by Britain. Its right to do so is vigorously disputed by Spain. Guantanamo Bay Naval Base is a 117 sq. km area of land in Cuba to which the USA has a 'perpetual lease'. The USA's right to occupy Guantanamo Bay is disputed fiercely by the Cuban government. It is deeply ironic that the USA should occupy an enclave territory run by a regime that it has done everything to overthrow. It is even more ironic that the USA should use it as a prison for 'Islamic terrorists' who allegedly attacked the United States, and that these prisoners should have been subjected to degrading treatment by the US government. Within the UK itself, the fact that the 'six counties' in the northern part of Ireland are part of the 'United Kingdom of Great Britain and Northern Island' has been a long-standing cause of controversy and periodic bouts of intense violence.

1. East–West Relations: Cooperation or Conflict?[3]

The freedom of capitalist globalization after the 1970s produced an immensely beneficial outcome for humanity. The unleashing of the full force of oligopolistic competition resulted in the most dramatic technical progress the world has ever seen, producing tremendous benefits for most of the human race. The explosion of international trade and the great increase in the international flow of capital helped to spread these benefits widely across the world. The era of capitalist globalization produced a global culture, which makes it seem impossible that there could be worldwide military conflict. The motto of the 2008 Olympics in Beijing, which took place immediately before the explosion of the global financial crisis, was 'One world, one dream'.

However, the unfolding of the capitalist free market brought profound contradictions. It was indeed, in Charles Dickens's famous words, both 'the best of times and the worst of times'. Dickens's own dialectical approach to writing admirably suited the double-edged character of political economy in this period. The contradictions resulting from the release of 'wild capitalism' included grave deterioration in the global ecology, a profound threat to the whole of humanity from global warming, a sharp rise in inequality within both rich countries and developing countries, an unprecedented concentration of global business power, and a growing dominance of a deregulated financial system over the entire trajectory of global political economy.

The contradictions of capitalist globalization erupted in 2008. The human species confronts a Darwinian challenge to its continued existence in anything like its present form. Although capital has never been more global, people remain rooted within the nation-state, with a sharp division of interests between those who live in high-income countries and the majority of those who live in the rest of the world.[4] There are many common points of outlook in the West and in China that may help to facilitate a peaceful resolution of their differences. In both cases there is a mystical tradition, with wonder and incomprehension in the face of the mystery of human existence. During one of our research trips we walked braced against the sea wind on the deserted sea shore near Shantou, an ancient port city in eastern Guangdong province. We looked out on the South China Sea, the beach awash with debris from a recent storm:

> To stand at the edge of the sea, to sense the ebb and flow of the tides, to feel the breath of a mist over a great salt marsh, to watch the flight of shore birds that have swept up and down the surf lines for untold thousands of years…is to have knowledge of things that are as near eternal as any earthly life can be. (Carson 1941, 3)

In his introduction to the *Tao Te Ching*, D. C. Lau wrote: 'The flood-like *qi*... is the basic ingredient of the universe...[and] when developed to the utmost, it fills the space between Heaven and Earth, and when that happens Man is in the same stream as Heaven and Earth' (Lau 2009). Is there any difference between the way people from the East and from the West feel at the edge of the shore, gazing at the ocean?

In the East and West there is a common ethical strand of 'benevolence' that tries to 'do unto others as you would wish them to do unto you'. Adam Smith's *Theory of Moral Sentiments* (1761) explores the critical importance of benevolence for a good society: 'To feel much for others and little for ourselves, to restrain our selfish, and to indulge our benevolent affections, constitutes the perfection of human nature; and can alone among mankind produce that harmony of sentiments and passions in which consists their whole grace and propriety' (Smith 1982 [1761], 25). Charles Darwin's *Descent of Man* (1871) argued that the key difference between man and the lower animals is the moral sense possessed by humans. He considered that the 'social instincts' are crucial to the survival of the species. These instincts include 'love', 'mutual love', sympathy', 'sympathetic feelings', 'instinctive sympathy', the all-important emotion of 'sympathy', 'sympathetic kindness to others', 'mutual aid', 'fidelity', and 'benevolent actions'. Darwin uses the word 'love' more than 90 times in *The Descent of Man*. In China the concept of benevolence is fundamental to the understanding of human nature. In 1694, Huang Liuhong wrote a manual on the education of local magistrates:

> Mencius said: 'All men have a mind which cannot bear to see the suffering of others. The ancient kings had this commiserating mind, and, likewise, as a matter of course, they had a commiserating government (*bu renren zhixin, bu renren zhi zheng*). This is in essence what this book is all about. In the administration of local government nothing is more important than this principle.' (Huang Liuhong 1984)

However, the core of Western ideology is much more strongly oriented than China's towards individual rights and freedom. In his famous and hugely influential book, *Capitalism and Freedom*, Milton Friedman asks the reader to imagine that there are four Robinson Crusoes marooned on desert islands. Three of them are on 'small and barren islands' while one of them is on a 'large and fruitful island':

> Of course, it would be generous of the Crusoe on the large island if he invited others to share its wealth. But suppose he does not? Would the other three be justified in joining forces and compelling him to share

his wealth with them? The unwillingness of the rich Crusoe to share his wealth does not justify the use of coercion by the others... [This] would make a civilized world impossible. (Friedman 1962, 165)

Such an answer would be inconceivable to most people in China. Eastern ideology is much more strongly oriented towards the common interest and a harmonious society: 'The ultimate purpose of government is the welfare of the common people. This is the most basic principle of Confucianism and has remained unchanged throughout the ages' (Lau 1976).

Traditional China and Europe had fundamentally different approaches towards overseas expansion. In the fifteenth century, under Admiral Zheng He, a huge Chinese fleet made seven epic voyages, taking as many as 28,000 men with it. The expeditions peacefully explored a vast territory as far as Madagascar, bringing rich information back to the Chinese emperor. No attempt was made either then or in subsequent periods to build an overseas empire, despite China's technological superiority over the West, until the nineteenth century. China's statecraft focused almost entirely on ways to maintain stability, peace and prosperity within the Chinese mainland. China devoted stupendous efforts over many generations to building a Great Wall to protect itself against land invasion from neighbouring territories. It did not seek to colonize the territories around the South China Sea, despite the fact that it was comprehensively dominant in East Asia for at least two millennia, and had military superiority over the rest of the region and deep trade links with these territories.[5] Wang Gungwu concludes that China did not seek to colonize Southeast Asia because it was a 'land-bound society', which had a 'continental mind-set' with a continual pull from its 'powerful political and cultural centre' (Wang Gungwu 2000, 23, 37). Over a long sweep of its history China has emphasized the importance of regulating the market in a non-ideological fashion to serve the interests of the mass of the population within its own territory. This philosophy has the potential to make an invaluable contribution to the survival of the human species in the face of the surging contradictions of capitalist globalization.

In the fifteenth century the government of Catholic Portugal also sent out a series of expeditions; these were to conquer the Canary Islands. The indigenous people were almost entirely wiped out in violent military conflicts. Portuguese settlers established sugar plantations with slaves from the African mainland. From then onwards the West undertook a long process of overseas conquest and rule, which culminated at the end of the nineteenth century in the wild 'scramble for Africa' and the frantic search for a 'place in the sun'. White Europeans considered themselves as the 'chosen people' of the Old Testament, with a God-given right to conquer the rest of the world. The people of the Caribbean,

Central America, South America, North America, Africa, the Middle East, South Asia, Southeast Asia, Australasia and China all were incorporated into the rule of white European Christians, often forcibly and with great violence, including the decimation of numerous indigenous peoples. By 1914, a large part of the world was ruled by white people of European origin.[6]

By 1900 all the territories surrounding the South China Sea were Western colonies, including the Philippines (a US colony), Indonesia (a Dutch colony), Malaya (a British colony) and Indo-China (a French colony). The Western countries' vast colonial empires were mostly not dismantled until the middle decades of the twentieth century. Decolonization was often accompanied by violent conflict with indigenous national liberation movements. For example, in Southeast Asia during World War II, most of the region was conquered by Japan, which replaced the region's European colonial masters. After Japan's defeat, the Western colonial powers, with Britain at the forefront, attempted to re-impose their colonial rule. Ferocious struggles against national liberation movements followed in Vietnam, Indonesia and Malaya.

Following the final dismantling of colonialism in the 1970s,[7] the Western-led ideology of wild capitalist globalization, crystallized in the Washington Consensus, brought about the comprehensive crisis of global political economy in which we now sit (Nolan 2009). Belief in the superior morality and efficiency of free markets lay at the core of the ideology. The chief figure in wild capitalist globalization was Alan Greenspan, chairman of the US Federal Reserve from 1987 to 2006. His self-proclaimed intellectual heroine was Ayn Rand. Her best-selling text, *Atlas Shrugged* (1957), was wildly popular among the leaders of free market fundamentalism after the 1970s. Its supporters claim that its sales in the USA are second only to those of the Bible. It is profoundly hostile to the state. Rand considers that taxation is immoral as it allows the government to appropriate private property by force. It champions the virtues of the free market and selfishness as the foundations of a good society:

> To love money is to know and love the fact that money is the creation of the best power within you... The lovers of money are willing to work for it. They know they are able to deserve it... The proudest distinction of Americans is...the fact that they were the people who created the phrase 'to *make* money'...The words 'to make money' hold the essence of human morality. (Rand 2007 [1957], 412–14)

Greenspan met Rand in 1952 and they remained close friends until her death in 1982. Greenspan found Rand's philosophy of 'unfettered free markets' to be 'compelling' (Greenspan 2007, 52).

A profound adjustment is required in the West if there is to be a fruitful cooperation between East and West in order successfully to build global institutions to meet the common interests of the whole of humanity ('all under heaven'). The West needs much better to appreciate the way in which it is viewed by the majority of the world's citizens. In recent years in the West the level of hostility towards China has grown steadily. In part, this has ideological roots in anti-communism. In fact, there was considerable debate in China at the time when the Chinese Communist Party (CCP) was founded in 1921 about the way in which to translate the term 'communism'. In the end the CCP adopted the Chinese term '*gongchang zhuyi*', which literally means 'common property-ism'. However, there were other suggestions. These included '*gongtong zhuyi*' ('common-ism'), '*gongxiang zhuyi*' ('sharing together-ism') and '*shetuan zhuyi*' ('mass-ism'). They also included the term '*datong zhuyi*', which harks back to the ancient Chinese concept of '*datong*', or 'great harmony' for 'all under heaven'. Using '*datong zhuyi*' as the translation of 'communism' indicates a society in which the pursuit of the 'common good' or the 'common interest' is the paramount goal, without specifying the particular means by which it might be achieved. Rousseau wrestled endlessly with this concept. In the *Social Contract and Discourses* he refers to the 'common interest', the 'common good', the 'general will', the 'will of all', the 'public will', the 'public interest' and the 'great society'. Ultimately, Rousseau regarded the supremacy of the great General Will as 'the first principle of public economy and the fundamental principle of government' (Cole 1993, xliii). Rousseau's profound concern for the 'common interest', however that might be defined, is one reason for the popularity of his writings in China. A 'communism' which pursues the 'common interest' of 'all under heaven', both East and West, is a philosophy that all human beings might agree to.

Unfortunately, the history of warfare is typically unconnected to ideology, but, rather, it is more often connected to national power and, especially, the struggle for scarce resources. The growing Western hostility towards China may have little to do with ideological hostility towards 'communism', and more to do with the West's fear that its position in the world, which it has occupied for hundreds of years, is threatened. The Peloponnesian Wars were not fought over ideology. Rome's conquest of Europe, the Middle East and North Africa was not driven by ideology. Nor was Napoleon's conquest of Europe.[8] The West's innumerable wars of colonial conquest and Japan's conquest of China were not ideologically driven. There was nothing to distinguish the ideologies of France and Germany in the Franco–Prussian War. The 'enlightened' European countries that ripped each other to pieces in 1914–18 were ideologically indistinguishable. The attempt by Germany, arguably the most 'enlightened' of all European countries, to conquer Europe after 1939 was not driven by ideology.[9]

The militaristic, violent, ideologically and economically dominant position of the West, including its Japanese protégé, is drawing to a close. China's rise is only one part of a general process of transition away from a global system that began with Portugal's military conquest of the Canary Islands in the fifteenth century and has continued in one form or another ever since. This process has been accelerated by the global financial crisis and is greatly complicated by the global nature of giant firms, for whom their home country is of ever-decreasing importance (Nolan 2012). Honestly coming to terms with this unfolding reality and engaging peacefully with China, and, increasingly with other latecomer countries, will require true 'enlightenment' from the politicians, people and mass media in the West.

2. The West and the South China Sea

The West has a centuries-long history of involvement with the countries around the South China Sea. The nature of this involvement is fundamentally different from that of China. The presence today of around 30 million people whose Chinese ancestors migrated peacefully to the region constitutes a critical difference from the West's historical relationship with the lands around the South China Sea.

The Philippines

The Philippines was a Spanish colony from 1565 until 1898. Spain's occupation of the Philippines involved many violent episodes. For example, in 1603 Spanish reprisals against an uprising by the Chinese community in Manila cost 23,000 lives (Fairbank et al. 1965, 26). At the end of the nineteenth century, the USA launched a 'looking outward' policy, 'in an era when doctrines of Social Darwinism and Nordic racial superiority provided a sanction for keeping up with other nations in the search for markets, colonies, and naval bases' (Fairbank et al. 1965, 475). In April 1898 the United States declared war on Spain over Cuba. At dawn on 1 May 1898 the American Asiatic squadron led by Commodore Dewey attacked the Spanish fleet in Manila at anchor in the bay. By lunchtime the whole Spanish fleet was burning or sunk. Eight Americans were slightly injured in the attack and around 400 Spanish sailors killed or wounded (Fairbank et al. 1965, 476). Many people view the Battle of Manila Bay as the moment at which the modern US Navy was born.[10] In 1898 the United States annexed the Hawaiian Islands, one-third of the way across the Pacific, and occupied Wake Island, 2,300 miles to the west of Hawaii. Under the 1898 peace treaty with Spain the USA took over Puerto Rico, Guam, which is almost all the way to the Philippines, as well as the Philippines itself, for which it paid $20 million. The Philippines became an American 'self-governing commonwealth' in 1935. Japan occupied the country in 1942–45. The Philippines only gained full independence in 1946.

After it annexed the Philippines in 1898 the USA faced a full-fledged rebellion, which continued until 1902. The United States used 70,000 troops, of whom 4,200 died, to suppress the rebellion (Fairbank et al. 1965, 728; Zinn 1999, 311–20). There was enormous loss of life among the Philippines' population, both directly in battle as well as through disease and starvation. A US captain wrote home: 'Caloocan was supposed to contain 17,000 inhabitants. The Twentieth Kansas swept through it, and now Caloocan contains not one living soul' (quoted in Zinn 1999, 315). A volunteer from the state of Washington wrote: 'Our fighting blood was up, and we all wanted to kill "niggers"... This shooting human beings beats rabbit hunting all to pieces' (quoted in Zinn 1999, 315). An American general returning to the United States from Southern Luzon said: 'One-sixth of the natives of Luzon have either been killed or have died of the dengue fever in the last few years. The loss of life by killing alone has been very great' (quoted in Zinn 1999, 315). In the US Senate in 1900 Albert Beveridge said:

> The Pacific is our ocean... China is our natural customer... The Philippines gives us a base at the door of all the East... There are not 100 men among them who comprehend what Anglo-Saxon self-government even means, and there are over five million people to be governed... It has been charged that our conduct of the war has been cruel. Senators, it has been the reverse... We must remember that we are not dealing with Americans or Europeans. We are dealing with Orientals. (Quoted in Zinn 1999, 314)

Vietnam

The French conquest of Indo-China in the late nineteenth century was particularly violent (Vien 1987). After Japan's defeat in 1945, the Vietnamese united front national resistance movement, led by the Viet Minh, declared Vietnam an independent country. President Ho Chi Minh announced:

> The French have fled. The Japanese have capitulated. Emperor Bao Dai has abdicated. Our people have broken the chains which have fettered them for nearly a century and have won independence for Vietnam. Vietnam has the right to enjoy freedom and independence and in fact has become a free and independent country. (Quoted in Vien 1987, 254)

Immediately the British sent a large force to occupy key parts of Southern Vietnam, paving the way for the return of French forces. By 1953 the number of troops in the French Expeditionary Force reached 250,000. The French effort to re-colonize Vietnam was supported increasingly strongly by the United States.

The French fought an extraordinarily bloody campaign, with enormous losses among their troops. The French forces systematically followed the 'First Way of War' (Grenier 2005), intended to destroy the will of the fighting force: 'Entire villages were burnt down, their inhabitants massacred, and tens of thousands of people were herded into concentration camps... [French troops] systematically destroyed crops and food reserves so as to starve the people and prevent food from reaching the resistance' (Vien 1987, 286). This was the same 'total war strategy' that the French invading force had adopted in their conquest of Algeria in the 1840s (Sessions 2011). It was the same strategy as that followed by British forces in Ireland in the sixteenth and seventeenth centuries and by the British colonists and their successors in North America (Grenier 2005). The French were finally defeated at Dien Bien Phu in 1954, which involved the deaths of around 22,000 French soldiers. A large proportion of the remaining French forces went on to fight for France against the national liberation movement in Algeria in a bloody war that lasted from 1954 until 1962, in which the French army employed the same techniques of 'total war' that they had used in Vietnam.

From 1954 to 1962, the United States provided massive support to the Diem regime in South Vietnam, including extensive provision of 'training personnel'. Despite this, resistance to the Diem regime intensified. In 1962 the United States sharply increased the number of 'advisors' in South Vietnam and stepped up its involvement in 'counter-insurgency' operations. In 1965 the United States' armed forces became fully involved in war against the communist regime in the north and communist resistance in the south. By 1965 there were 190,000 US troops in Vietnam, and a decade of 'total war' began. During the war in Vietnam, large areas of the country were declared 'free fire zones' which American planes bombed at will. By the end of the war seven million bombs had been dropped on Vietnam, more than twice the total dropped in Europe and Asia in World War II. Haiphong and Hanoi were fire bombed more than once by the US Air Force. Large quantities of poisonous sprays were used to destroy trees and any kind of vegetation in the large areas on which they were dropped. Horrific attacks on Vietnamese civilians were carried out by US troops on the ground, including the infamous My Lai massacre, in which 450–500 people, mostly women, children and old men, were shot. At least two million people died in the Vietnam War, of whom a significant number were civilians who died as a result of the direct and indirect effects of US bombing.

Indonesia

The Dutch conquest of Indonesia, which spread over a long period of time, involved great violence by the occupying forces. For example, in the Javanese Rebellion of 1820–25, led by the devout Muslim, Prince Diponegoro, around 8,000 European troops and 200,000 Javanese died (Fairbank et al. 1965, 722). In the decades prior to the Japanese invasion in 1941 Indonesia experienced a ferment of cultural debate, closely akin to that in the Arab world.[11] The *pergerakan* movement involved a flowering of artistic endeavour and a renewed search for a Muslim identity in the face of colonialism and modernization. Following the Japanese defeat in 1945, the national liberation movement, led by Sukarno, declared Indonesia an independent state. There was widespread popular support for Sukarno's declaration, with massive 'ocean rallies' across the country. President Sukarno was able quickly to establish a relatively stable bureaucracy and army. However, the Dutch made clear that they wished to re-assert their position as colonial rulers of Indonesia, and they were fully supported in this goal by Britain, by far the most powerful military force in Southeast Asia. Britain took responsibility for the country until such time as the Dutch armed forces could return in strength. British troops landed in September 1945. The British intervention was seen, both by critics at the time and by historians since, as a 'calculated war of imperial conquest' (Bayly and Harper 2007, 170).

Part of the British forces landed at Surabaya, the largest naval base in Southeast Asia after Singapore. The landing stimulated a violent uprising. Several civilians and 230 British troops were killed as well as their commander, General Mallaby. The commander of the British forces in Indonesia announced: 'Crimes against civilization cannot go unpunished... I intend to bring the whole weight of my sea, land and air forces and all the weapons of modern warfare against [the rebel forces] until they are crushed' (quoted in Bayly and Harper 2007, 179). He launched an attack on the city with 24,000 troops, as well as tanks and aircraft. There followed the Battle of Surabaya, in which around 600 British troops were lost. The British government officially estimated that there were 10,000 Indonesian casualties, but Indonesian estimates of the number of dead are as high as 15,000. In 2001 the British government issued a formal apology for the attack on Surabaya. The battle constituted an 'epiphany' for the Indonesian independence movement deeply reinforcing the widespread wish for national independence, or *merdeka*. British troops were involved in further, less dramatic conflicts until the Dutch troops arrived in March 1946. The Dutch forces launched a full-scale military attack on the republican forces as well as conducting 'savage police action'. However, in the face of intense popular opposition the Dutch government realized that it would be impossible to contain the independence forces, and in 1949 Indonesia became fully independent. In 1955 Indonesia hosted the first meeting of the 'Non-Aligned Movement'. It took place in Bandung and included representatives from 29 African and Asian non-aligned countries. China's premier Zhou Enlai led the Chinese delegation at the conference.

Malaya

British colonial rule over the diverse states of Malaya was achieved more peacefully than colonization elsewhere in Southeast Asia. However, British armed forces intervened repeatedly in support of one or other local ruler, before the various Malay states were united under colonial rule. Britain's undisputed naval strength lay behind its interactions with Malaya. In 1901 Britain had 25 naval stations in the East Indies and China, with a fleet of 37 'big-gun' naval vessels (Dalziel 2006, 66–67). The Malay Federation was the core of the pre-1941 British empire in Southeast Asia. It formed a 'vast crescent of land', that 'stretched from Bengal, through Burma, the southern borderlands of Thailand, down to Singapore island' (Bayly and Harper 2007, 8). The economic resources of this region were considered by Britain to be 'so vital to its domestic recovery that it was willing to expend an unprecedented amount of blood and treasure in its re-conquest' (Bayly and Harper 2007, 11). Prior to the Japanese occupation Malaya had produced around one-half of the world supply of tin and rubber. Immediately after the Japanese defeat in 1945, British troops returned to Malaya in force. By September 1945, the British Southeast Asia Command had 61 warships in Singapore and 100,000 troops in the Malayan peninsula.

Among both Malays and Chinese the desire for independence intensified during the Japanese occupation. After their re-occupation of Malaya the British faced an increasingly intense struggle with different segments of the movement for independence. Throughout this struggle the British nurtured a close relationship with UMNO (United Malays National Organization), which had its main basis of support among the Malayan middle class and which rules Malaysia to this day. After 1948 UMNO was the only legal political party permitted by the British. During the British re-colonization young non-communist radicals formed Angkatan Pemuda Insaf (API), the 'Generation of Aware Youth', which called for 'independence through blood' (*merdeka dengan darah*). At the same time a powerful Islamic independence movement emerged, with its own political party, Hizbul Muslimin. It called for immediate *merdeka*. Its goal was to build an 'Islamic society and the realization of a Darul Islam, an Islamic state' (Bayly and Harper 2007, 418). The secular API was banned in 1947 and Hizbul Muslimin was banned in 1948.

However, by far the most serious challenge to British rule came from the Malayan Communist Party (MCP), which had its main support among the Chinese community, which comprised around one-third of Malaya's population. In the first half of the twentieth century, a flood of poor Chinese migrants had come to Malaya to work on the rubber plantations and mines. During the Japanese occupation, the MCP led the Malayan People's Anti-Japanese Army (MPAJA) in its struggle against Japanese occupation, with the main base of their support among Chinese workers. The Japanese occupying army carried out 'systematic screening and execution of Malayan Chinese', with a total of around 50,000 Chinese people killed, in the 'biggest single atrocity of the war in Southeast Asia' (Bayly and Harper 2007, 25). After 1945, the MCP led the struggle against the British re-colonization of Malaya.

The anti-British resistance surged in 1948. A major factor in the surge of anti-British feeling was the effort to re-impose control over the rubber plantations. During the Japanese occupation a large-scale squatter movement had occurred, mainly among the Chinese workers. Backed with arms and police powers, the planters were able to reclaim their fiefdoms largely unchallenged (Bayly and Harper 2007, 495). The British strongly supported the forcible eviction of squatters. This in turn provoked violence against plantation owners: 'The spark that lit the Malayan revolution came from below and caught both the British and the communists unawares' (Bayly and Harper 2007, 428). The British responded by banning the MCP and declaring a state of emergency across the whole peninsula. It lasted for twelve years, even beyond independence in 1957.

There followed several years of brutal warfare between the British forces, mainly with Indian soldiers, and guerrilla forces of the MCP. The main basis of support for the MCP was the Chinese plantation and mine workers. The British were unsure what to call the guerrillas: 'Above all officials were desperate to avoid any words which might suggest a genuine popular uprising… They settled on "bandit"…and by 1952 had shifted to "communist terrorist" (CT)' (Bayly and Harper 2007, 437). By the end of 1948 the Malayan public was becoming conditioned to the violence by British forces being reported in a clinical statistical form, as 'kills of bandits', or later CTs: 'The culture within the military was such that British units kept tallies of "kills"; in military memoirs hunting metaphors abound… Bodies were routinely placed on public display to cow local people… The Emergency was a war by any other name' (Bayly and Harper 2007, 455–56). British forces used 'large-scale bombing with 1,000 lb bombs', though they found that it was 'not as effective as in Iraq' (Bayly and Harper 2007, 478).

'Only' 226 people were executed during the state of emergency. Capital offences required the inconvenience of a public trial. However, the emergency regulations allowed the British to detain 'suspects' for up to two years without trial. In 1949 the British introduced Emergency Regulation 17D, which allowed for collective detention in de facto concentration camps, an instrument that the British had devised during the Boer War. By May 1950, 26,741 detention orders had been signed. Families were routinely divided and conditions in the camps were admitted to be 'worse than that experienced by internees under the Japanese regime' (the deputy commissioner of police, quoted in Bayly and Harper 2007, 483). Trade unions were 'devastated'. The Special Branch openly attended union meetings and 'RAF police terrorized trade unions on their bases in Singapore' (Bayly and Harper 2007, 495).

The British attempted to break the foundation of popular support for the MCP-led anti-British struggle by massive forcible re-settlement of mainly Chinese squatter communities. Between 1951 and 1954 official government reports recorded that 572,917 people were 're-settled' in 480 'New Villages' and a further 560,000 were 're-grouped' in towns and rubber estates: 'This was the largest planned population re-location in recorded history' (Bayly and Harper 1957, 490). The forcible re-settlement divided families and broke up old communities. In their new locations strict curfews, travel restrictions and strict control over food supply were imposed. The most notorious case of re-settlement concerned the 'shy, forest-dwelling' Orang Asli people. They were viewed by the British as a 'vital link in the MCP supply chain'. They were uprooted and sent en masse to concentrated settlements in lowland areas. Of the 25,000 Orang Asli who were re-settled, between 5,000 and 7,000 died in their new locations (Bayly and Harper 2007, 494).

3. America's Re-balancing towards the Western Pacific

In 2011–12 the United States announced a major shift of strategic direction towards an emphasis on the Asia-Pacific region:

> US economic and security interests are inextricably linked to developments in the arc extending from the Western Pacific and East Asia into the Indian Ocean region and South Asia, creating a mix of evolving challenges and opportunities. Accordingly, while the US military will continue to contribute to security globally, *we will of necessity rebalance toward the Asia-Pacific region.* (US Department of Defense 2012, 2)

US secretary of state Hillary Clinton affirmed that 'the twenty-first century will be America's Pacific century, just like previous centuries have been' (Clinton 2012). She enlarged on the shift in US strategic direction:

> The future of politics will be decided in Asia, not Afghanistan or Iraq, and the United States will be right at the centre of the action... One of

the most important tasks of American statecraft over the next decade will therefore be to lock in substantially increased investment – diplomatic, economic, strategic, and otherwise – in the Asia-Pacific region. (Clinton 2011)

Constructing a network of Asian political and military alliances is a critically important part of US international relations strategy in the decades ahead. The United States believes that its renewed involvement in Asia is vital to the region's future:

The region is eager for our leadership and our business – perhaps more than at any time in modern history. We are the only power with a network of strong alliances in the region, no territorial ambitions, and a long record of providing for the common good… Our challenge now is to build a web of relationships across the Pacific that is as durable and as consistent with American interests and values as the web we have built across the Atlantic. (Clinton 2011)

As part of the 're-balancing towards Asia' the US government announced a new military strategy termed the Joint Operation Access Concept (JOAC). It is unimaginable that the United States could win a land-based war with China. The JOAC signalled a shift from a land-based strategy to a strategy based on air- and sea-focused military strategies. It is self-evidently aimed at China. The concept was first presented to the public in the 2010 Quadrennial Defense Review: 'The Air Force and Navy together are developing a new joint air-sea battle concept for defeating adversaries across the range of military operations' (US Department of Defense 2010). One of the Pentagon documents released on the subject recommends that in the event of a conflict with China, the US should 'attack enemy anti-access/area denial defenses in depth'. In the case of China's land-based anti-ship missiles that would mean preparing for a large strike on military bases in mainland China (*FT*, 1 June 2012). James Cartwright, a retired US general and former vice chairman of the Joint Chiefs of Staff, said: 'The air-sea battle concept is demonizing China' and 'that's not in anybody's interest' (quoted in the *FT*, 1 June 2012). Officially the air-sea battle concept is not aimed at China. However, in private Pentagon officials acknowledge that the Pentagon has been alarmed by China's investments in the 'access-denial' weapons that air-sea battle is designed to address, from ballistic missiles to submarines and Beijing's emerging cyber-war capabilities (*FT*, 1 June 2012). In 2012, the Pentagon linked together China and Iran as the two key threats to US 'power projection capabilities' in terms of asymmetric warfare (US Department of Defense 2012, 4–5).

The United States is massively dominant in terms of military strength. Official US military spending is around $3,200 per person compared with around $113 in China. US military spending amounts to 69 per cent of the military spending of the whole of NATO, which has 26 European member countries, and it amounts to 46 per cent of total global military spending (IISS 2011, 476). A consistent theme of the US government in recent years has been the insistence that China should be more open and transparent about its true level of military expenditure. China's officially reported military spending in 2011 was $91.5 billion. However, according to the US–China Economic and Security Review Commission, China's actual military spending in 2011 was over $150 billion (USCESRC 2011, 160). The official figure for US government military spending in 2013 is $525.4 billion. However, there is a wide range of military expenditure that is not included in the official budget (Wheeler 2012). These include $19.3 billion on 'nuclear warhead research and upkeep'; $88.5 billion on 'overseas contingency operations', i.e., the wars in Afghanistan and elsewhere; $26.8 billion on military retirement costs; $137.7 billion on veteran affairs, i.e., the human consequences of past and present wars; and $46.3 billion on homeland security. If all the items of military expenditures not included in the official budget figures are added together, they amount to $468.9 billion, and the 'real' total US military budget for 2013 amounts to $994.3 billion, which amounts to no less than 25.7 per cent of all US federal government expenditure and around 7 per cent of America's GDP (Wheeler 2012). In other words, 'real' US military spending is around seven times greater than 'real' Chinese military spending. The main elements of the US armed forces include 10–11 aircraft carriers; 88 large surface combatants (e.g., cruisers and destroyers), of which up to 32 are 'ballistic missile–capable'; 55 attack submarines; over 1,000 airlift and air re-fuelling aircraft; 800 theatre strike aircraft; and 500 long-range strike bombers (IISS 2011, 43).

The United States and its allies in northeast Asia have enormous armed forces on China's doorstep. They have the world's most advanced weaponry, produced by giant US arms manufacturers, including Boeing, Lockheed Martin, Northrop Grumman and Raytheon (IISS 2011). The US Pacific Command in Japan has around 36,000 military personnel. The US Seventh Fleet is dedicated to operations in the 'Western Pacific', with its headquarters at Yokosuka in Japan. At the core of the Seventh Fleet is a nuclear-powered aircraft carrier, as well as seven destroyers and two cruisers, all with guided missiles. The US Air Force bases in Japan at Okinawa-Kadena and Misawa have over fifty fighter and fighter ground attack aircraft. The US Pacific Command in Korea has around 25,000 military personnel. The US Seventh Air Force has its headquarters at Osan. There are around 180 American attack aircraft at the Osan and Kunsan airbases in Korea. In addition to the

USA's own massive military forces in the region, its allies have large amounts of US-supplied weapons. Its three main allies in the region, Korea, Japan and Taiwan have a total of over 1,000 US-supplied fighter and fighter ground attack aircraft (IISS 2011). The fact that the air forces of Japan, Korea and Taiwan consist mainly of US-supplied equipment greatly facilitates their coordinated operation. In addition to its forces in China's immediate vicinity, the US also has a massive fighting capability of its Third Fleet in the 'Eastern Pacific', based in San Diego, and large bases in the British territory of Diego Garcia and the USA's own Guam island in the Western Pacific. The Third Fleet includes 4 aircraft carriers, 8 nuclear-powered ballistic missile submarines, 2 nuclear-powered guided missile submarines, 29 nuclear attack submarines, 8 cruisers and 21 destroyers.

To this day, the USA retains an extensive array of directly ruled territories in the Pacific, including not only Hawaii and Guam, but also American Samoa, the North Mariana Islands, and numerous small islands, such as Midway Atoll, Kingman Reef, Palmyra Atoll, Baker Island, Navassa Island and Johnston Atoll. The United States and Japan are building joint military training ranges on the North Mariana Islands. There are also a variety of islands that are closely associated with the United States. For example, the Federated States of Micronesia and the Republic of Palau became fully independent of the United States in 1986 and 1994 respectively, but the United States 'provides defense and some financial assistance in return for military use of the islands' (US Department of the Interior 2012).

The Ryukyu Islands are the most strategically important of all the world's small island groups.[12] They stretch out over 700 miles to the southwest of mainland Japan into the East China Sea. They culminate in a group of tiny uninhabited islands, called the Diaoyu in Chinese and the Senkaku in Japanese. The largest of the Ryukyu islands is Okinawa, which is 70 miles long. It is around 400 miles from Okinawa to China's Fujian province and around 800 miles to Tokyo. For centuries Ryukyu was a tiny independent kingdom inhabited by seafaring traders, similar to those in Japan's southern islands (Kerr 2000 [1958]). However, the culture of the Ryukyu was arguably more strongly influenced by Chinese than by Japanese tradition.[13] Five years after the Meiji Restoration in 1868 Japan asserted its authority over Ryukyu and in 1879 it forcefully incorporated the Ryukyu kingdom into Japan as 'Okinawa prefecture', ruled by Japanese officials. At the end of World War II Japan had around 100,000 troops on Okinawa as a last line of protection against the possible invasion of the Japanese mainland by American troops. In April 1945 the United States landed half a million troops on Okinawa. Around 100,000 people died in the ensuing 'rain of fire and steel', around one-half of whom were Okinawa civilians.

After the Japanese defeat US troops continued to occupy Okinawa. In 1951 the San Francisco 'Treaty of Peace' gave the United States 'all powers of administration, legislation and jurisdiction' over the territory, 'including the inhabitants and their territorial waters'. The US constructed massive military facilities on Okinawa, using it as a key base in both the Korean and the Vietnam wars. In 1972 the Ryukyu Islands, including Okinawa, as well as the Diaoyu Islands, were 'returned' by the US to Japan. However, Japan agreed to pay the United States an 'annual host nation support fee', in order to help finance the continued American military occupation. Today this amounts to around $4 billion annually. The US military presence on Okinawa continues to grow. The largest US facility on Okinawa is Kadena airbase, with 18,000 US Americans, and there are numerous other US military installations on Okinawa. Moreover, the US controls large areas of sea and air space around the Ryukyus (Johnson 2000, 36). US occupation is hugely controversial in Okinawa itself as well as in mainland Japan. The American bases completely dominate the island's geography and the presence of so many American troops has had a devastating effect on the culture of the island's population:

Few Americans who have never served abroad in the armed forces can have any conception of the nature or impact of an American base complex, with its massive military facilities, post exchanges, dependents' housing estates, swimming pools, and golf courses, and the associated bars, whorehouses, and venereal disease clinics that they attract in a land like Okinawa. (Johnson 2000, 35)[14]

Hostility among the Okinawa population and large sections of the Japanese population reached fever pitch in 1995 when three US servicemen abducted and brutally raped a 12-year-old girl. The commander of the US forces in the Pacific, Admiral Richard C. Macke, commented: 'I think that [the rape] was absolutely stupid. For the price they paid to rent the car, they could have had a girl' (quoted in Johnson 2000, 35).[15]

In 1995 when Joseph Nye was defense secretary, the US government produced a strategy document (US Department of Defense 1995) for the Asia-Pacific region. He enunciated a policy of 'deep engagement' (Nye 1995), which he argued was necessary on the grounds that 'rising powers create instability in the international state system': a 'forward-based troop presence ensures the US a seat at the table on Asian issues' and 'enables us to respond quickly to protect our interests, not only in Asia but as far away as the Persian Gulf'. For the foreseeable future, Japan and the Okinawa base would serve as the 'cornerstones of our security strategy for the entire region'. The governor of Okinawa remarked that Nye spoke of Okinawa as if it were

'American territory'. In 2006, Japanese prime minister Koizumi agreed to replace the ageing Futenma US Marine base on Okinawa with a massive new state-of-the-art military facility at Henoko, also on Okinawa. The new base would cost $16 billion and be completed by 2014.

In August 2009 the centre-left Democratic Party (DPJ) won an historic landslide victory to end over half a century of continuous rule by the Liberal Democratic Party. The new prime minister, Hatoyama Yukio, announced that the country was setting out a new path:

> The era of US-led globalization is coming to an end... The recent economic crisis resulted from a way of thinking based on the idea that American-style free-market economics represents a universal and ideal economic order... Globalization has progressed without any regard for non-economic values, or for environmental issues or problems of resource restrictions.

He raised doubts about the permanence of the dollar as the global reserve currency. He urged Japan not to forget its identity as a 'nation located in Asia'. He said that Japan should 'aspire to move towards a regional currency as a natural extension of the region's rapid economic growth', and argued that Japan should 'spare no effort to build the permanent security framework to underpin currency integration'. He spoke of working towards an 'autonomous East Asian Community' and towards 'a more equal relationship with Washington'. The new government declared that it would not accept the Koizumi government's agreement to build a new US Marine base at Henoko. Nor would it continue to pay the annual 'host nation support fee' to fund US bases on Japanese territory.

The US foreign policy establishment responded with a concerted attack on the Hatoyama government. Joseph Nye derided the DPJ as 'inexperienced and still in the thrall of campaign promises' (*New York Times*, 6 January 2010). Richard Armitage, former assistant secretary of state, stated that the DPJ was 'speaking a different language to the rest of the world' when it came to deterrence. Richard Bush, director of the Brookings Institute's Centre for Northeast Asia Policy Studies,[16] said the US government should try to 'broaden the views of the new government and shape its policy in ways that fit US interests' (Bush 2010). He said that the US should continue to 'shape China's intentions over time so that they move in a benign direction, so that it has more to gain from cooperation than a challenge'. This required both 'engaging and incorporating China as much as possible, and maintaining the strength and willingness to define limits'. Bush stated that US bases on Okinawa were vital because Okinawa is 'relatively close to mainland Japan, to Korea, to the South China Sea, and to the Strait of Malacca'. President Obama's defense secretary, Robert Gates, threatened 'serious consequences' if Tokyo did not carry through the agreement. Pentagon press secretary Geoff Morrell said that the US would 'not accept' a negative response from Japan. Kurt Campbell, assistant secretary of state, said that the Japanese public would 'have to understand' the need to keep US forces on Okinawa. Prime Minister Hatoyama visited the United States in April 2010. The *Washington Post* described him as the 'biggest loser of all world leaders', and noted that some Obama officials described him as 'hapless' and 'increasingly loopy'. At an official dinner he was 'rudely rebuffed' by President Obama.

Shortly after his return to Japan, Hatoyama capitulated and announced his government's support for the Koizumi agreement. On 28 May the agreement was formally incorporated in a US–Japan joint statement. On 2 June Hatoyama resigned as Japanese prime minister, and was replaced by Kan Naoto. Prime Minister Kan immediately rang President Obama to reassure him that his government would honour the 28 May agreement. Kan was rewarded immediately with a photo opportunity with President Obama. The US House of Representatives passed a resolution which expressed 'appreciation to the people of Japan, and especially on Okinawa', for their continued hosting of US bases. These sentiments did not fit easily with the comments made by Kevin Maher, head of the State Department's Office of Japan Affairs, in a lecture in Washington in March 2011, in which he said that the Okinawans were 'masters of manipulation and distortion' (*New York Times*, 10 March 2011).[17]

The Hatoyama vision of fraternity and an autonomous East Asian Community had disappeared and was replaced by Japan's 'traditional subservience to Washington'. The United States pressed ahead with its long-term goal of integrating Japan's 'Self-Defense Forces' (SDF) under US command: 'The next generation of leaders in the DPJ is made up of realists who want a more effective Japanese role in the world and are not afraid to use the Self-Defense Forces or to stand up to China or North Korea on human rights' (Michael Green, quoted in McCormack 2010, 24). In 2004 Japan installed its first US-made advanced anti-ballistic missile defence radar system and in September 2012 it was announced that Japan was installing a second such system. Senior Chinese officials and scholars commented that the US-supplied missile defence system had contributed to greater Japanese boldness in relation to the dispute with China over the Diaoyu Islands: 'Japan would not have been so aggressive without the support and actions of the US.'

In 2012 an open dispute erupted between China and Japan over the Diaoyu Islands, the group of uninhabited islands located at the extreme southwestern end of the Ryukyu Islands. They are 1,000 miles from Tokyo, but only 200 miles from the Chinese mainland and just 120 miles from Taiwan. They appeared on Chinese maps as the 'Diaoyu' islands as early as the fifteenth century. The uninhabited islands were annexed by Japan in 1879 when it annexed the rest of the Ryukyu island chain. In 1895 after China was defeated by Japan they were formally ceded to Japan under the Treaty of Shimonoseki. Around 1900 the Japanese government allowed ownership of the islands to pass to an entrepreneur who ran a small bonito processing plant on one of the islands until 1940. The islands have been deserted ever since. Ownership formally remained in private Japanese hands. In 1972, when the United States gave up control over the Ryukyu Islands, the entire body of the islands, including the Diaoyu Islands was returned by them to Japan. The islands are included in the US–Japanese Security Treaty. Theoretically, the United States is required by the treaty to provide military support if China were to occupy the islands. The United States' decision to return the islands to Japan was deeply resented among the Chinese population and was formally protested by the Chinese government. The issue of Japan's invasion of China is extraordinarily sensitive, quite independently of the views of the Chinese government.[18] Over a long period China pursued a peaceful resolution of the dispute over ownership of the islands. However, in 2012 the governor of Tokyo decided to buy the islands through public subscription. The attempt was forestalled by the Japanese government's decision to keep the islands in the hands of the Japanese state by buying the islands themselves, but this decision also stimulated strong antagonism in China as it reaffirmed the determination of the Japanese government to keep the islands in Japanese hands.

Hillary Clinton also toured East Asia in 2012, and delivered a series of warnings to China about its policy towards the countries that surround the South China Sea. She said: 'We believe the nations of the region should work collaboratively to resolve disputes without coercion, without intimidation and certainly without the use of force.'[19] In September 2012 Hillary Clinton spoke of her tour of East Asia: 'Time and again, I had leaders – I mean, I'm talking about the highest leaders – essentially say: "Thank goodness. I thank you. I'm so pleased you're here"' (quoted in *International Herald Tribune*, 21 September 2012). America's 're-balancing towards the West Pacific' and the warnings delivered by Hillary Clinton commanded wide support among the high-income countries. In fact, as we have seen, today's high-income countries have a long record of intervention in the region around the South China Sea, frequently involving the use of massive military force to achieve their objectives.

Conclusion

The long history of interaction between the West and the territories around the South China Sea could not be more different from China's interaction with the region. China's principal interaction was through trade and the peaceful migration of people, some of whom became leading business figures, but most of whom were ordinary workers, typically in low-income occupations. The vulnerable Chinese 'sojourner' communities often experienced discrimination and were frequently attacked.[20] Over several centuries the European powers fought to build colonial empires in the lands around the South China Sea. Between 1941 and 1945 their collective empire was violently snatched away from them by their 'East Asian pupil', Japan.

The draft of the Universal Declaration of Human Rights was put before the first General Assembly of the United Nations in 1946. The declaration was formally approved by the General Assembly in 1948. For centuries prior to the declaration and for decades thereafter, the actions of the West in the developing world were repeatedly contrary to the 'Enlightenment' principles embodied in the declaration. The climax of the war against Japan involved America's prolonged 'total war' against Japan's civilian population.[21] Following Japan's defeat, the West fought a prolonged and immensely bloody succession of wars to re-establish their rule over the lands around the South China Sea, against a succession of national liberation movements, including those of a secular, Muslim, communist and 'united front' nature.

The Western media routinely ridicule China's fears of 'encirclement' by the US and its East Asian allies. Today the United States is poised with an overwhelming military presence around the region, with massive naval and air forces in bases stretching from Britain's Diego Garcia in the west, through Japan and Korea, to Guam in the east. The island of Okinawa has been a de facto US colony since 1945. It has 36,000 US military personnel and bristles with vast amounts of high-technology military equipment. It is literally on China's doorstep and on the edge of the South China Sea. The US has conducted tenacious and aggressive diplomacy to sustain its tight diplomatic and military relationship with its allies, especially in Japan and Korea.

The long historical record of the 'West', including Europe, Japan and the United States, in its interaction with the lands around the South China Sea, are grounds for grave concern at the prospect for peace in the region in response to China's 'rise'. America's 're-balancing towards the Western Pacific' is taking place in the context of economic stagnation and socio-political dislocation in the high-income countries. It increases the likelihood of a 'new Peloponnesian War'. In order to avoid this outcome China will need to demonstrate great diplomatic skill and forbearance in the face of the West's provocation and its collective amnesia about its own history in the region, as well as its ignorance of the nature of China's historical relationship with the region. Should China itself 'repay injury with injury' (*yi yuan bao yuan*), 'repay injury with kindness' (*yi de bao yuan*), or 'repay injury with firmness' (*yi zhi bao yuan*)?

Notes

1 Western universities are now replete with heavily funded centres of 'rising powers', which is a code name for 'the China threat'.

2 International disputes over fishing rights are common. For example, the UK fought a series of 'cod wars' with Iceland from the late 1950s through to the 1970s.

3 For a full discussion, see Nolan (2009).

4 There is, of course, a significant minority of the population of developing countries that is affluent and 'globalized'. In China today it is estimated that the top one per cent of households have over 60 per cent of total household wealth. The relationship of the top one per cent to the mass of the Chinese population is complicated. However, a truly global 'middle class' remains a minority of the population in developing countries, including even in China.

5 The only significant exception to this is the fact that for around 1,000 years China ruled over North Vietnam, which is contiguous to the southwest Chinese border province of Guangxi. North Vietnam broke away from Chinese rule at the end of the Tang dynasty in 907 AD.

6 The question of the extent and nature of economic development under colonial rule is a much more complex issue. The view is widely held by 'Marxist' economists that colonialism was the basic cause of underdevelopment and was widely accompanied by 'deindustrialization' in developing countries (see, e.g., Bagchi 1982; Baran 1957; Frank 1967). In fact, Marx's own view of the impact of colonialism was quite different (see, e.g., Marx and Engels 1952; Avineri 1968). He deplored the hypocrisy and violence of the colonial powers, but argued that colonialism was a progressive force that would permit the development of capitalism in countries ruled by 'Asiatic despotisms', such as China and India. This would in turn permit industrialization, with the accompanying economic and social progress. Although his view of the developing world as mainly ruled by stagnant 'Asiatic despotisms' is highly problematic, there is an abundance of evidence that colonialism was accompanied by extensive economic progress. Warren (1980) provides an overall appraisal of the progressive character of colonialism. In the case of Southeast Asia, Allen and Donnithorne's (1957) careful analysis provides a positive overall evaluation of the region's economic development under colonial rule. Whether development would have been faster without colonialism is an unresolved counter-factual speculation.

7 In fact, numerous colonial territories still existed after this date, including the United States' territories in the Pacific. Britain did not return Hong Kong to China until 1997 and it retains a highly significant set of dependencies of immense strategic value. These include the British Indian Ocean Territory (which contains the United States' military base at Diego Garcia), Gibraltar and several Caribbean territories. In the South Atlantic, thousands of miles from the UK, British dependencies span almost the whole area, with Ascension Island and St Helena in the north, the South Sandwich

Islands, South Georgia and the Falkland Islands in the south, and even further south, the South Orkneys and the South Shetland Islands, which form the British Antarctic Territories.

8 It's true that Napoleon's wars of conquest began with the motive to spread revolutionary ideas to the rest of Europe but this motive quickly faded: 'Motivated at first by a desire to carry revolutionary freedoms to the subjects of neighbouring kingdoms, the French ended by committing themselves to a permanent military programme of national aggrandizement' (Keegan 1993, 349).

9 However, the resistance to German fascism had a strong ideological element.

10 The US victory in the Battle of Manila Bay is celebrated on American patriotic websites.

11 On the intellectual ferment in the Arab world in the late nineteenth and early twentieth centuries, see Hourani (1983 [1962]).

12 Unless otherwise indicated the following paragraphs are taken from McCormack (2010), which provides a deeply illuminating analysis of US–Japan relations in connection with Okinawa.

13 'The [Ryukyu kingdom] was a toy state, with its dignified kings, its sententious and learned prime ministers, its councils and its numerous bureaux, its organization of temples and shrines, and its classical school, its grades in court rank and its codes of law, all developed in an effort to emulate great China' (Kerr 2000 [1958], 15–16).

14 It is a moot point whether the destructive social impact, especially on young women, of the presence of US troops across the world, is greater than the former social impact of British or French troops in their respective colonial possessions.

15 The servicemen were tried and jailed. Admiral Macke was 'permitted to retire' following his comment.

16 Bush was formerly a national intelligence officer for East Asia at the US National Intelligence Council.

17 Maher was removed from his post by Kurt Campbell for these 'unfortunate remarks'.

18 One of the most powerful accounts of Japan's occupation of mainland China was written by an American citizen, Iris Chang. Her account of the Japanese Army's occupation of Nanjing in December 1937 is one of the most terrifying accounts of war atrocities written in modern times (Chang 1997). Iris Chang committed suicide in 2004 at the age of 36.

19 This sentence appeared in various forms throughout Hillary Clinton's Far Eastern tour in 2012.

20 The most notable attacks were in Indonesia in the 1960s and again in the late 1990s during the Asian financial crisis.

21 Several hundred thousand people died in these attacks, which were explicitly aimed at civilians in Japan's major cities. American submarines sunk almost 2,000 Japanese merchant ships, killing over 100,000 civilians. America's nuclear bomb attacks on Hiroshima and Nagasaki killed over 300,000 people.

BIBLIOGRAPHY

Allen, G. C. and A. Donnithorne. 1957. *Western Enterprise and Economic Development in Indonesia and Malaya*. London: Macmillan.

Allison, G. 2012. 'Thucydides' Trap Has Been Sprung in the Pacific'. *Financial Times*, 22 August.

Augur, P. 2000. *The Death of Gentlemanly Capitalism*. London: Penguin Books.

_____. 2005. *The Greed Merchants*. London: Penguin Books.

Avineri, S. 1968. *Karl Marx on Colonialism and Modernization*. New York: Doubleday.

Bagchi, A. K. 1982. *The Political Economy of Development*. Cambridge: Cambridge University Press.

Bain. 2010. *China's Luxury Market*. New York: Bain & Co.

Baran, P. 1957. *The Political Economy of Growth*. New York: Monthly Review Press.

Bayly, C. and T. Harper. 2007. *Forgotten Wars: The End of Britain's Asian Empire*. London: Penguin Books.

BERR (Department for Business Enterprise and Regulatory Reform [UK]). 2008. *The 2008 R&D Scoreboard*. London: BERR.

BIS (Department for Business Innovation and Skills [UK]). 2009. *The 2009 R&D Scoreboard*. London: BIS.

_____. 2010. *The 2010 R&D Scoreboard*. London: BIS.

BoCom (Bank of Communications). 2010. *Interim Report*. Shanghai: BoCom.

BP. 2011. *Statistical Review of World Energy*. London: BP.

Broome, R. 2010. *Aboriginal Australians: A History Since 1788*. Revised 4th edition. Sydney: Allen & Unwin.

Bush, R. 2010. 'Okinawa and Security in East Asia'. Brookings Institution, 10 March.

Bushnell, A. O. 1993. *Gifts of Civilization: Germs and Genocide in Hawaii*. Hawaii: University of Hawaii Press.

Carson, R. 1941. *Under the Sea Wind*. London: Penguin Books.

CBRC (China Banking Regulatory Commission). 2012. *Annual Report, 2011*. Beijing: CBRC.

Chang, I. 1997. *The Rape of Nanjing: The Forgotten Holocaust of World War II*. London: Penguin Books.

Chang Song. 2005. 'Consolidation and Internationalization in the Global Banking Industry since the 1980s, and the Implications for Chinese Banking Reform'. University of Cambridge, doctoral thesis.

Chen Qingtai. 2012. 'Turning from State-Owned Enterprise Reform towards State-Owned Assets Reform'. *Caijing* 322 (May).

Clinton, H. 2011. 'America's Pacific Century'. *Foreign Affairs* (November).

_____. 2012. 'Forrestal Lecture'. Naval Academy, Annapolis, January.

Cole, G. D. H. 1993. 'Introduction'. In J.-J. Rousseau, *The Social Contract and Discourses*. London: Everyman.

Confucius. 1976. *The Analects*. London: Penguin Books.

Cook, J. 1999. *The Journals*, selected and edited by Philip Edwards. London: Penguin Books.

Dalziel, N. 2006. *Penguin Historical Atlas of the British Empire*. London: Penguin Books.

Darwin, C. 2004 [1871]. *The Descent of Man*. London: Penguin Books.

Directorate-General for Economic and Financial Affairs. 2011. *European Economic Forecast*, November.

DTI (Department of Trade and Industry [UK]). 2007. *The 2007 R&D Scoreboard*. London: DTI.

Dunn, J. 2005. *Setting the People Free: The Story of Democracy*. London: Atlantic Books.

Euromoney. 2011. *Euromoney FX Survey*. May.

Fairbank, J. K., E. O. Reischauer and A. M. Craig. 1965. *East Asia: The Modern Transformation*. London: Allen & Unwin.

Finley, M. 1978. 'The Fifth-Century Athenian Empire: A Balance Sheet'. In *Imperialism in the Ancient World*, edited by P. Garnsey and C. R. Wheeler. Cambridge: Cambridge University Press.

Frank. A. G. 1967. *Capitalism and Underdevelopment in Latin America*. New York: Monthly Review Press.

Friedman, M. 1962. *Capitalism and Freedom*. Chicago: University of Chicago Press.

Friedman, T. 2005. *The World is Flat: A Brief History of the Twenty-First Century*. New York: Farrar, Straus & Giroux.

Gao Yuning. 2011. *China as the Workshop of the World*. London: Routledge.

Garnsey, P. and C. R. Wheeler, eds. 1978. *Imperialism in the Ancient World*. Cambridge: Cambridge University Press.

Goldman, M. 2003. *The Piratization of Russia*. London: Routledge.

Greenspan, A. 2007. *The Age of Turbulence*. London: Penguin Books.

Grenier, J. 2005. *The First Way of War*. Cambridge: Cambridge University Press.

Haines, M. R. et al., eds. 2000. *A Population History of North America*. Cambridge: Cambridge University Press.

Hong Kong Research. 2012. 'Sino–Japanese Tensions and Why the Economics Matter to Hong Kong'. Hong Kong Trade Development Council, 5 October.

Hourani, A. 1983 [1962]. *Arab Thought in the Liberal Age*. Cambridge: Cambridge University Press.

Huang Liuhong. 1984. *A Complete Book Concerning Happiness and Benevolence: A Manual for Local Magistrates*. Tucson: University of Arizona Press.

Hu Jintao. 2012. Report to the 18th Party Congress, 8 November.

Hymer, S. 1975 [1972]. 'The Multinational Corporation and the Law of Uneven Development'. In *International Firms and Modern Imperialism*, edited by H. Radice. Harmondsworth: Penguin Books.

IEA (International Energy Agency). 2007. *World Energy Outlook*. Paris: OECD.

IISS (International Institute for Strategic Studies). 2011. *The Military Balance: 2011*. London: IISS.

IMF (International Monetary Fund). 2011a. *World Economic Outlook*. Washington DC: IMF.
_____. 2011b. *Financial System Stability Assessment*. Washington DC: IMF.

Johnson, C. 2000. *Blowback: The Costs and Consequences of American Empire*. New York: Metropolitan Books.

Kagan, D. 2003. *The Peloponnesian War*. London: HarperCollins.

Kaufman, H. 2009. *The Road to Financial Reformation*. Hoboken: John Wiley & Sons.

Keegan, J. 1993. *A History of Warfare*. London: Pimlico.

Kerr, G. 2000 [1958]. *Okinawa: The History of an Island People*. North Clarendon, VT: Tuttle Publishing.

Keynes, J. M. 1936. *The General Theory of Employment, Interest and Money*. London: Macmillan.

Kotz, D. M. and F. Weir. 2007. *Russia's Path from Gorbachev to Putin*. London: Routledge.

KPMG. 2011. *Mainland China Trust Survey 2011*. Beijing: KPMG.

Krugman, P. 2000. *The Return of Depression Economics*. Harmondsworth: Penguin Books.

Lao Tse. 2009. *Tao Te Ching*. London: Penguin Books.

Lau, D. C. 1976. 'Introduction'. In Confucius, *The Analects*. London: Penguin Books.

_____. 2009. 'Introduction'. In Lao Tse, *Tao Te Ching*. London: Penguin Books.

Lenin, V. I. 1968 [1917]. *Imperialism, the Highest Stage of Capitalism*. Moscow: Progress Publishers.

Li Jinming and Li Dexia. 2003. 'The Dotted Line on the Chinese Map of the South China Sea'. *Ocean Development and International Law* 34: 287–95.

Lyons, G. 2007. *State Capitalism: The Rise of Sovereign Wealth Funds*. London: Standard Chartered.

Marshall, A. 1920 [1890]. *Principles of Economics*. 8th edition. London: Macmillan.

Martin, J. 2012. 'Hero Pilot Who Opposed War in Vietnam only to be Crushed by Nixon'. Obituary, *Financial Times*, 22 October.

Marx, K. 1967a [1886]. *Capital, Vol. 1*. New York: International Publishers. [First published in German in 1867.]

_____. 1967b [1886]. *Capital, Vol. 3*. New York: International Publishers. [First published in German in 1867.]

Marx, K. and F. Engels. 1952. *Manifesto of the Communist Party*. Moscow: Progress Publishers. [First published in German in 1848.]

McCormack, G. 2010. 'Obama versus Okinawa'. *New Left Review*, July–August, 5–28.

McKinsey. 2009. *Global Capital Markets*. London: McKinsey.

Meeks, G. 1977. *Disappointing Marriage*. Cambridge: Cambridge University Press.

Morehead, A. 1968. *Fatal Impact: The Brutal and Tragic Story of How the South Pacific was 'Civilised', 1767–1840*. London: Penguin Books.

Nolan, P. 1995. *China's Rise, Russia's Fall*. Houndmills: Macmillan.

_____. 2009. *Crossroads: The End of Wild Capitalism and the Future of Humanity*. London: Marshall Cavendish.

_____. 2012. *Is China Buying the World?*. Cambridge: Polity Press.

Nye, J. 1995. 'The Case for Deep Engagement'. *Foreign Affairs*, July–August.

Obama, B. 2011. 'Remarks to the Australian Parliament'. Parliament House, Canberra, Australia, November.

OECD (Organisation for Economic Co-operation and Develoment). 2012. *China in Focus: Lessons and Challenges*. Paris: OECD.

Penrose, E. 1995. *The Theory of the Growth of the Firm*. 2nd edition. Oxford: Oxford University Press.

Pew Trust. 2012. *Sea Around Us Project*. Washington DC: Pew Trust.

Radice, H. ed. 1975. *International Firms and Modern Imperialism*. Harmondsworth: Penguin Books.

Rand, A. 2007 [1957]. *Atlas Shrugged*. London: Penguin Books.

Rice, C. 2012. 'America Must Remember That It Is Not Just Any Other Country'. *Financial Times*, 27 September.

Roberts, C. 2007. *The Unnatural History of the Sea*. Washington DC: Island Press.

Romney, M. 2012. Speech at the Republican Convention, September.

Rousseau, J.-J. 1993 [1923]. *The Social Contract and Discourses*. London: Everyman.

Ruigrok, R. and R. van Tulder. 1995. *The Logic of International Restructuring*. London: Routledge.

Sessions, J. E. 2011. *By Sword and Plough: France and the Conquest of Algeria*. New York: Cornell University Press.

Shirk, S. 2007. *China Fragile Superpower*. New York: Oxford University Press.

Smith, A. 1982 [1761]. *The Theory of Moral Sentiments*. Revised edition. Indianapolis: Liberty Classics.

SSB (State Statistical Bureau [China]). 2009. *China Statistical Yearbook*. Beijing: State Statistical Bureau.

_____. 2010. *China Statistical Yearbook*. Beijing: State Statistical Bureau.

_____. 2011. *China Statistical Yearbook*. Beijing: State Statistical Bureau.

Standard Chartered. 2009. *Annual Report*. London: Standard Chartered.

Steinfeld, E. 2010. *Playing Our Game*. Oxford: Oxford University Press.

Thomas, N. 2010. *Islanders: The Pacific in the Age of Empire*. London: Yale University Press.

Thornton, R. 'Population History of Native North Americans'. In *A Population History of North America*, edited by M. R. Haines et al. Cambridge: Cambridge University Press.

Thucydides. 1972. *History of the Peloponnesian War*. London: Penguin Books.

Tocqueville, A. de. 1994 [1863]. *Democracy in America*. 2 vols. London: Everyman.

Towers Watson. 2010. *The World's 500 Largest Asset Manager*. New York: Towers Watson.

UNCTAD (United Nations Conference on Trade and Development). 2010. *World Investment Report*. Geneva: UNCTAD.

_____. 2011. *World Investment Report*. Geneva: UNCTAD.

US Chamber of Commerce. 2006. *China's WTO Implementation and Other Issues of Importance to American Business in the US–China Commercial Relationship*. Washington DC: US Chamber of Commerce.

USCESRC (US–China Economic and Security Review Commission). 2010. *Report to Congress*. Washington DC: US Government Printing Office.

_____. 2011. *Report to Congress*. Washington DC: US Government Printing Office.

US Department of Defense. 1995. *United States Security Strategy in the East Asia-Pacific Region*. Washington DC: US Government Printing Office.

_____. 2010. *Quadrennial Defense Review*. Washington DC: US Government Printing Office.

_____. 2012. *Sustaining US Global Leadership: Priorities for 21st Century Defense*. Washington DC: US Government Printing Office.

US Department of the Interior. 2012. *Territorial Acquisitions of the United States*. Washington DC: US Government Printing Office.

Vien, N. K. 1987. *Vietnam: A Long History*. Hanoi: Foreign Languages Publishing House.

Wang Gungwu. 2000. *The Chinese Overseas*. Cambridge, MA: Harvard University Press.

Warren, B. 1980. *Imperialism: Pioneer of Capitalism*. London: Verso Books.

Wen Jiabao. 2007. *Report on the Work of the Government*. Beijing, 5 March.

_____. 2008. *Report on the Work of the Government*. Beijing, 5 March.

Wheeler, W. 2012. 'The Real "Base" Pentagon Budget and the Actual "Defense" Budget'. Public Intelligence Blog.

WB (World Bank). 1995. *Bureaucrats in Business: The Economics and Politics of Government Ownership*. Washington DC: World Bank.

_____. 2000. *World Development Report: Entering the Twenty-First Century*. Washington DC: Oxford University Press.

_____. 2002. *World Development Report: Building Institutions for Markets*. Washington DC: Oxford University Press.

_____. 2008. *World Development Indicators*. Washington DC: World Bank.

_____. 2010. *World Development Indicators*. Washington DC: World Bank.

_____. 2011. *World Development Indicators*. Washington DC: World Bank.

_____. 2012. *World Development Indicators*. Washington DC: World Bank.

Winchester, S. 1985. *Outposts: Journeys to the Surviving Relics of the British Empire*. London: Penguin Books.

Wolf, M. 2004. *Why Globalization Works*. New Haven: Yale University Press.

Woodworth, D. C. 1994. 'The Exclusive Economic Zone and the United States' Insular Areas; A Case for Shared Sovereignty'. *Ocean Development and International Law* 25: 365–90.

Yan Xuetong. 2011. *Ancient Chinese Thought, Modern Chinese Power*. Princeton. Princeton University Press.

Zheng Bijian. 2011. *My Observations*, London: Routledge.

Zinn, H. 1999. *A People's History of the United States, 1492–Present*. New York: HarperCollins.

INDEX

Page numbers followed by *t* indicate tables.

Lightning Source UK Ltd.
Milton Keynes UK
UKOW03n0634260114

225269UK00001B/2/P